Endorsements for
When Language Meets Blockchain

Language is the basis for communication. It enables every human interaction and fuels every business activity. Blockchain provides traceability and security for transactions that require it. Peggy strides the worlds of language and blockchain, and helps us understand where these worlds meet.

Renato Beninatto
CEO
Nimdzi Insights

Language is a symbol of a country. Language has value and its value is positively correlated to the political and economic status of a country. Dr Peng presented the concept of language capability where language data are collected and shared on blockchain. These data will be circulated systematically driven by tokens and be applied to the IOL (Internet Of Language) platform. With this, we can look forward to profound changes to the translation profession and these changes will give great impetus to the transmission of global culture.

David Lee
Professor
Singapore University of Social Sciences

Translation is a domain that has not changed fundamentally in over a thousand years. Dr Peng has conducted a thorough analysis on integrating blockchain application with the translation industry and presented the innovative concept of language capability. She has applied language blockchain products Wordpower and Twinslator to translation practices and created the IOL (Internet Of Language) ecosystem. It is worth looking forward to the realisation of barrier-free communication for mankind.

Yu Jianing
President
Huobi Education,
Leading Blockchain Educational Institution in China
Chairman
On duty of the Blockchain Committee of China Communications Industry Association

I am shaken to witness such an extensive transformation of the translation industry in the era of blockchain. With her distinct and profound knowledge on language, Dr Peng has done a marvellous job on her explorations. This book is a must-read for every translation professional.

Wei De Han
Renowned Russian Sinologist
Translator for more than 10 Chinese ancient classical stories which include *The Art of War by Sun Tzu* and *Book of Changes*

Blockchain technology is not only applicable to recording financial transactions but has also been applied to other fields. Dr Peng has done a meaningful job probing the applicability of blockchain into the language service domain.

David Cane
Founder and CEO, Memsource a.s.

This book explores the possibilities that could result from the integration of language with the latest technology. "Blockchain + Translation" is "Internet + Translation" and "Artificial Intelligence + Translation". This is a model overlaid with new and infinite possibilities awaiting to be explored.

Fang Jun
Founding Member, Token Economy Industry Alliance
Consultant Partner, Huobi University
Author of *Introduction to Blockchain*

It is an innovative initiative to combine the study of language and blockchain. The concept of "language capability" presented in the book creates value for language within blockchain. This is an innovation out of human's innate capacity for language. It will be the beginning of a new domain.

Ye Kai
Founder of Han Tuo Technology
Author of *Token Economic Design Pattern*

Dr Peng adopts deductive reasoning for her product and deduced a solution supported by blockchain technology which could resolve the perplexing phenomenon of high output efforts reaping low returns faced by translation professionals, otherwise quoted in Gresham's Law as "Bad money drives out good".

Zhu Hongbing
Chairman
Singapore Blockchain Technology Foundation

Many people in the language services industry feel that blockchain is just a solution, but Dr Peng thinks that language and blockchain are correlated, and similar correlations exist for blockchain, artificial intelligence and language. I recommend that everyone should read this book to prepare for the near future.

Jaap van der Meer
Director
TAUS, Language Data Networks

This masterpiece moved me out of my industrial perspective and walked me into the essence of blockchain. We communicate daily with our fluent mother tongue which in fact, is equivalent to a chain executing its application. This book is a steady push to the language services industry.

Chen Caigen
Founder, Daily Shakes

Language is the basis of common understanding for human development. Aided by blockchain, contributions by language creators could be identified, quantified, recognised and gain due returns which will give an impetus to the development of language and civilisation.

Sun Zhiyong
Senior Partner
Beijing Tian Tai Law Firm

The translation profession is going through an industrial reform in the era of blockchain and Dr Peng is in the vanguard for both the theory and the practical aspect. Besides a systematic exploration into the theory, the latest research and development results of blockchain are also brought into university classrooms, helping students to be linked seamlessly with the latest technology of the translation industry.

Susan Xu
Head, Translation and Interpretation Programme
Singapore University of Social Sciences

When Language Meets Blockchain

When Language Meets Blockchain

PENG Zhihong
IOL (Internet Of Language) Research Institute, China

Translated by TAN Mui Yan Winnie

NEW JERSEY · LONDON · SINGAPORE · BEIJING · SHANGHAI · HONG KONG · TAIPEI · CHENNAI · TOKYO

Published by

World Scientific Publishing Co. Pte. Ltd.
5 Toh Tuck Link, Singapore 596224
USA office: 27 Warren Street, Suite 401-402, Hackensack, NJ 07601
UK office: 57 Shelton Street, Covent Garden, London WC2H 9HE

and

The Commercial Press Ltd.
No. 36, Wangfujing Street, Beijing, P.R. China 100710

Library of Congress Cataloging-in-Publication Data
Names: Peng, Zhihong, author. | Tan, Mui Yan Winnie, translator.
Title: When language meets blockchain / Peng Zhihong, IOL (Internet Of Language)
　　Research Institute, China ; translated by Tan Mui Yan Winnie.
Other titles: Dang yu yan yu dao qu kuai lian. English
Description: New Jersey : World Scientific, [2022] | Includes index.
Identifiers: LCCN 2021047915 | ISBN 9789811237843 (hardcover) |
　　ISBN 9789811237850 (ebook) | ISBN 9789811237867 (ebook other)
Subjects: LCSH: Translating and interpreting--Technological innovations. | Translating services--
　　Technological innovations. | Language and languages--Philosophy. | Blockchains (Databases)
Classification: LCC P306.97.T73 P46 2022 | DDC 418/.020285--dc23/eng/20211122
LC record available at https://lccn.loc.gov/2021047915

British Library Cataloguing-in-Publication Data
A catalogue record for this book is available from the British Library.

当语言遇到区块链
Originally published in Chinese by The Commercial Press Ltd.
Copyright © The Commercial Press Ltd., 2019

Copyright © 2022 by World Scientific Publishing Co. Pte. Ltd.

All rights reserved. This book, or parts thereof, may not be reproduced in any form or by any means, electronic or mechanical, including photocopying, recording or any information storage and retrieval system now known or to be invented, without written permission from the publisher.

For photocopying of material in this volume, please pay a copying fee through the Copyright Clearance Center, Inc., 222 Rosewood Drive, Danvers, MA 01923, USA. In this case permission to photocopy is not required from the publisher.

For any available supplementary material, please visit
https://www.worldscientific.com/worldscibooks/10.1142/12303#t=suppl

Desk Editor: Jiang Yulin

Typeset by Stallion Press
Email: enquiries@stallionpress.com

Dedication

Dedicating this book to Mr He Enpei. Our encounter forms a beautiful chapter of my life for which I will be eternally grateful. You are the one who ignite the spark to bring out the best in me.

Peng Zhihong

Contents

xiii	**About the Author**
xvii	**About the Translator**
xix	**Foreword 1** A Fusion of Language and Blockchain
xxiii	**Foreword 2** Linguistic Capability — The Catalyst for Human Civilisation
xxvii	**Foreword 3** The Token Economy and Language Services
xxxi	**Preface**
xxxv	**Introduction**
1	**Chapter 1** To Know Macro from Micro — Innate Similarities Between Language and Blockchain
39	**Chapter 2** A Sudden Revelation — Everyone Lives Within His Own Language Chain
75	**Chapter 3** A Perpetual Deadlock — The Language-Based Translation Services Industry Retains a Workshop-Style Existence
109	**Chapter 4** Unrecognised Gifts — The Lack of a Suitable Model for Bilingual Talents to Actualise Potential

CONTENTS

xi

143 **Chapter 5**
Wide Recognition — Blockchain Reveals the Value of Bilingual Talent

183 **Chapter 6**
A Perfect Match — The Wonderful Union of Language and Blockchain

217 **Chapter 7**
The Born Child — Cross-Linguistic Capability as a Fundamental in the Blockchain Era

255 **Chapter 8**
A Beautiful Evolution — A New World Free from Language Barriers

287 **Chapter 9**
The Journey with Language — A Mutually Fulfilling Partnership

325 **The Conclusion: Once in a Thousand Years**

327 **Epilogue**

331 **Index**

About the Author

Email: peggy.peng@transn.com

Peng Zhihong obtained a Doctor of Philosophy (Ph.D.) in Education and was named Associate Professor of Huazhong University of Science and Technology at the age of 33.

Dr Peng immigrated to Singapore in 2000 and since then has been committed to the research and promotion of Chinese language and culture in Singapore, and has facilitated cultural exchange between Singapore and China. She led the development of a textbook series entitled "Business Chinese Today" under the auspices of the then Workforce Development Agency (WDA) of Singapore and the textbooks have been incorporated into its training programme "Workforce Skills Qualifications".

She returned to her hometown Wuhan, China in 2013 to join China's leading artificial intelligence language service platform Transn IOL Technology Co., Ltd as a top management personnel.

Since 2018, she has been focusing on the theoretical research and practical explorations of how blockchain applications can transform the language field and has explored ways to integrate artificial intelligence, blockchain, big data and other cutting-edge technologies for intelligent organisation and scheduling of integrated language service capacity. Her team members, under her leadership, have proposed the concept of language blockchain products, have developed Twinslator and WordPower and have entered the phase of practical applications for these blockchain products. They are set to enhance the capacity and organisational efficiency of the language services industry through an ecosystem on a language networking platform known as IOL (Internet Of Language). The demand and supply parties of language services will be empowered to provide basic support for fast, accurate, low cost and large-scale delivery of multilingual services.

Dr Peng loves language. Having a career in the language domain allows her to tap on technology to inject power into languages and contribute to the development of the language services industry.

Currently, Dr Peng is the deputy director of IOL (Internet Of Language) Research Institute, the following is a brief introduction to the IOL ecosystem:

IOL is a leading language service platform driven by AI, blockchain and other technologies to gather resources from translators around the world. The entire blockchain is AI empowered, from pre-translation planning, capacity resource matching, translation and editing to post-translation follow-up. IOL strives to be the industry infrastructure to propel language service enterprises to take a big leap forward to the new translation era. The translation workflow and industry chain will be reshaped with increased translation capacity, greater efficiency and lower costs.

IOL overcomes the obstacles of a traditional quality control model to improve operation efficiency of the translation services industry.

It is competitive in terms of resource capacity planning, production efficiency, cost effectiveness and quality. It has achieved industry-wide recognition by end users and various industry players. The current delivery speed of IOL is 100,000 words per hour, millions of words per day, and billions of words per week.

IOL is progressing to alter the ecosystem of the language industry by transforming existing industry structure, operation mode and stakeholder relations. It will act as a model for the integration and development of AI and blockchain technology to promote intelligent digital upgrading of the language service industry.

About the Translator

Tan Mui Yan Winnie is a freelance English and Chinese translator. She is a Singaporean Chinese with two grown-up children. Winnie graduated from the Singapore University of Social Sciences in December 2021 with a Bachelor of Arts in Translation and Interpretation (English and Chinese). She has five years of translation experience and has translated commercial documents, literary works, web novels and marketing materials.

Winnie had ten years of industrial work experience which include eight years as a Research Officer with the Government of Singapore Investment Corporation. Her role was to gather and interpret data to perform analysis on equities markets, company performance, economic developments, and technology trends. Her research contributions supported the generation and execution of investment decisions. She also had experience in a sales and marketing position in an import and export trading environment.

Winnie appreciates the opportunity to translate *When Language Meets Blockchain* to benefit English readers and in particular, language professionals. She believes that all linguists and especially translators like herself will benefit from Dr Peng's work on Cross-Linguistic Capability. It has been a pleasurable challenge working on the translation and the production of this book, and Winnie anticipates the positive impact of blockchain application to the translation services profession. She hopes to see the potential of translators being fully recognised and duly rewarded, enabling a fulfilling language service profession.

Foreword 1

A Fusion of Language and Blockchain

I was delighted when Peggy asked me to provide the foreword to her new book *When Language Meets Blockchain*. We are living through such an exciting period of change in the language industry and the arrival of blockchain will, without a doubt, have an impact on the way we conduct our business. Our industry has traditionally been slower to adopt new technology but blockchain checks many boxes for us, especially in the translation supply chain.

Peggy and I met in Boston, MA, in June 2018. We connected on many topics, but the most innovative discussion was related to blockchain. It was great to learn more about the concept and about its benefits, such as tokenisation. At the time I was looking to test the application of blockchain technology to address the multiple micro-transactions that are made in the language industry. I believe 70% of our transactions are small and that blockchain technology will increase efficiency.

Blockchain is still quite a new thing and China could be the first country to apply it to the language industry. When we met, Peggy was just starting to think about how language services providers could combine with blockchain in China. I found her direction interesting and gladly accepted her invitation to be advisor to her Language Information Communication Chain (LIC), the world's first language public chain.

Since then, we have frequently exchanged views on blockchain and she has proven to be highly perceptive. She intuitively understand the environment and current challenges facing translators, companies communicating to global markets, and the language services industry as a whole.

An additional point to note is that blockchain could bring more transparency to compliance processes. Imagine a world where linguists' work would be traceable, auditable, and confidential; this is where Peggy says we are heading, and her book is perfectly timed.

In this book, Peggy discusses how blockchain can support translators to realise their full potential, how language and blockchain are perfect partners to achieve greater efficiency, and how combining the two can lead us to a world without language barriers. That is an interesting concept for global M&A which is where my expertise comes into play — I have spent over two decades accumulating IPO experience in the course of my career in financial communication and compliance.

The Legal and Regulatory Environment
Until July 2018, I was managing the leading language services provider Donnelley Language Solutions, a specialist in supporting customers with their Initial Public Offerings. We worked successfully with companies for decades to raise capital and bring them to market while helping to negotiate the regulatory environment of the SEC (US Securities and Exchange Commission) and the other national financial authorities.

Investor Trust
Developing investor trust by teaming up with established professionals in the financial industry, major banks and legal experts, all of whom undertake due diligence, is key. This can include background checks and review of supporting documents

such as the business terms and white paper of the offering, and the purchase agreement.

Multilingual Documentation

Money talks — in every language in the world. While English is the lingua franca of the IPO market, companies are required to take a long path through local regulations and multilingual adaptation to local markets. To further investor trust (not to mention the trust of the regulatory authorities), documents in all languages must be accurate and transparent, with a comprehensive description for an investor to make an informed decision.

It is here that the language and finance industries find themselves at a crossroads. For instance, the finance industry is being disrupted by Fintech and the increasing prevalence of language technology is bringing us ever closer to a world without language barriers. With the arrival of compliance initiatives, such as the General Data Protection Regulation in Europe, the world is tightening up its online privacy standards across the board. Moving forward, it will not be just the highly regulated industries, such as finance, legal, and life sciences, that are impacted by stringent laws around data and information, but everyone. And all these industries too will need solutions for their various pain points.

Clarity in a Constantly Shifting Regulatory Environment

In her book, Peggy has succeeded in bringing clarity and new ideas to blockchain, a challenging and fascinating subject in equal measures. And with the rise of AI, the conversation is more relevant and urgent than ever, allowing us an unprecedented insight into human thinking and intelligence, and offering a valuable glimpse into the new society that we are moving towards.

Christophe Djaouani
SDL Senior Vice President

Foreword 2

Linguistic Capability —
The Catalyst for Human Civilisation

Language and blockchain are representations of civilisational existence that have emerged from the process of human evolution and development.

Language was created out of the need for interpersonal communication; it is necessary for transmission of thoughts. Language enriched and continues to enrich the world surrounding mankind. Language is a part of culture; it is a distinctive form of cognition and expression of the world around us. As society progresses, cross-linguistic and cultural exchange arises, and translation has become the basis for realising cross-linguistic and cultural communications.

Blockchain is a revolutionary technology that transforms human collaboration models, it enables the transmission of values. Blockchain's distributed ledger system may seem like an emerging technology, however, it is in fact, the origin of the universe. With societal advancement, mankind has surpassed the stage of self-sufficiency. The exchange of labour and values amongst individuals are becoming more common, the disadvantage of coordinated efforts in productivity and value exchange in a centralised productivity framework is becoming more apparent. Blockchain is, therefore, the foundation for realising the freedom of value transmission and establishing a network of trust.

In human history, language has lasted for thousands of years; blockchain, on the other hand, is an emerging technology. They appear to be completely unrelated, but in fact, they complement and integrate mutually to boost human civilisation in the new era.

This work *When Language Meets Blockchain* offers a perspective beyond the traditional, it elevates the role of language from a general tool to a driving force with linguistic capability. In the process of accelerating globalisation, linguistic capability will be a helping hand for blockchain to play a pivotal role in cross-linguistic and cultural communications. Linguistic capability is a key concept introduced and the book further elaborates on the value of cross-linguistic capability. It also explores solutions for cross-linguistic and cultural communications in the era of blockchain, to enable the convergence of linguistic capability with blockchain technology and artificial intelligence. Just as electricity empowered mankind with energy, linguistic capability will service different domains. Not only will it enable people across the globe to reach a larger consensus, it will also support collaboration on a larger scale, with more intensity and at deeper levels. It will expand the scope and depth of mankind's cognition, making civilisations more colourful through communication and richer through mutual appreciation. All these will bring about changes in business models through changes in the way information is transmitted and will result in tremendous economic impact for the benefit of mankind.

From the perspective of blockchain, the book further demonstrated that language is more than just a tool, it is also a resource and a form of capability. The more users there are for language as a resource, the greater the differences between users, and the more it is used, the higher the value generated and capabilities produced. Language is an outcome of human civilisation, it embodies history, culture and ways of thinking of individual ethnic groups as depicted by the quote adopted from the Buddhist scriptures "one language, one world; one word, one bodhi". This means that we can see the world through a language, and we can validate the truth through a word. Blockchain is able to unlock this capability in different languages; share extensively through worldwide circulation, with exposure beyond the native language community; as well as reach a consensus and enable capabilities exchange, with direct involvement from everyone, whether as a contributor or a beneficiary. The compatibility of the natural attributes of language and blockchain will enable blockchain to document and fuel human civilisation naturally.

With language as basis and technology as enabler, the author's perspective on how the language services industry may adapt to the times by embracing blockchain technology for industrial transformation, is both forward-looking and value enhancing.

In this book, profound rules are made simple, there is minimal elaboration in the conclusion, however, the key points in each chapter are well explained; without excessive argumentation, all reasoning has been skilfully integrated into a simple story.

Language and blockchain, well integrated, will drive advancement in civilisation.

He Enpei
Founder and CEO
Transn Technology Co., Ltd

Foreword 3
The Token Economy and Language Services

Over the years, we have been pondering if blockchain possesses any commercial value and how it can be empowered with capabilities applicable to all trades and industries. Blockchain is essentially a "digital data-distributed ledger". This technology could in the long run reshape the rules of society and business networks. However, the implementation comes with great difficulties. Besides being unable to keep up with the advancement of technology infrastructure, it is also disruptive to the existing work order of current social and business networks, as well as human lives. Therefore, the adaptation has to be done slowly.

Teacher Yuan Dao and I were among the first to shift our attention to the organisational and collaborative models of bitcoin, Ethereum, and other internet communities. We discovered that among them, tokens and a set of transparent algorithmic rules surrounding the allocation and circulation of tokens have major and practical commercial significance. Therefore, at the end of 2017, we proposed that the "token economy" will be the main direction for blockchain application.

The token economy is about the creation of values through a set of tokens that are issued and circulated on the blockchain and regulated by open and transparent algorithmic rules (smart contracts) and incentive systems so as to organise large-scale community collaboration on the internet.

Nevertheless, the token economy is not applicable for all domains, they must fulfil the following basic conditions:

1. Be an activity that creates value. Essentially, before the token economy can gather millions of people into collaboration, the primary motive must be to create value, whether to generate profits for businesses or the creation of conceptual products through broad consensus, similar to Bitcoin.
2. Embody free will and choice. In organised collaboration within an internet community, the majority of members are free willed individuals and most collaborative activities are freely traded and exchanged.
3. There is a direct correlation between the size of the community population and the level of collaboration. The larger the scale of collaboration, the higher the intensity and level of collaboration and the more efficient the value created.

The above three conditions may not be fulfilled in all domains. The third condition, in particular, is not a characteristic of many collaborative activities. Take the example of core technology research and development and its breakthrough, efficiency is not boosted by the number of people involved. A motley crew of people around a scientist will only reduce efficiency. Which then are the areas that will fit this profile? Telecommunications networks, social media marketing, advertising, and finance etc. are industries that have the so-called Metcalfe's Law characteristics and are known to meet all three conditions, this makes them more suitable for the token economy.

On the basis of these three prerequisites, there is a problem concerning the design of the token incentive system. The entire goal of the design for the token incentive system is to reduce transaction costs, increase transaction efficiency, and to promote the magnitude, strength and frequency of community collaborations.

This is a simple logic, when a project attracts a high rate of participation and the combined efforts contribute to high earning capacity, we will then set up an incentive system to attract influx of involvement where everyone can work together to generate higher value. While others may adopt traditional models to set up an entity, their enormous efforts would only be able to garner interest from hundreds or thousands. The token economy on the other hand, with the use of tokens and smart contracts, could possibly gather thousands, tens of thousands or even millions to join in the collaboration, this is true competitive advantage. Basically, this is about how one can make the best out of the token economy and its incentive system as tools and allow the "invisible hand" to assist in gathering an internet community to work together to think bigger and achieve more.

Before I read Dr Peng Zhihong's book, it did not occur to me that language services can be linked to both blockchain and the token economy framework. However, I have gained new insights through its vivid storytelling and the lucid and concise theoretical exposition. Indeed, language and blockchain have certain structural similarities and the language services sector could very well fulfil the three conditions I mentioned. The use of the token economy to stimulate language services, particularly in the translation services community, through a reasonable token reward scheme to create a high value concept product is indeed a fascinating idea and I believe, highly achievable.

There is no doubt that everything needs to be tested and be put into practice. I have seen initial successes and embryonic forms of new project models in many industries and hope to see Dr Peng achieving pioneering success in the integration of language services and the token economy.

Meng Yan
*Vice President of Technology & Academy,
Chinese Institute of Digital Assets
Founding Partner of Ruixin Capital
Initiator of Token Economy in China*

Preface

Blockchain is an emerging technology as well as an ideology. It is a new species and the mother lode for new species. It allows participants who are strangers with no trusting relationships to associate and collaborate because of economic interests.

Regardless of the field in which blockchain is applied, it will ultimately require human involvement. Human collaboration requires communication, and communication cannot be done without language. Blockchain was designed to be "decentralised", but language groups formed their own centres. If the language barrier is not broken, the blockchain application will essentially still be circulating within, but not across individual language groups, thus making it polycentric and not truly "decentralised".

The internet makes it possible for information from around the world to be delivered easily to everyone's computer. However, such information exchange is predominantly performed in one's mother tongue and/or first language which I define as the main language a person uses daily which may not necessarily be his/her native language. Thus, a great deal of information in other languages, although available, is largely inaccessible. Due to language barriers, people are blind to the vast array of information that comes in other languages. The information in the mother tongue/first language is the only valid information for them. The distance between people and the world is essentially the distance between their computer screen and their eyes.

Blockchain technology is an essential part of the internet of value. If the language barrier is not broken, it will be difficult for people who speak different languages to communicate effectively, it will also be difficult for them to collaborate efficiently. Thus, the transfer and exchange of value will not be possible, and the power of blockchain will be reduced significantly. Therefore, blockchain needs language as support and breaking the language barrier is imperative in the blockchain era.

The conversion of information between different languages, commonly known as translation, has been a major problem that has bothered people for thousands of years. Even after several industrial revolutions, the industry has not changed fundamentally and has so far remained a workshop-style industry. Companies that offer translation services are typically intermediaries, and typically, 80% of these companies outsource more than 80% of their work to part-time translators. Due to the diversity of language expressions and cultural richness, it is difficult to measure and control the quality of translation, and it is difficult to reflect and measure the value of the translator as a producer of creative work. Moreover, big data is fragmented and difficult to produce on a large-scale basis, and more than 90% of the information flow still takes place within the respective native language circles.

Tokens are the soul of blockchain. With a token, a translator's capability can be quantified. Quantification is the foundation of order, the extent to which a translator can be quantified in all aspects will provide a firm basis for order; large-scale and flexible collaboration can then take place. The resulting big data can be contributed to artificial intelligence to allow the aggregation of global language resources, both human and machine, and the generation of powerful language conversion capabilities, i.e., cross-linguistic capabilities. Language capabilities empower all trades and industries. Breaking language barriers to enable global, barrier-free communication will transform existing communication and business models, bringing a new world to our work and lives, one that is free from language barriers.

Different languages reflect different ways of thought, and if the barriers to language conversion are broken, the amount of information that we can have access to will increase significantly and the thinking modes of different languages will be more fully demonstrated. We will have more channels for transmission of ideas and have opportunities to develop stronger cognitive abilities. We will also be able to experience the world in more ways than one, hopefully, our perspectives will then be broadened and we can become wiser.

Language is the shared wealth of humanity. In fact, language carries culture. Each language condenses the worldview of its users and is a symbol of their community. Different languages reflect different ways of perceiving the world, each language encapsulates the rules, traditions and beliefs of its community of users; when a language becomes extinct, a part of human civilisation disappears forever. There are more than five thousand languages in the world today, but only a dozen is actually spoken, some by only a few thousand or even a few hundred people, and the vast majority of languages are on the verge of extinction. This is impossible to salvage with only a limited number of language workers. But the birth of blockchain may very well enable conservation and impartation of these languages and cultures.

It is evident, even undeniable that new technologies and achievements that affect the progress of mankind have increasingly been accomplished through teamwork instead of individual creativity. Team members are predominantly from the same language group, even if they are from different language groups, they are capable of communicating with each other in a common language, or they would not be able to work together to achieve their goals. If the language barrier is broken, flexible cooperation between different language groups on a global scale will be possible, and new technologies will emerge at an unprecedented pace, accelerating the progress of human civilisation.

The natural fit between blockchain and language lies in the fact that the global value exchange on blockchain requires language to support it, as well as enable it to reach its full potential. Language, on the other hand, also needs the support of blockchain to show its worth in preserving human civilisation and conveying information.

Why is blockchain and language a perfect fit rather than a simple union? "Cross-Linguistic Capability" is the love child of blockchain and language, how will it be generated and how will it be of value? What sort of a new world will be built after language empowers all trades and industries? Each chapter of this book begins with a story and is followed by a summary. It is structured in a way that allows for easy reading and perception of the key points.

The protagonist is Peggy, a graduate with a master's degree in translation who moved to Singapore to work in a translation services company. In this multiracial and multicultural country, she became fascinated by the infinite wonders of language, but at the same time, also disturbed by the backwardness of the translation services industry, which led her to embark upon an extensive reflection and exploration on language. At a blockchain conference, Peggy, who was the interpreter, met her childhood friend Henry, who was the keynote speaker, and they complemented each other's knowledge on language and blockchain. During their lively discussions, they discovered that blockchain and language were such a natural fit and in fact, mutually required — to aid in each other's accomplishments and maximise each other's value. They were convinced that language would not only be the most successful application on the blockchain, but would also create a whole new world. They felt a deep sense of commitment to a sacred mission and were thus inspired to start a business together to build a better future.

Introduction

Before we begin to explore the relationship between language and blockchain, let us first step into the respective worlds of language and blockchain. We use language every day at high frequency. Language is indispensable throughout life and it is also a unique human ability.

Man, being one of the many species on earth, is not as strong as an elephant, not as agile as a monkey, not as fast as a leopard; man does not have a tiger's strong teeth, a dog's keen sense of smell, an eagle's sharp eyesight, or a bat's keen hearing. But man has evolved to stand out from the rest of the species to become the most dominant force on earth. This is because human beings are born with a special ability — the ability to create and use language.

Human can quickly use language to transmit information in a crowd, create the same cognitive image in a group of strangers and even elicit strong emotional resonance. This allows individuals who do not know each other to spontaneously organise themselves for a common goal, to divide tasks and collaborate, to bring their own views, values and ideas into play, and to form an incredible force to achieve seemingly unattainable goals together.

The charm of a country's culture and the cohesion of a nation are expressed and transmitted mainly through language. Language is distinguished based on fundamentals, global context, social forms, and universality. Language is a national symbol, and it underpins the power of a country. We can go beyond conventional linguistic perceptions to look at language from varying perspectives.

We can view language as an operating system. Each of us acquired a certain language from the environment in which we were raised, it is equivalent to being fitted with this operating system. Language and culture are inextricably linked: as people acquire a language, they simultaneously embrace the culture that is embedded in it and its way of viewing the world. Regardless of the operating system that is installed in the human brain, that is, regardless of the language acquired, all languages share some basic characteristics.

Language is an agreement; it is a consensus. Through the acquisition of language, people establish a common understanding of both the objective and the subjective world. This is how we can communicate and collaborate. When we talk about a cloud, a tree, a mountain, we are presented with the same object and image in our minds.

Ideas that are unseen and untouchable are also felt and transmitted through language, giving rise to common perceptions and even shared emotions. Language is an accepted practice of expression that has been developed over time and is accepted and used by the members of a linguistic community. Some of the common words or phrases used in our daily living that are culturally understood may mean differently to people from other cultures. For example, when we say an item "costs an arm and a leg", it does not mean paying for something with an arm and a leg literally. In fact, it is an idiom to indicate that something might be overly priced. Regardless of whether this expression is scientific, people agreed and accepted it, and so it continues to be used today.

Language development is the result of new consensus reached by a linguistic community. Languages evolve, not as a result of authoritative bodies setting and imposing requirements but due to a certain level of psychological approval by the linguistic community for spontaneous dissemination, use and accumulation. For a long time, "vermicelli (粉丝 fěn sī)" has been known among Mandarin speakers as a type of noodles made from starch. Subsequently, people who show admiration for celebrities, sport, etc. became known as "fans" and it was transliterated to "粉丝 fěn sī" in Mandarin. The meaning of "粉丝" continues to expand to include people who are interested in a myriad of activities and topics, such as fans of dance and Disney, as well as online supporters for Chinese communication platforms like Weibo and Baidu Tieba. Corresponding to the development of the meaning of "fans" in English, "粉丝" has been given a new meaning by the members of the Mandarin language community. When a linguistic community reaches a certain level of acceptance of an expression, it will spread quickly and be used extensively to form a new consensus. This is a natural process in which everyone in the language community is both a participant and a witness.

Language records history. People record the various phases of history with words from different perspectives; we can also find historical footprints in language. The vital aspects of social life that change constantly are naturally reflected in language. The keyword of the year is a mirror that reflects the current state of social life, the annual keywords of the last ten or twenty years could very well outline the general trajectory of society's development over this period.

Language is an open system; it is available to all of us. Regardless of social status or wealth, a baby can lie in its mother's arms to learn to speak, acquire vocabulary and understand sentence structures. Language is in everyone's mind, it can be made accessible to everyone equally, and it is the common heritage of humanity.

Language is a resource that becomes more valuable when used more frequently. Language resources are not exhausted or depleted by increased usage leading to competition. Rather, every language community encourages people from other countries or races to learn its language, the more a language is spoken globally and the more widely it is used, the higher its value.

Language is established through its natural attributes such as popular usage, consensual development, historical traces, and being an open system. These allow the language to develop in a self-driven and continuous manner. Members of a language community can communicate effectively with one another, express ideas, understand one another and collaborate to create value.

Blockchain is a buzzword and a trend that has been receiving a high level of attention. It is becoming clear that blockchain, as the infrastructure for the next generation of the internet, will lead to tremendous technological innovations and industrial transformations around the world.

Blockchain is a technology that expresses system ontology, i.e., systematic forms are expressed directly through technical means without any proxy. Arguably, blockchain is a technology for processing complex information to reduce transaction costs.

Blockchain is powerful because it has some fundamental characteristics.

Blockchain is "decentralised". "Decentralisation", the opposite of centralisation, is the removal of the advantage enjoyed by the central node of centralisation. In a "decentralised" blockchain system, in terms of data possession, the data centre or data management centre in the original system will be removed. In terms of business process, with the realisation of data sharing and the reconstruction of business process, the former centralised business links and nodes that are no longer needed will also be removed.

Blockchain is autonomous. Blockchain allows multiple participants and polycentric systems to follow publicly available algorithms and rules. It operates based on an automatic consensus mechanism that allows all nodes in the system to exchange, record and update data freely and securely in an environment that does not need a trusted central authority, therefore, no human intervention whatsoever.

Blockchain is tamper-proof. Blockchain consolidates the data for each time period sequentially by means of joint bookkeeping of multiple nodes in the network, and forms a single traceable, non-tamperable block of data that is connected and recorded in the chain, much like a complete record of history as time moves on.

Blockchain is a form of shared distributed ledger technology. It is an immutable, time-ordered cryptographic ledger database with a unified consensus mechanism that is jointly maintained by multiple nodes.

Blockchain is an open system. Apart from the fact that the private information of the parties to the transaction is encrypted, blockchain's data is open to everyone, anyone will be able to inquire about blockchain data and use it for relevant applications through a public interface, with a high degree of transparency in the entire system.

The characteristics of blockchain: decentralised, distributed, non-tamperable, consensus and openness allow for the aggregation of data scattered around the world through the invisible hand of the token, and can thus lead to the evolution of autonomous artificial intelligence of all sorts.

Language is the product of human civilisation, the carrier of civilisation from one generation to the next. It is also a fundamental ability of human beings to relate to each other and to organise ourselves to dominate over other species on earth.

All scientific achievements can be understood as the result of human collaboration with previous generations through language.

It is also language that enables human cognition and allows thoughts within the brain to be expressed beyond the brain, by individuals to groups. Blockchain differs from other innovations in the history of technology. Historically, technological innovations have been associated with increasing productivity, whereas blockchain is about revolutionising production relationships and changing the model of collaborative exchange and distribution of benefits among people.

Language and blockchain seem to have no intersection, yet they are bewilderingly similar in a certain way. Can language and blockchain be on the same frequency and resonate with each other sufficiently to ignite sparks? Please follow us on our exploratory journey...

———— Chapter 1 ————

To Know Macro from Micro

Innate Similarities Between Language and Blockchain

Like many others before her, Peggy had left China to pursue a career overseas. A love for languages had led her to pursue a master's degree in translation. After graduation, she sought employment in multilingual and multicultural Singapore and was offered a job with a translation services company. As she began her new life in Singapore, Peggy was excited to observe and experience the language culture in Singapore. At the same time, she also found herself missing her life back home. She continued to read widely and realised that she was able to observe in real life, many of the language characteristics described in the books she had read. Stimulated by a common language, our brains process and churn out similar images and models. Language is a consensus; it is not controlled by any centralised body. Language is "decentralised"; it has a distributed storage system. Language is an open system, individuals have complete freedom of usage of any word or phrase. Language creates and develops within a community, every language group is an autonomous community.

1   Language is a consensus.
2   Language is "decentralised", a distributed storage system.

3   Language is an open system.
4   Language development is the result of community autonomy.

***

As the cabin lights dimmed, Peggy closed her book, switched off her reading lights, adjusted her blanket and pillow and put on an eye mask; she was ready to sleep. But the turbulence did not allow her to do so. Instead, imagery of the Tower of Babel described in her book began to take shape in her mind.

A congregation of men speaking the same language, the builders had a common desire for mankind to never suffer from a flood again by building a tower, tall enough to reach the heavens. With this goal in mind, a united human race set out to work systematically with bricks and tar, striving to build a glorious tower to soar into the heavens and connect directly with or even challenge god himself.

But as the story goes, this act was against the will of god who had instructed the people to worship him and spread out across the earth, rather than congregate and build to make a name for themselves. And so god confounded human language which broke the unity of the people and separated them from one another. The human race was thus scattered and construction of the Tower of Babel abandoned. In her dreamy state, Peggy could almost reach out and touch the incomplete Tower of Babel, she saw the originally joyous group of people scattering in frustration as a result of the language barriers that had been so suddenly erected between them.

The cabin lights flickered on, the plane began its descent.

Looking out of the cabin window, the island of Singapore shone from afar like a brightly coloured gem on a piece of black silk. As the plane approached the terminal, appearing in front of Peggy was a sea of lights upon infrastructure, splendid and orderly, glittering in the dark.

The plane touched down at Changi Airport Terminal 2. Peggy had heard of its good reputation, still, she was stunned by the beautiful airport. Stepping onto the clean and soft carpeted floors, she followed the human traffic into the arrival hall. There, she was greeted by the themed flower displays of sunflowers and orchids; inadvertently, her footsteps slowed. The unique landscape of flowers was rich, varied, and charming. Peggy was mesmerised but before she knew it, she had cleared the immigration check and her baggage was waiting.

She stepped out of the airport terminal and was immediately assaulted by the hot and humid air typical of tropical Singapore. The night was bright and clear, and with the moon shining in the sky, it was especially enchanting. There were many taxis waiting to pick up passengers and in no time, her heavy luggage was swiftly loaded into the clean and tidy boot of a taxi.

On the way to the apartment, Peggy saw that the roads were neatly lined with trees and bushes. The scenery flew past Peggy's vision like whirlwind along the way, relics of World War II and together with historical monuments told the story of Singapore's soaring history.

> The same words "小姐 xiǎo jiě" used in different places have different connotations. In China, unlike Singapore, "小姐 xiǎo jiě" has a negative connotation. Instead, the more common way of addressing a lady who is a stranger is "beauty (美女 měi nǔ)".

Immersed in a rich modern urban atmosphere, Singapore also has its arts and cultural flavours. Peggy was deeply attracted by all that she saw, Singapore had displayed its unique charm to visitors, on first contact.

Full of curiosity, Peggy was taking everything in quietly when her driver suddenly asked, "Young lady (小姐 xiǎo jiě), where are you from?"

"China!" Peggy paused for a moment before she replied. She glanced at the rear-view mirror to take a closer look at the driver.

He was a middle-aged man in his late fifties or early sixties, with dark coloured skin and a friendly smile on his face.

"I am right! I knew you were from China. Beijing or Shanghai?" asked the driver.

"China is huge. I am from Hangzhou, Jiangxi Hangzhou," Peggy replied proudly.

"Hangzhou? Where the West Lake is located? Where Xu Xian and Bai Niangzi (characters from the Chinese legend Madame White Snake) lived?" The taxi driver seemed familiar with China and Chinese culture.

"You are correct. However, that is just a romantic Chinese folktale."

"I have seen the West Lake from internet websites, beautiful indeed! But I have not been to Hangzhou, I would like to visit if I have the chance to."

Hearing praises about her hometown from a stranger, Peggy replied with a smile, quoting a Chinese saying, "Up above, there is heaven, down below, there is Suzhou and Hangzhou (上有天堂下有苏杭 shàng yǒu tiān táng xià yǒu sū háng). You will be very welcomed in Hangzhou."

The driver replied by quoting another famous Chinese saying, "Different places cultivate different people (一方水土养一方人 yī fāng shuǐ tǔ yǎng yī fāng rén), ladies from Suzhou are beauties too." Before Peggy could respond, the driver continued, "Is this your first trip to Singapore? I see that you are not heading to a hotel, judging from the baggage, it does not look like you are on a tour. Are you here to study or work?"

Peggy replied, "I am here to work for a translation services company."

"Translation services company…what is there to be translated at the translation services company? Singaporeans are bilingual due to our education system," the driver looked at Peggy in bewilderment.

"Bilingual education for all?" It was Peggy's turn to be puzzled.

"Indeed, everyone knows English, English is the language of business in Singapore. Besides English, we also speak our mother tongue language, the Malays speak Bahasa Melayu, the Chinese speak Mandarin and the Indians speak mainly Tamil or Hindi…" the driver explained.

"I knew before I came that there are four official languages in Singapore," Peggy started racking her brain for the information she had gathered on Singapore prior to her trip.

"Indeed. However, this was implemented by the government only after Singapore gained independence in 1965. In Singapore, although the official business language is English, many people, including non-Chinese, can speak Mandarin too. Afterall, the Chinese make up the majority of the population, about 77%," the driver clearly knew his figures when he spoke.

Seeing that the driver was already warmed up for further conversation, Peggy initiated a question, "Uncle, don't mind me asking, but why are you still driving at this age?"

"Because I need to put food on the table. Besides, Singapore is small, unlike China." The driver laughed, seemingly hapless.

"Do you not have any pension?" Peggy was curious.

"I have CPF,[1] every month I will get a small amount of my CPF from the government, however, to solely depend on the CPF is not enough, I have to plan for a rainy day. While I am still mobile and able to drive, I should continue to work and accumulate savings. I cannot pin my hopes on my children for survival, life is not easy for them as well," the driver replied, in a matter-of-fact manner.

"So how has economic development in Singapore been for the last few years?" Peggy was keen to hear a local's perspective.

> Language reflects life in a society.

"Singapore is a little red dot, incomparable to China. Everyone lives with apprehension and caution. You will see that Singaporeans are working very hard," the driver commented, much like a social critic.

Peggy had done a fair bit of "homework" before her relocation to Singapore, she had read that despite Mandarin being widely spoken in Singapore, from the elites to ordinary working-class folks, only a few actually possessed a high level of proficiency in the language. Peggy was amazed by how articulate the taxi driver was through his use of Chinese idioms, but she held herself back from further questioning since it was their first and probably last meeting.

Before long, Peggy arrived at her destination. She paid and thanked the driver, holding on to her bulky luggage and aided by the GPS on her mobile phone, she located the HDB[2] apartment unit which she had rented online. There are no restrictions for foreigners on housing rental in Singapore, it can be done by engaging a

---

[1] The Central Provident Fund also known as CPF is a compulsory comprehensive savings plan for working Singaporeans and permanent residents, primarily to fund their retirement, healthcare and housing needs.
[2] Public housing from the Housing and Development Board (HDB).

professional property agent or by exploring the real estate listings in newspapers or on websites.

Cost effectiveness and comfort are often part of the consideration factors for renters, and in these aspects, the HDB apartment is an ideal choice. These are public housing subsidised by the Singapore government and they are found all over Singapore, well-equipped with amenities and well-connected to the public transport system.

In Singapore, 80% of the population resides in HDB flats, HDB dwellers comprise Singaporeans, permanent residents and foreigners like Peggy. The difference is that Singaporeans are given housing grants to buy a leasehold HDB apartment and acquire property rights, whereas foreigners can only rent a housing unit without enjoying any form of subsidy.

Rental costs for HDB apartments vary according to location, remaining lease and furnishings, as well as the flat types. Peggy had chosen a three-room HDB apartment with two bedrooms of different sizes, a living room, a kitchen and a toilet.

Living under the same roof were study mama[3] (陪读妈妈 péi dú mā mā) Doreen and her daughter who was studying in a primary school. When Peggy was deciding on lodging matters, she had considered the fact that she liked the company of children and that it would be a safer option to co-rent with another female tenant. She had also considered the location before settling on her final choice of accommodation.

Just as she stepped out of the elevator and approached the flat, Peggy remembered that she had not contacted her parents yet, she quickly sent a WeChat message to her parents, "Dad, Mum, I had

---

[3] Study mamas are foreign women who accompany their children to Singapore while their offspring receive primary- and secondary-level education. Most of the study mamas are from mainland China.

a smooth journey and have arrived at my place of accommodation in Singapore. All is well, do not worry." She pressed the doorbell.

After a couple of rings, the door opened. Doreen looked at Peggy with her heavy luggage and knew who she was immediately. She welcomed Peggy into the house and helped her with the luggage. "You are here, how was your journey? Was it smooth?"

A pot of brightly coloured orchids and an open book were on the living room table. Pots of green plants sat upon the windowsill, the windows were wide opened and their leaves rustled in the gentle breeze.

Looking around, Peggy saw that it was a modest-sized apartment. However, thanks to Doreen, the place was neat and cosy with furnishings like those in China. That gave Peggy a feeling of home.

"Thank you, Aunt Doreen. It was a smooth journey."

"Did you take a taxi?"

"Yes, the driver was friendly and welcoming, we had a good chat on the way here."

"Then you must have seen Singapore's night scenery, how did you find it?"

"I feel that Singapore is very beautiful and clean, it is also modernised, at least on the surface it looks as good as I had imagined. I will explore the rest of it slowly," Peggy replied as she put her bag on the sofa.

"I believe Singapore will definitely live up to your expectations."

"I really am looking forward to it."

Amidst their conversation, a young girl walked out from the master bedroom. She had fair skin and her hair was tied up in a ponytail, casually clad in a t-shirt and shorts, she seemed a little shy as she blinked her big eyes.

"This is my daughter, Candice. Candice, say hello to sister Peggy."

"Hello sister Peggy," the young girl whispered shyly.

"She has just started Primary Three. After she completed pre-school back home, I brought her to Singapore. Our children face keen competition in schools today, since it was within our capabilities and for the sake of the child, I made the harsh decision to quit my job and brought her here to receive a bilingual education. My husband and I really hope that she does not follow her parents' path. We studied for more than a decade only to be dumbfounded when it comes to the English language." Peggy noticed that Doreen's eyes displayed resentment but also perseverance as she spoke.

> The economic value of language.

"On the way here, the taxi driver told me a little about the bilingual education system in Singapore," Peggy replied simply.

"Oh yes! Environment is a very important factor for learning language. When I was studying in the university with my husband, we put in great effort but still did not do well enough for English. However, put the child in an English-speaking environment and they pick up the language fast," Aunt Doreen began to smile.

"Yes, and Singapore has a system with good teaching methods and curriculum," Peggy saw the chance to bring the conversation to more neutral ground.

"Yes, it is also near China which makes it convenient to go back home in just a few hours. Besides, the public security system is good, with just me and my daughter here in Singapore, her father will have peace of mind too," Doreen's voice took on a more relaxed tone.

"Uncle did not come to Singapore together with you?" Peggy asked.

"He has never been here, what will we live on if he comes here with us?" Doreen smiled, "He stayed in Qingdao to make a living."

"What does Uncle do for a living?" Peggy queried.

"He is a businessman. In doing business, connections are important. He is a stranger to Singapore and not fluent in English. He is in a better position to utilise his skills and showcase his abilities in the familiar environment of China. With a stable income, he can support our life and learning here."

Doreen continued, "You mentioned on WeChat that you are a master's degree graduate who will be working in Singapore. What exactly do you do?"

"I majored in translation. I will be working for a translation services company in Singapore as a project manager. I planned for an early arrival with the intention to familiarise myself with the environment before reporting for work at the company," Peggy did a brief introduction of herself.

"Generally, it seems that girls are more suitable than boys to do language studies," Aunt Doreen remarked on a common feature of language learning in colleges and universities.

"Hah! That does seem to be the case, it was obvious that the girls outnumbered the boys in our translation classes," Peggy affirmed right away.

Peggy had graduated from a top university in Wuhan, under the sponsorship of Project 985.[4] As an undergraduate, she had

---

[4] Project 985 was a Chinese government project to promote the development and reputation of the Chinese higher education system by founding world-class universities in the 21st century.

majored in mechanical engineering, it was a popular field with a high demand for graduates and Peggy had thought that she would have good job prospects. However, as she progressed through her course, Peggy realised that she was not particularly enthusiastic about the field of mechanical engineering. Whilst she did not hate it, she could not say that she liked it, and deep down, she did not want to compromise and settle for a job that she did not actually like. Fortuitously perhaps, in her second year of studies, Peggy joined a student club for language activities. Her experience at the club developed her interest in languages. As such, upon graduating from the mechanical engineering programme, she chose to pursue a master's degree in translation at the same university. The learning journey for the master's degree led her to develop appreciation for the profundity and beauty of languages. Hence, she decided that she wanted to work in a language-related field. Naturally, the multicultural and multilingual city of Singapore became an ideal place for Peggy to begin her career. After several attempts, a translation services company in Singapore managed to secure a work permit for her.

Doreen on the other hand, hailed from Qingdao, Shandong province in China. Doreen and her husband had graduated from the local university and she had originally been employed by a law firm in China. However, she had given up her job to accompany her daughter in Singapore.

The economic value of language.

Besides the legal knowledge which she had acquired in Mandarin, Doreen did not have any other special skills. Limited by her proficiency in English, she was not able to obtain certification to practise law or work in the legal industry in Singapore. Being unable to find any suitable employment, she could only provide Mandarin tuition lessons for children living in the same apartment block to supplement the family income.

Looking at Doreen who was only slightly younger than her mother, Peggy was suddenly filled with an indescribable feeling of warmth. Perhaps it was the older woman's warm smile and kind words. After all, when one is in a foreign land, even small acts of kindness from strangers feel extremely precious, not to mention that they would both be living under the same roof in the days to come.

"Oh yes, Aunt Doreen, while in the taxi, I noticed that the taxi driver was rather fluent in Mandarin, he used several Chinese idioms effortlessly in conversation, such as 'preparing for the rainy season' (未雨绸缪 wèi yǔ chóu móu), 'trembling with fear' (战战兢兢 zhàn zhàn jīng jīng)' and 'walking on thin ice' (如履薄冰 rú lǚ bó bīng)'. Before I came to Singapore, I was under the impression that there are not many with high proficiency in Mandarin," Peggy remarked.

"This is not surprising. In Singapore, these few idioms that you highlighted are in fact commonly used phrases known by many people and they are part of the examinable phrases for the PSLE.[5] The land area of Singapore is only one twentieth that of Beijing; cramped into this small yet metropolitan island nation, everyone feels stressed out, afraid of losing out and falling behind. As such, life in Singapore is very fast paced, people speak and do things carefully but also directly."

"This reminds me of a lesson I had in school where the teacher told us that language is, on a certain level, the epitome of a society, it reflects its spirit as well as habits and customs, it is true then. Due to Singapore's small size as a country, the locals are used to being prudent and vigilant in times of peace and stability which

---

[5] The Primary School Leaving Examination (PSLE) is a national examination in Singapore administered by the Ministry of Education and taken by all students near the end of their sixth year in primary school before they move on to secondary school. The examination tests a student's proficiency in the English language, their respective mother tongue language, mathematics and science.

leads to higher frequency in the use of these particular phrases," Peggy immediately recalled the knowledge she had gleaned from her education.

"You have summarised it very well, and injected depth and flavour to even a simple observation. Well, I believe you are tired from the travelling, do some simple unpacking and have a good night's rest, you can finish the rest of the unpacking tomorrow before we go out for a walk," Doreen replied thoughtfully, concluding their conversation, just as the hands of the clock on the wall inched towards midnight.

Peggy did not feel that she had travelled a long distance. It had only been a few hours on the plane and just that morning she had eaten breakfast at home in China, yet, she was about to go to bed in a different country. Everything felt slightly surreal.

Gazing out of the window, she could still see an endless flow of cars on the road, moving forward like a wriggling and winding tape, Peggy felt a deep sense of emotion welling up in her throat: "Singapore certainly lives up to its name as a city that never sleeps." Exhausted from her long day, she fell asleep quickly.

The next day, Peggy finished unpacking while Doreen sent her daughter to school. With time on their hands afterwards, they went for a walk around the neighbourhood and Peggy was able to take good look at the exterior of the HDB apartment blocks in daylight for the first time.

HDB apartments are generally more than ten-storey high, and the apartment blocks in each cluster are painted in their own group of vivid colours. Clusters are often separated by a main road, so by standing at the side of the main road in a HDB estate, it is often possible to see blocks that are painted in different hues. The individual blocks are usually connected by sheltered walkways on the ground floor, which is basically empty public space and several buildings share a common green space that is often also outfitted with exercise equipment and playground infrastructure for children.

Peggy lived in an estate with conventionally designed HDB blocks. However, there are also blocks that have special design features, such as being circular, Y-shaped, or with sloped roofs. Every few years, based on specific requirements, residents in each cluster vote for a new colour scheme for repainting of the exterior walls and common areas, and the respective town council undertakes maintenance/improvement works to common infrastructure, e.g., staircases, elevators, corridors, lights, and so on.

If Singapore by night may be described as calm but active, by day it is bright and bustling, filled with energy and vitality. The sky is blue, the grass green, and the roads are filled with continuous traffic; but it is orderly and seldom congested. With a mere 728 square kilometres, land is especially precious, tall buildings are within sight nearly everywhere, but it is neither monotonous nor depressing because Singapore has made much effort to green the urban landscape with shade-giving foliage and contiguous green spaces. Tall trees lining the sides of roads provide shade for pedestrians. Overhead bridges with covered shelters have shrubs and flowers planted on each side, bridge piers are covered in green leaves and vines. Multi-coloured flowers bloom under the azure sky and in pockets of green. Residents can choose to avoid the noisy dusty roads and walk in shady green spaces if they so prefer.

"Singapore certainly lives up to the title of 'Garden City', it is so clean and beautiful!" Peggy could not hold back her heart-felt admiration as she took in the sights and sounds of her new neighbourhood.

A Chinese idiom says that "food is the first necessity of the people" (民以食为天 mín yǐ shí wéi tiān). Since food is a primary need, it would undoubtedly be a window to understand the customs and living habits of a community. As Doreen and Peggy strolled around and chatted, they realised before long that it was time for lunch. Doreen suggested they go to the nearby "Pasar".[6] Peggy saw that the Pasar was much like the food market back in China, however, the variety of small shops was more comprehensive. Besides selling all kinds of raw food and dried ingredients for cooking, there were also stalls selling cooked food and drinks, as well as smaller stores selling supplies of daily necessities and apparel.

Doreen and Peggy looked around until they found a free table. It had coloured stools fixed to the ground. Large ceiling fans were switched on at full blast to keep the air cool. Peggy checked out the stalls selling various types of drinks and cooked food, she noticed that there were usually two people running a stall. One was the chef while the other took charge of cashier duties, apportioning of ingredients and serving food to customers.

The air teamed with the aroma of various foods, there was a feast for the eyes at one glance: roti prata (crispy, crusty Indian pancake made of fat, flour and water), nonya kuehs (bite sized sweet dessert made by Peranakan[7] women known as nonyas), char kway teow (broad white noodles fried with dark sweet sauce, egg, bean sprouts, fish cake, cockles and Chinese sausage), Taiwanese oyster omelette, Hong Kong dim sum, satay (stick-skewered marinated meat grilled over a charcoal fire), laksa (rice noodles in spicy coconut curry gravy with shrimp, egg, chicken and cockles), bak kut teh (pork ribs served with peppery and clear

---

[6] Pasar is a term for wet market in Singapore. It is basically a market selling fresh meat, seafood and other perishable goods. In Singapore, the Mandarin word used is 巴刹 bā shā, a variation from the equivalent of 农业/菜市场 nóngyè/cài shìchǎng in China. Very often, markets in Singapore also have a hawker centre under the same roof, where affordable cooked food is sold.

[7] Peranakan is a layered term, most commonly used (but not limited) to refer to an ethnic group formed by intermarriage between south Chinese settlers and indigenous Malays in key ports along the Straits of Malacca.

soup or darker soya sauce coloured soup), Hainanese chicken rice (steamed chicken with fragrant rice cooked in chicken stock), fried carrot cake (steamed cake made of rice flour and shredded white radish that is stir-fried with sweet sauce, egg, garlic and pickled radish), fish head curry (a spicy dish comprising a huge fish head and vegetables served with rice or bread), chilli crab (hard shelled crabs cooked in thick tomato and chilli gravy) and butter prawns, to name but a few. Diners could pick and choose freely from the smorgasbord of local specialties.

As someone with more "experience", Doreen, who had been in Singapore far longer than Peggy, chose an authentic Singapore food court and recommended that Peggy should try Old Chang Kee fried food and bak kut teh. Old Chang Kee is a chain store, it can be found in most high-end shopping complex and at traditional stores, Peggy placed orders for cuttlefish on a skewer, fish balls, sotong[8] balls and curry puffs.

Peggy found the food that she tried unexpectedly tasty, not only did she have her craving for good food satisfied, but she was also able to acquaint herself with the language differences and profundity, as well as understand some of the history and cultural aspects behind the various food types.

The story started from a conversation with the service personnel of this Singapore food court.

Differing language expression due to cultural differences.

When the hot food was served, the waitress gently told Peggy, "Be careful, it is hot (烧 shāo)." Peggy was stunned for a moment and did not know how to respond. Doreen explained, "She is telling you to be careful not to be scalded (烫 tàng) by the hot food." "So that's it!" Peggy felt a little

---

[8] Sotong is the Malay word for squid.

silly for not understanding and wanted to thank the waitress but she had already left.

Peggy looked at the bowl and examined it in detail, there were two or three pieces of pork ribs with a few cloves of garlic. Sipping a spoonful of the soup, she could taste garlic, angelica, star anise, liquorice; with the addition of some slices of red chilli mixed with soya sauce, it was indeed a delicate, yet not overwhelming mixture of flavours. The soup was fragrant, and the meat was delicious.

Seeing that Peggy enjoyed the soup and rice, Aunt Doreen began to tell Peggy the story about the origins of bak kut teh. Although there were a few versions Doreen chose the most widely accepted version:

During the Ming and Qing Dynasties, the Southeast Asia region including the Malay Archipelago and the islands of the Philippines and Indonesia were known as Nanyang. From the Ming Dynasty to the Republic of China, thousands of people in Guangzhou, Fujian and other coastal areas suffered from political chaos, poverty and famine. Many people volunteered or were forced to go to Nanyang to earn a living by doing hard physical labour. These workers were very poor and could not afford to eat well, but they needed the nourishment; furthermore, their working environment led to the accumulation of 'dampness' in their bodies. Therefore, to strengthen and remove moisture from their bodies, the workers came up with the idea of cooking pork bones containing just small silvers of meat with Chinese herbal medicine as a dish.

History and culture behind the cuisine.

Subsequently, the quality of the pork ribs used for bak kut teh improved, and more ingredients were added to complement the soup dish. With bak kut teh becoming the national food, the price has also increased, but in general, it is still affordable for the general public at S$5 for a small bowl, and S$7 for a large bowl at a hawker centre.

After dinner, Peggy wanted a drink. She browsed through the menu before proceeding to place her order with the middle-aged female F&B assistant at the counter, "Ah Yi (阿姨), I want a glass of lime juice, with ice added."

"Ah Yi? Are you calling me?" The assistant smiled as she took her order, "Young lady, you must be new to Singapore. In Singapore, you can just call me Auntie."

"Auntie?" Peggy was puzzled.

"Indeed, Auntie or Uncle, in English," The assistant replied in a friendly manner.

"Auntie, Uncle..." Peggy murmured to herself as she wondered, a country's language is indeed a window of reflection for its unique characteristics. In a multicultural and multiracial country like Singapore, the collision of different languages could potentially ignite many sparks.

> Differing language expression due to cultural differences.

"Please get a straw (水草 shuǐ cǎo) from there," The assistant told Peggy as she pointed to the other side of the counter.

Peggy was baffled, she turned to Doreen in confusion and queried, "What is that?"

"In Singapore, 'shui cao' refers to drinking straws," Doreen explained to Peggy as she walked over to pick up a straw for Peggy. She consoled Peggy, "Do not worry, within a week you will pick up everything naturally."

Thereafter, Doreen took Peggy to a few more places. With everything that she encountered being novel, Peggy was able to form a more distinct impression of Singapore in just the short span of a day.

Peggy's decision to work in Singapore had to a great extent been influenced by Zenna, a teacher whom she had befriended during her days in the university. Zenna was a young female teacher, after completing her undergraduate studies in China, she went to Singapore to pursue master's and doctorate degrees. Upon graduation, she returned to China to become a teacher.

When Peggy was in her second year of the master's programme, she helped to organise an international friendship get-together at the university. It was at this event that she met Zenna; they connected with each other easily and kept in touch with each other thereafter. Before long, they had become good friends.

As a young Chinese student who returned from abroad, Zenna had shared with Peggy her experiences and knowledge gained while she was in Singapore. Gradually, Peggy became more interested in Singapore, and wanted to know even more about Singapore. Hence, she decided to work in Singapore after her graduation.

To help Peggy adapt to life in Singapore quickly, Zenna introduced her to Charles Cai, the president of a local association in Singapore. Charles invited Peggy to join his group of fellow Chinese nationals in Singapore.

The so-called local association was in fact a WeChat interaction group. On any one day, everyone would chat in the group, and activities such as meeting up for chats or sightseeing would be organised for group members. This was a way to provide emotional support for members who were living far from home. The association had a president and a vice president, but their roles were mainly as organisers of activities.

A few days after Peggy had arrived in Singapore, Charles sent an invitation to the group for a barbecue at his house. "Folks, we have not met up in nearly three months. Come to my house this Sunday for a barbecue, at the ground floor barbecue area. Just the same old place with the same old rule: potluck."

Peggy was excited when she saw the invitation and signed up for the barbecue without hesitation, but she did not know what was meant by the old rule, she decided to just introduce herself and ask, "Hello everyone, my name is Peggy. I just arrived in Singapore to start a new job. This will be my first time joining you all, what should I bring?"

"It is very casual, you can either buy some barbecue ingredients or make your own specialty dish. It is mainly for everyone to get together," Charles replied immediately.

On that Sunday morning, Peggy got up early to make a soft and fragrant chiffon cake with Doreen's electric rice cooker and set off for the condominium where Charles lived. In Singapore, only about 20% of Singaporeans live in private condominiums. As soon as Peggy arrived, she saw a smiling, plump looking security guard standing at the entrance. HDB flats do not have security guards. "Condominiums are indeed different!" Peggy thought to herself as she registered at the security guardhouse to enter.

Looking around, there were three swimming pools of different sizes between the two buildings, the water in the pools was crystal clear. The smaller children's pool was shallow, with fountains and recreational facilities, and the larger adult pools had reclining chairs and sunshades surrounding them.

The area in the condominium was surrounded by walls. On the side of the main entrance there was also a waterfall and the car park. On the other side were the leisure and entertainment areas.

Peggy moved towards the barbecue area where a few Chinese people were mingling. People streamed in, one after another, there were those who had settled in Singapore for many years just like Charles, young people who had only been in Singapore for a year or two, study mamas with children in tow…all of them brought with a variety of food, tender boiled duck with soya sauce, braised chicken claws, sweet and sour pork ribs, baked biscuits and more. All kinds of food filled the table, it was a feast that was more than enough for all present.

Joining this "big family" for the first time, Peggy naturally became the focus. She was not a natural extrovert and had not liked social gatherings very much previously, however, after being in Singapore for a few days, she had begun to miss her family and home. From time to time, Peggy felt heart-warmed by the Chinese dialects she heard from the conversations of the people around her.

"Peggy, what is your main area of studies?" Charles approached her and initiated a conversation.

"As an undergraduate, my major was mechanical engineering, but I majored in translation for my master's degree," Peggy replied.

"It would have been such a breeze to get a job in the mechanical engineering field, why did you opt to further your studies in languages?" Charles asked.

"Interest!" Peggy blurted out without thinking.

"What is so interesting about languages?"

"Oh, I love languages. Take dialects as an example, I just heard someone speak in the Hangzhou dialect, I feel so familiar and close to that person now. We have children among us at the gathering today, in Hangzhou, children are called 'Tiny Teeth' (小牙儿 xiǎo yá ér)," Peggy shared, revealing her passion for languages.

"'Tiny teeth', such an adorable way to address the children indeed," Charles' wife, Sarah remarked as she walked towards them.

> Language is an important window of reflection for local culture.

"Dialect is not only interesting, but it reflects many characteristics of a language. When I was studying in Wuhan, there was a dialect phrase, 'to start working between 5am to 7am (卯起搞 mǎo qǐ gǎo)'. It means to hold on and carry on with determination. Wuhan is a city that has experienced extreme weather conditions as well as severe natural disasters like droughts and floods. The dialect phrase reflects the indomitable and unremitting spirit of the people of Wuhan."

When Peggy started talking about language, she had so much to say, she felt she could talk forever.

Sarah exclaimed, "Yes, of course! I do know some people from Wuhan who indeed have such distinguishing characteristics. Instead of literally saying 'to start working between 5am to 7am', relating it with 'to do with an all-out effort' (铆起搞 mǎo qǐ gǎo) is more representative of the image of the Wuhan people, what better way to express the proverb 'The unique features of a local environment always give special characteristics to its inhabitants (一方水土养一方人 yì fāng shuǐ tǔ yǎng yì fāng rén)'."

Charles and Sarah were truly hospitable hosts and took pains to look after the well-being of every one of their countrymen. Soon it was time to start the fire and everyone helped with the food preparation, some placed food on skewers and grilled them on the iron racks while others marinated the meat.

"There are several ways to do a barbecue, we are doing it over an open fire with skewers. Heat is easily accumulated over an open fire and it is necessary to frequently turn the food to allow heat to spread evenly, otherwise, it will be charred on the outside and raw on the inside. Another way to barbecue with open fire is with a fork grill. A fork grill uses one or two prong sticks to fork the food which makes it easier to rotate over the fire. This method is more suitable for roasting whole chicken, duck, fish or meat in bigger pieces." Sarah explained. Peggy nodded in understanding and she worked with Sarah and a few other ladies to barbecue the food.

"Aunt Sarah, what jobs do you and Uncle have in Singapore?" Peggy asked curiously.

"I teach Mandarin at an adult learning institute in a local university. This is to cater to the needs of the society, there are people from all walks of life, regardless of age and nationality, who wish to learn Mandarin. Charles is working in a research institution and he is much like a scientist in the materials field." Sarah answered with a smile.

"Scientist? I guess Uncle Charles must be very competent in scientific research. It is not easy to identify a research direction in engineering, however, when a focal point is established, the research can progress very swiftly, simply because research methodology in engineering fields is matured and standardised. I am actually a mechanical engineering graduate, but I am not too keen to specialise in this field, so I switched to translation instead," Peggy was full of admiration.

"Oh, translation? Your current job must be related to language then?" Sarah was pleasantly surprised.

"Oh yes, I am a project manager with a translation services company. But I have not reported for work, so I am not exactly sure what it will be like," Peggy replied.

"Interest is the best motivation for a job. I chose to study English due to the prospects of this profession. Foreign languages were not as popular at the time and were also not given much attention, but knowing English has been a tool for me. Subsequently, the more I studied, the more I appreciate the profundity of languages," Sarah said in all sincerity.

"Yes, since I was young, I studied English under the examination-oriented education system. I sat for examinations like the English test band 4 and band 6 at university, but I did not feel that learning a foreign language was fun. It was only after I joined a language related community in school that I changed my mind. In order to learn English, I read some foreign English magazines and books. I gradually overcome the prejudiced mindset of 'Chinese is the most beautiful language' and realised that every language has its profundity. I remember I was reading an English article and came across a phrase 'juicy eyes', describing the eyes of a lady. In the Chinese language, this would probably be 'bright and watery big eyes (水汪汪的大眼睛 shuǐ wāng wāng de dà yǎn jīng)', this is a beautiful Chinese phrase too, but at that point, the phrase 'juicy eyes' touched me intensely, I found it simple and beautiful!" Peggy's eyes sparkled as she talked about her passion.

> Every language displays its unique characteristics.

"You are absolutely correct. Language is not just beautiful, acquiring proficiency in a foreign language can also provide one with a unique perspective of viewing one's native language from the angle of another language. Don't be mistaken, such words of acuity were not said by me, I heard it online from a professor of Tsinghua University. Undoubtedly, if a person's mastery of the Chinese language is not high, it will be difficult to learn a foreign language to a qualified level. Well, Tsinghua University has a long history of countless graduates who become masters well versed in both Chinese and foreign languages, so this is a very good example. For someone who studies translation, it is even more important to maintain your individual proficiency in both Chinese and the foreign language concurrently," Sarah commented while sorting the barbecued skewers.

"Indeed, translation is not just about the language, but also about the background of the culture and ways of thinking, it encompasses a great deal of knowledge. When I was an undergraduate, I had a friend who was of Xinjiang Uighur nationality. After she finished the second draft of her graduation thesis, she realised she had a problem. The structure of the Uighur language is more like English, with sentences of inverted word order. My friend had written everything in Mandarin but the sentence structure was more similar to that of her native language and thus her entire work was not so easy to read. Hence, she approached me for help," this incident came to Peggy's mind suddenly.

> Different languages view the world with different perspective.

"Indeed, a language is a way of looking at the world, it can provide a different way of thinking too," Sarah nodded.

"I will have to continue to study diligently," Peggy gave a mock sigh of resignation.

"Youngsters like you have time and energy, and you will learn quickly as long as you work hard. Oh yes, if you are keen, we can find a time for you to visit the adult learning institute where I work. It is related to your language profession, a place where people from different racial, language and cultural backgrounds gather to learn; the experience is not something you can get from reading books, Peggy. By the way, please pass the cumin and barbecue sauce!" Sarah replied, she had clearly taken a liking to Peggy.

Just then, Charles walked towards them, "Sarah, go easy on the marinate, too much salt is not healthy. Peggy, how do you feel about Singapore since you got here, have you adjusted to the environment?"

"Hello Uncle Charles, all aspects of living are very good. Aunt Doreen, who is my co-tenant, is very friendly. There is no issue of jet lag, the living environment and weather are very comfortable. The only concern I have now is about reporting to the company, I am feeling a little apprehensive as I am not sure about what the working conditions will be like," Peggy smiled as she replied.

Charles laughed, "Just address me as Charles like everyone else. Do not worry, young people should have the belief that everything can be done well if you are willing to work hard. Times are different now, children of your generation are so blessed, you just had to follow the structured education system to complete your studies in China, and you are now able to explore the world outside China while you are still in your prime, unlike us who had to suffer..."

"Uncle Charles...Oh, no, Charles, when did you come to Singapore?" Peggy stuck out her tongue, as she caught herself.

"I entered the university in 1979 and went to Belgium in 1985 where I studied for a master's degree and a doctorate in materials science. After 10 years in Belgium, I came to Singapore with my wife and children," Charles recalled.

"Charles, Charles, I can hear you from a distance, contrasting your past misery with the present generation's fortune. We have more stories to tell as the 'Old Three Grades (老三届 lǎo sān jiè)'. Talking about difficulties, we did experience difficult times. But as we look back now, it was nothing really, most of us managed to overcome the difficulties. We should understand that every generation will face a set of problems relevant to their time. It is not any easier for youngsters today." Peggy looked in the direction where the voice was coming from, it was Andrew Chen, vice president of the association.

> Language bears the imprint of time.

"Old Three grades?[9] What is the Old Three Grades?" Peggy could not understand.

"I belong to the generation of the Old Three Grades," Charles replied.

"Why?" Peggy probed.

"The 'Old Three Grades' are related to the background of our time. The 1966 to 1968 batches of middle and high school students all graduated in the same year, this created a huge crisis for employment. The six batches of students were named the 'Old Three Grades'. It is no wonder that you do not understand, this is history for you," Andrew laughed.

"Now that you mentioned it, I seem to have some impression of this term." In the spur of the moment, Peggy was enlightened.

> Language bears traces of history which cannot be tampered with.

"While this is not a phrase that is being used today, it was embedded in the minds of people of our generation. Many of the literary works that wrote about the 'educated youth (知青 zhī qīng)' at that time contained this phrase, and their work recorded and reflected the state of our lives and our mindset," Andrew seemed lost in his thoughts.

"If I have the opportunity, I would definitely read those books and find out more about your generation," Peggy was intrigued when she heard about the books.

---

[9] This is a specific group of middle school and high school students who had graduated in 1966, 1967 and 1968. Due to the commencement of the cultural revolution in China, they could not continue with their education and many were sent to work as agricultural labourers in the countryside.

"It was much harder for us to leave China then, and there were not many mainland Chinese immigrants in Singapore. We were one of the earliest batches of Chinese nationals to be here," Charles concluded.

As Charles and Andrew spoke about their past experiences, people around them also began to recall their own rationale and experiences for coming to Singapore.

"Although everyone had different starting points, identities, ages, purposes and course of events, we all ended up in Singapore. Today we are gathered here as fellow Chinese nationals, toasting each other, chatting and laughing merrily and sharing experiences and feelings, there is definitely a natural affinity amongst us." Many thoughts ran through Peggy's mind as she listened to the conversations from the people around her.

Just as Peggy was beginning to feel emotional, Sarah the chef invited everyone to eat, "The first part of the grilling is almost done, come over and help yourselves to the barbecued food, take whatever you want on the table, it is a buffet." Sarah handed Peggy a skewer with some barbecued chicken wings that were fresh from the grill, sizzling hot and gleaming with oil; they looked so tempting that Peggy could not wait and took an eager bite. "Charles, I almost forgot. Can you go upstairs and bring the sea coconut dessert which I had prepared last night from the fridge? Look at what else is good in the fridge and bring it down with you," Sarah called out to Charles for help.

> The way of expression differs for different cultural backgrounds. People in China will say a son and a daughter instead of a boy and a girl.

Sarah continued from where Charles had stopped previously, "When Charles and I were undergraduates, I was studying English. We met and fell in love and subsequently went abroad together. We have two children, a boy and a girl, they are older than you. They have worked for several years. Unfortunately, they are not home today. I will find an opportunity to introduce them to you. Young people like you all will have no problem mingling."

The aroma of the barbecued food gathered everyone to the table. As everyone ate with great relish, the aromas of the various barbecued meats and other prepared dishes filled the air.

"I say, knowing how to barbecue is really a skill. It is not healthy for the meat to be charred. Sarah was skilful enough to ensure that the meat is crisp on outside and tender on the inside. It is so delicious. Our dear Charles is indeed blessed. He married such a capable wife and can enjoy delicious food anytime! He doesn't have anything to complain about!" Everyone laughed at this comment by one of the guests.

After everyone's appetites had been satisfied, they cleaned up and adjourned to Charles's home for tea, dessert and more interaction.

Peggy took the chance to speak to some other people.

There was a little boy, Aden who was there with his mother. He looked to be the same age as Doreen's daughter Candice. Peggy observed that when Aden and his mother communicated, his speech would be peppered with one or two sentences in Shanghainese. In fact, Aden's mother, Stella often replied to him in Shanghainese.

"Stella, is Aden new to Singapore and for how long has he been here? He seems to speak Shanghainese very fluently," Peggy was curious.

"Oh no, Peggy, my husband and I are from Shanghai. We came to settle down in Singapore, our children were also born here. At home, my husband and I often speak Shanghainese and teach our children to speak the dialect as well. Language is like a tool, it will become rusty if it is not used. Although it is the dialect of my hometown, I will lose touch if I don't use it, it is better to speak more of it, and it feels heart-warming for my husband and I to hear our native dialect at home," Stella said with a smile.

"Yes, I felt fine for the last few days since my arrival in Singapore, but just now, as I was eating, I heard someone speak in the Hangzhou dialect and I was suddenly struck by a feeling of homesickness. I suddenly longed for my mother's homecooked meals. Although there are many Chinese restaurants here, I believe the taste will be very different. It is the same for dialect, it arouses certain emotions in us," Peggy said, feeling a little sentiment.

"We felt strongly about this when we first came. Language carries cultural and emotional elements, we do not want our children to forget where their roots are, so we try our best to take them back to Shanghai for a few days every year to expose them to an environment where they immersed in the Shanghai dialect," Stella nodded, agreeing with Peggy.

> Language bears emotional attachment.

"In many places, there are now fewer people who can speak dialects, especially children who have received Mandarin education in schools since childhood. In fact, I really think certain emotions can only be expressed in dialects," George joined their conversation.

> Language is an open system, people can learn any language, use words and phrases, as well as sentence structure freely.

George was a young man who had been to many countries. He could converse in simple sentences in many languages. During the course of his studies, he had lived in the United States and Germany briefly as an exchange student. He had also been to India and Japan to attend international academic conferences. He was in Singapore to work, just like Peggy, but he was not in the language industry.

Being smart and widely exposed to many countries, George shared vividly with everyone his experiences and the knowledge he had acquired while he was abroad; very soon, he became the focus of the conversation. Everyone joined in the fun and asked George to say the same few words in many languages one after another, not only did he have to change the language he was speaking, he also had to speak in the particular style or accent of the country in question. It became evident that while George had no problems switching languages, he was not very skilled in mimicking the actual accent and tone of the languages as they were spoken in different places.

> Language is an operating system. The language that is learned from young leads to specific perspectives and observations of the world around.

"Although I have been to many places and can speak a little in many languages, I have never lived abroad on a long-term basis. Therefore, I have only acquired the instrumental nature of language but have not learned the essence. In some American families, I saw Chinese children who were adopted from a young age. They spoke perfect American English. If only their voices could be heard and their faces not seen, no one would guess that they were Chinese," George sighed.

"When I was still studying, I encountered some African schoolmates who spoke fluent Chinese. Many foreign students study in China with their families. Their children are exposed to the Chinese language since childhood and they can speak Chinese fluently," a guy beside Peggy commented.

This made Peggy recall a similar story, "The university where I studied had a campus radio station that broadcasted various kinds of self-produced radio programmes. One evening while I was walking in the campus, a female host on the radio did an interview with a male student. The male student was competent and fluent in Chinese. As I continued listening, I realised that he was not a native Chinese, I was quite surprised then. Actually, I realise now that my school had quite a number of foreign students. Indeed, many could speak Mandarin well."

"Sometimes I feel that having studied our mother tongue for so many years, my Chinese is still not of the same standard as foreigners. What a shame!" a middle-aged uncle with a Singaporean Mandarin accent suddenly blurted out.

"Hahaha…" Everyone laughed.

The conversation continued, but Peggy got up and walked to the windows. Sarah saw her staring blankly at the stream of traffic on the road and walked over with half a dragon fruit for her. "A penny for your thoughts?"

"Aunt Doreen, my co-tenant, told me that Singaporeans live life at a fast pace. I have been walking around the last few days and had met some locals. I feel that people in Singapore are indeed hardworking, very motivated at least. Late in the night, there are people on the MRT[10] who have just left their workplaces. I once saw someone who looked like a teacher marking a student's homework in the MRT. I had no idea why, but looking at them makes me feel a little nervous and I do not feel 'buddha-like' (佛系 fó xì) anymore," Peggy shared openly with Sarah.

"What is this term 'Buddha-like'?" Sarah was puzzled.

---

[10] Mass Rapid Transit (MRT), the railway network in Singapore.

"Oh, it is widely used in China. I have no idea who came up with this phrase, but whether it is on the internet or in our daily lives, everyone is using it. You will be deemed behind the times if you do not know how to use this term. The term 'Buddha-like' refers to someone who feels indifferent about everything and typically it is to describe young people who do not buy into aspirational society. Young people ridicule themselves for being 'Buddha-like'. Sometimes it also signals a form of helplessness that they must lower their expectations for life altogether. However, my understanding of being 'buddha-like' is not so negative. It bears the meaning of being happy-go-lucky. Do Singaporeans not use this term?" Peggy suddenly recalled where she was.

> Language development is the result of collective choice and communication of language groups, having gone through a certain cycle of psychological stimulation.
>
> Language is autonomous.

"I have not heard these words before, maybe the term has not reached Singapore yet. The common language used in Singapore's corporate and learning environments is English, Mandarin speakers in Singapore do not get to know these popular internet slang as fast as compared to mainland China. Generally, there will be a time lag," Sarah analysed.

"However, the internet is connected to the whole world, with a device on hand, my presence will be felt in the world. Afterall, internet buzzwords know no borders," Peggy replied as she waved the mobile phone in her hand.

Sarah was amused.

"For people like us who are in our 50s and 60s, our parents are no longer around, so we don't visit our hometown as much now, and therefore, we are unable to keep up. I already knew there is a generation gap between us and you young people, this makes it even more obvious," Sarah exclaimed.

"No, no, I don't feel uncomfortable chatting with you at all, Aunt Sarah!" Peggy winked at Sarah, and seeing Sarah's doubtful expression, Peggy smiled and explained, "If I encounter someone whom I cannot connect with, every minute of the chat is a drag. It is as if I have encountered a caveman who does not know any new words, however, if due to circumstances, I have to continue with the chat, such an awkward chat situation is called 'embarrassed chat (尬聊 gà liáo)' by netizens."

"Hahaha..., this young lady here is really eloquent," Sarah clearly liked the sunny natured and witty Peggy very much.

Time flies when one is having fun, the visitors rose one after another and left after saying goodbye to Charles and Sarah.

Before Peggy left, Sarah invited Peggy to visit her workplace once more. Peggy agreed with full anticipation.

Summary:
To Know Macro from Micro

We are surrounded by language from the moment that we were born. It seems like a natural, proper, and rightful process and thus, people would feel that language is something that we know very well. But do we really understand what is language?

Human beings are born with linguistic ability but the language that one speaks depends on the environment that one grows up in. Language is like an operating system installed in the human mind from young which controls the mode of thinking and working styles. A European kid who learns Mandarin in China from young will think and speak like a Chinese person, even though he is genetically Caucasian. Vice-versa, children from China who are adopted by Americans and grow up in an American family will not have any imprints of China on them other than the genetic factors. However, for languages, they may be different, but they bear certain characteristics that are similar.

Language itself is a form of consensus. From birth, babies in their infancy are already surrounded by languages, "are you hungry?", "have you wet yourself?", "are you sleepy?" and so forth, and languages accompany the babies in their daily lives. Whether or not the baby understood, people will be interacting with them through language. This is the process where the baby will gradually learn the language and build up the connection with the material world and be moulded mentally, from a 'natural person' to a 'social man'. Language allows people to shape similar images and models in their minds. The community that speaks a common language will reach a form of consensus.

Language is a decentralised distributed storage system. Language is not released by any institution nor is it any form of compelled usage. Some examples of the latest expressions such as 'koi fish' (锦鲤 jǐn lǐ) which is a symbol of luck, 'buddha-like' (佛系 fó xì) which means to feel indifferent, and 'official announcement' (官宣 guān xuān) are popular phrases which can be applied to anyone or any situation as long as they resonate with the majority users and it will be widely disseminated. Given that the process of dissemination is spontaneous, new expressions will be established by popular usage. Every user is a node of the language community, a record keeper and a disseminator. Language is a form of group memory — even when an expression is dying out, its traces will not be erased from history. If it has been used, it not only exists extensively in all language medias, but it will also be distributed and stored in people's memory.

Language is an open system. Everyone has the freedom to learn any language in this world. Almost all countries adopt an open attitude and actively promote their own language culture. The United Kingdom set up the "British Council" in 1934, Germany established the "Goethe Institut" in 1951 and China set up "Confucius Institute" in 2004. These are the efforts by individual countries to popularise their language culture. Other countries did not have such big-scale efforts but there are policies in place in the form of subsidies to give support. The openness for language is also displayed as being liberal and transparent. Language is not owned by any organisation, group or individual; it is shared wealth, with everyone having equal rights and freedom to use every word and phrase.

Language development is the result of group autonomy. The emergence of new expressions will only be spread widely and be used frequently when they received approbation by a significant number of people in the group. This process is all spontaneous; no organised publicity is required, nor is there a need or even a possibility of compelled usage if the expression is in line with the style of the group. This is an objective process of group decision-making and implementation. Language development and updating iteration of vocabulary is completed in this process of group autonomy.

The creation of a new technology will not bring about changes in all domains. Whether the technology can be applied effectively in a particular domain to bring about changes is related to the compatibility between the natural characteristics of that field and the characteristics of the technology. The higher the compatibility, the greater the change. The creation of mechanisation brought about fundamental change in the cultivation and harvesting of wheat and rice on the plains. But it will not be possible to achieve the same for harvesting tea though it is also an agricultural product.

Language and blockchain bear great similarities in their genetic characteristics, and they resonate at the same frequency, effortlessly.

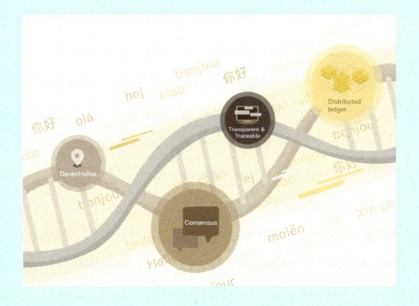

Note

———— Chapter 2 ————

A Sudden Revelation

Everyone Lives Within His Own Language Chain

The translation services company where Peggy assumed her position as a project manager was in a remote location in an industrial estate. The office was outmoded and small in scale, a sharp contrast to the comprehensive and aesthetically pleasing company website. Though disappointed, Peggy was self-motivated and able to fulfil her job assignments independently. Spending her spare time to visit the Adult Learning Institution where Sarah taught, Peggy was able to reflect on her experience from attending Sarah's courses on "Introduction to Mandarin" and "Commercial Translation", which led her to new realisations about the profundity of languages.

Each and every one of us lives within our own language chain. Each language has its own phonetic, lexical and grammatical system to define civilisation in its own way, forming an independent entity. Different languages provide different ways to perceive the world. The world is flat in terms of commerce where all competitors have an equal opportunity, yet it is not flat in terms of language communication because different languages are like intangible nets, dividing the world into different segments.

1 Everyone is a node on the language chain.
2 Everyone can participate in the building of common understanding.
3 A different language represents a different public chain.
4 Everyone can receive, generate and produce output for language data.

***

Upon deciding to search for a job in Singapore, Peggy began to do extensive research on possible job opportunities for master's degree graduates in translation. At the same time, she also tried to find out more about life and working conditions in Singapore from Zenna.

When Peggy was an undergraduate, she had attended a forum and learnt from an outstanding female instructor that there were basically three ways to decide on a career: Firstly, be company oriented and identify a stellar company to work for. Secondly, be industry oriented and identify a target industry that suits one's individual interest. Lastly, be career oriented and identify a target profession based on individual career planning.

The batch of students who were studying translation together with Peggy all took different career paths after graduation. Some decided to join the management teams of internet companies to give full play to their bilingual advantage, some were constantly travelling around the world as employees of foreign trade companies, some opted to become teachers and of course, there were also those who chose to be freelancers. Translation services companies are usually small-scale and in general, the job does not pay well, thus not many of Peggy's schoolmates chose to work for companies specialising in translation services.

However, Peggy was an exception. She felt that the translation profession was the closest to her field of study; although it would not generate great wealth, it would allow her to deal with languages, which was to her liking. Peggy also desired to see the world outside of China, therefore, she decided to find work in Singapore.

Finding the right job is like finding the right spouse. After a few interviews conducted through videoconference, Peggy received job offers from three companies and eventually accepted the offer from the company she was to work for, after much deliberation. There were many reasons that contributed to Peggy's decision. Initially, it was a very trivial detail that attracted Peggy — the website of the company was aesthetically pleasing and user-friendly. If resumes are the facades of job seekers, then corporate websites make or break the first impressions of companies. The official website of this company not only looked good, but everything from information search to submission of resume and acceptance of interview, could be smoothly executed, making a good first impression on Peggy.

David, the boss of the company, was a Chinese immigrant. He personally conducted the interview with Peggy. David was impressed by her and Peggy too had a good impression of this native Chinese employer who had a very respectable and gracious demeanour, so she decided to accept his offer.

On her first day of work, Peggy changed into a semi-formal outfit which she had specially prepared, put on high heels, light makeup and tied up her hair neatly.

Peggy studied her reflection in the mirror. She looked well-groomed and pleasant but not quite like her usual self who was usually dressed very casually, with a loosely tied ponytail and in flat shoes.

"You can do it! Do your best to make a good first impression on the boss and fellow colleagues." Peggy gave herself a final pep talk before leaving the flat.

It was not easy to locate the company. Even with the help of the GPS in her mobile phone, it still took Peggy awhile to find her destination. When it led her to a factory building, Peggy could not help but doubt if she had found the right place. She rechecked the GPS to confirm the location. It was correct.

Mixed feelings welled up in Peggy as she walked into the building, she moved slowly, carefully taking in the place where she would be working.

She saw that it was a U-shaped factory building with three storeys; it looked old and drab and the paint on the walls were peeling off. The factory area was not large, it was small and narrow in fact.

Several workers were moving in and out on the ground level, they wore a blue coloured uniform printed with a company's logo and were pushing trolleys loaded with stacks of printed matter wrapped in brown paper. They did not talk much, but when communication was necessary, they spoke loudly. Their voices echoed around the factory building and reverberated in Peggy's ears.

Although the factory was surrounded by greenery, Peggy could still feel the scorching heat indoors. "It must be the hot weather." Peggy tried hard to suppress the sense of disappointment that was growing inside her. She went around the U-shaped building and found a flight of stairs and a lift with a big door.

When the lift door opened, the wide internal space revealed that it was a cargo lift. Peggy was surprised as she had not seen such a spacious lift of more than ten square metres before.

The cargo lift soon reached the third storey. After making two turns and walking a few more steps, Peggy found the company.

David, the boss of the company, stood up to welcome Peggy, he looked exactly the same as he did in the videoconference. He was in his fifties and dressed in a neatly ironed long sleeve shirt tucked into tailored pants, which is the standard business casual attire.

"Hello Peggy, how are you? I am David, we met during the videoconference. I am glad you have come to join us." There was a polite exchange of handshakes. The other employees saw that there was a newcomer and stood up one after another to welcome Peggy aboard.

In actual fact, there were only three other employees, apart from Peggy and David. Initially, Peggy had thought these three were just part of a larger team of employees which included others who were handling external business matters outside the office. It was not until David introduced the company structure and everyone that Peggy realised this was the company's composition, four people in all, including the boss; with Peggy being the fifth.

> 70% of translation services companies have staff strengths of less than 10 people.

"Let's welcome Peggy, our new employee, she is a graduate of our profession."

Looking at the unfamiliar faces and knowing that the official business language in Singapore is English, Peggy gave a self-introduction in fluent English: "Hello everyone, I am Peggy and I am from China. I graduated with a master's degree this year and I studied translation in China. My job position is project manager, I am glad to be here to work with all of you." Peggy smiled even though she was actually feeling perplexed.

"Hi Peggy, I am Jason, Singaporean. I am in-charge of website management and market development. Welcome aboard, I hope we will get along." Jason had a dark skin tone and a small build but appeared energetic.

"I am Lily, also from China and I am a project manager like you, in-charge of managing and developing the resources within the company and the industry. The boss will brief you on the specific job responsibilities of a project manager, you are welcome to approach me if you have any doubts. This is Juliana, also a project manager, she is a Malaysian-Chinese who knows three languages Malay, English and Chinese." Lily looked only a little younger than Peggy's mother, her voice was pleasant and she appeared to be a competent career woman.

Juliana extended her hand to Peggy, "I am Juliana, nice to meet you, Peggy."

Peggy felt slightly consoled that all her colleagues were ethnic Chinese.

"Boss, what other business does the company have?"

"Don't address me as boss, call me David. We do mainly translation and interpretation as well as licence translation."

"Interpretations too?" Peggy was surprised.

"Indeed, in Singapore, many are bilingual but being bilingual does not mean having the knowledge of translation. Singapore is an international financial centre and an international port of call, a significant number of global 500 corporations have set up their Asia headquarters in Singapore. Huge volumes of trade activities create the need for translation and part of these are interpretations. For instance, if a team of Chinese delegates are in Singapore for observation and study trips, they will require interpreters," David replied.

"Does interpretation make up a big portion of the total business volume?" Peggy asked.

"Approximately 30%. Our core business is translation, it makes up more than 50% of the total business volume. When firms in the global 500 lists look to enter the China market, Singapore is often the stepping stone. Similarly, when Chinese businesses plan to expand beyond their local markets, they often choose to start from Singapore and therefore translation is required. Singapore is definitely the pivot for Chinese and Western culture," David replied with just a hint of pride in his voice.

"I guess licence translation is in demand due to Singapore being a typical country of immigrants," Peggy looked pensive.

"That's right, translation for certain licences is essential for immigration, this is also a stable part of our business and constitutes about 20% of the business volume." David confirmed Peggy's thoughts and went on, "I take care of the sales and marketing aspect, as well as the overall planning relating to company matters. I am also responsible for linking up and communication with clients and confirming of quotations etc. Jason is in charge of the website which is a very important part of the business. He must constantly maintain and optimise the website, as well as pay close attention to the bidding of Google AdWords, to enable target users to locate our website easily in the search process and possibly increase our market share and client base."

"Indeed, the company's website looks very professional and is user-friendly." Peggy replied as she recalled her experience as a user of the website.

"As for Lily and Juliana, they are project managers like you. The company's business is expanding, so they will have problems coping with the increased workload; furthermore, we are getting more businesses from China, hence this is my reason for employing you, a project manager with a Chinese background." David continued.

"What exactly does a project manager do? I did some research on the internet and David, you also mentioned a little about the job during the interview, but I guess my understanding is still not thorough and I do believe that different companies will have their own specific requirements? I hope you can give me more direction so that I can get started quickly," Peggy asked again.

"Project managers will be widely exposed to all aspects of our business and will require well-rounded abilities." David nodded his head.

"I'd love a challenging job," Peggy assured the boss.

"Specifically, a project manager is responsible for communicating with clients on the progress of individual projects. You must fully understand each client's requirements and assign suitable translators to do sample translations for some of the content provided by the customer. The client will then decide on the preferred translator after a review."

"We are equivalent to an intermediary," Peggy concluded.

A translation services company is a typical intermediary.

"This word is used correctly, but the job of an intermediary is not as simple as it sounds. For instance, finalising the choice for a translator after reviewing his or her sample translation does not mean everything will work out well. This is because the standard of the sample translation may not always be representative of the standard of the final translation. On one hand, the translator may have put in special effort to complete the sample assignment. On the other hand, translation is a dynamic skill where the quality of the finalised translation can be affected by many objective factors," David explained.

"Communications are mostly done online?" asked Peggy.

"Yes, most companies will not allow clients and translators to meet at their premises. If there is a need to meet up, a café is the best choice," said David.

"Where do we get the translators then?" Peggy queried again.

"There are many channels where we can source for translators. Our company has been operating for some years, so we have accumulated a pool of translators. More specifically, we have a name list with basic information of the translators such as name, contact information, area of specialisation, language domain, charges and also reviews of the translator's past projects and clients' comments. You must remember that these information on the translators are very important to every company, theoretically, they are not to be shared with other companies," David stressed.

"What else is necessary besides the pool of translators?" Peggy felt that she had a lot to learn.

"The next thing will be to expand your personal network and channel as a project manager. You have just arrived in Singapore and may not know too many people. However, after working for some time in this industry and living in Singapore long enough, you will slowly build up your connections with local translators. Bear in mind that a translation services company must safeguard the interests of the translators. Translation services companies will have working relations with many translators, and vice versa, translators will also work with more than one translation services company to maximise the work they can get. Generally, translators will prioritise working on projects from the companies with the best reputation and shortest payment cycle, especially those with many assignments and/or which pay a higher rate of fees," David replied.

"I understand. So, project managers must strive not only to expand the number of translators they can call on, but also to know in detail the strengths and weaknesses of their regular translators, which will then speed up and increase the efficiency of matching each client's requirements and also ease the process of subsequent negotiations with the clients," Peggy was clearly thinking while listening.

"Smart, that's it. Do remember that the client and the translator must not have any direct contact with each other in the process. Once they have a direct connection, we will likely lose the client. Afterall, translators have their own client base too," David warned.

"What about the pricing? Does the project manager handle that as well?" Peggy asked again.

"This is how pricing works, when the project manager discusses the project with the client, price plans will also be discussed, but take note that all transactions will be through the company account. Currently, translation rates are based on the number of words involved, there is a basis for reference which is adjusted according to the nature of business and the expectations on the quality of translation in order to decide on a comprehensive pricing package."

"Who will decide the price?" asked Peggy.

"We will first agree on a price with the client, this is the price that the client is willing to pay. Based on this price, we will then quote a lower price level for the translator, when the translator accepts our quote, we can then work together. Generally, for first time clients, translation services companies will request for a deposit, for regular clients with good credibility, especially the big clients, they can make payment after translation is done," David explained.

"I understand now," Peggy nodded.

"This is the situation in general but in the process of execution, it is inevitable that you will encounter special circumstances, these will have to be dealt with specifically, based on the individual issues.

We will have to cope with changes as they come." David replied. He seemed pleased with Peggy's desire to learn.

After David's introduction, Peggy took a good look at the office environment. The interior furnishings and decor were slightly newer and cleaner looking than those outside the office, but as a whole, the space still looked outmoded. The office space was compact, but everyone had their own workspaces which they kept neat and tidy. The boss worked in the same room as everyone else, except he had a slightly bigger desk.

"Our company rented this office space from the printing house; their offices are just next to ours. The first and second floors are their printing workshop and warehouse. Peggy, anything else you'd like to know?" asked David.

Peggy shook her head, "Nothing else at the moment."

"Alright then, go ahead to get your workspace ready. Take some time to familiarise yourself with the environment and the workflow, observe how everyone works and consult them anytime you have questions," David concluded.

At the end of her first day, Peggy boarded the same spacious cargo lift. As the lift began its slow descent, many thoughts filled Peggy's mind. The company had such a great, professional-looking website, but its on-site office conditions were a sharp contrast: simple and shabby, in a remote location and only employing a handful of people. The only thing that Peggy thought she could look forward to was the content of the job itself.

Peggy's heart felt as empty as the lift she had just stepped out of. She became more eager than before to pay a visit to the adult learning institution where Sarah was teaching. While her original objective to visit was to better understand Singapore society, Peggy keenly felt at that moment that she needed to be prepared to upgrade her level of knowledge in order to have more choices in the future.

Well, any new job is hectic at the beginning, so it was only two weeks later that Peggy had time to meet Sarah. In those two weeks, Peggy was diligent and eager to learn, very quickly, she was able to handle all her required tasks independently.

Sarah's workplace was part of a university but not located in the main campus, instead, it was in a city campus. Peggy and Sarah arranged to meet on a Wednesday evening after work, at the entrance of the campus. In order not to be late, Peggy left the office at 6pm sharp and rushed to the university without having dinner. She reached the campus 20 minutes before 7pm; Sarah was already waiting at the entrance.

"Have you had dinner?" Sarah asked as she handed Peggy a bottle of chrysanthemum tea and a home-made meal in a box.

"Oh, thank you Aunt Sarah!" Peggy was touched and surprised by Sarah's thoughtfulness.

"Today's lesson will be for the 'Introduction to Mandarin' course, it is on the fundamentals of the Chinese language. Besides this course, I am also teaching 'Commercial Translation' which is more difficult in comparison," said Sarah.

"Is 'Introduction to Mandarin' equivalent to primary school level Mandarin in China?" Peggy was puzzled.

"Almost," Sarah nodded her head.

"I see..." Peggy looked around the city campus as she spoke, "this city campus is smaller than I had imagined."

"This is rightfully so as it is not the main campus, the main campus is bigger and more beautiful, it is on a list of the most beautiful university campuses in the world, you must find time to explore it. This city campus in fact only has a main building and two annexes, there is a restaurant serving Western food and a biological science park beside the buildings. During weekends, members of the alumni will come here for talks, high tea, fitness and spa sessions or bring their children to swim and have fun, there is something for everyone in the family to enjoy."

The city campus was situated on a small slope and built into the terrain. The main building was squarish in shape, hidden among the tall green trees and the whole campus was surrounded by lawns. They walked along the flagstone pathway that led to the academic building and could smell the lovely scent of grass in the air.

"Although it is small, the design does give me the feeling that it is a university campus. Aunt Sarah, who are the people attending this class?"

"I have taught many batches of students, people from all walks of life, professionals, management staff from the global 500 firms who have headquarters in Singapore, civil service officers, staff of multinational corporations who are on posting assignments, as well as counsellors in embassies and many others. In any case, the students have diverse backgrounds and they are here in Singapore for different purposes, but their common goal is to learn Mandarin well."

> Everyone can freely own a right to a language.

"How many lessons are there every week?" Peggy asked.

"There are two time slots for the lessons, one is the evening class where lessons are held from 7pm to 10pm; the other is held on Saturday afternoon. Students will usually attend class on two of the evenings every week, either on Mondays and Wednesdays or Tuesdays and Thursdays. They have work commitments in the day, it is tough to have lessons every evening."

They arrived at the classroom, stepping in, Peggy saw that there were about 10 students already inside. At one glance, they were of different age groups, skin tone and appearance, indeed a rich and diverse group.

The students greeted Sarah one after another upon seeing her, in turn, Sarah introduced Peggy to the class, "Good evening everyone, this is my friend Peggy, she is from China and is currently working in Singapore. She is your classmate for tonight, I hope all of you will cherish the opportunity to learn together for these few hours. She speaks both English and Mandarin well, please interact with her during our lesson breaks." Peggy found a seat amidst the welcoming "hellos" from the students.

There was still more than ten minutes before the start of the lesson, more students streamed into the classroom one after another. Peggy noticed that almost everyone had a cup of coffee and some food, such as buns and fried food on skewers. Peggy thought to herself, "It seems that everyone is like me who rushed here after work and had no time for dinner. The coffee must be to help them stay awake!"

Before the lesson started, Sarah played a music video titled "confession balloon" which had been produced in fourteen languages by five universities and was being widely circulated on the internet.

"Everyone, let's start with a warm up activity. Say 'I love you' in your native language to the person next to you," Sarah assigned a task.

"あいしてる" (Japanese) "Saya cintai mu" (Malay) "사랑해" (Korean) "Aku cinta kamu" (Indonesian) "Je t'aime" (French) "Main tumse pyar karta hoon" (Northern Indian)…The students responded gamely, it was an interesting scene, much like a mini language party.

"Earlier on, everyone expressed 'I love you' in your native languages, if we were not in this classroom, we would not have understood a single word, would we? Isn't it amazing that languages can be so diverse and beautiful? More importantly, we have the opportunity to learn from each other today, let's start!"

The lesson began. It was then that Peggy noticed that Sarah's appearance was quite different from the first time they had met, at the barbecue. She was dressed in a white chiffon blouse tucked into a pair of black coloured wide-legged pants, with black leather wedge heels and sporting a light lip colour, altogether a very professional and elegant look.

Sarah also spoke differently, with precise pronunciation in a mellow voice and with an obvious effort to slow down when speaking in Mandarin. It sounded unnatural but considering that her students were still beginners, it was not surprising either. Speaking in this manner on any other day to a fluent Mandarin speaker would have sounded awkward.

Sarah's priority for the day's lesson was to teach everyone how to use the Chinese word "把 bǎ" in a sentence. "把 bǎ" is a preposition used to shift the object ahead of the verb and must be accompanied by some other words.

"Today we will learn the application of '把 bǎ' in a sentence, this is frequently used in our daily life. The '把 bǎ' structure has eight different usage patterns; we will learn the first type which is 'to see changes in position'." Sarah turned around to write the words on the white board, carefully and neatly. At the same time, she sketched an apple and a table below those words.

Sarah pointed at the apple on the whiteboard, most of the students could accurately say "apple" in Mandarin, "table" had the same response from the students as well. Sarah then wrote the Chinese characters for "apple" and "table" under the two drawings and drew a right pointing arrow from "apple" to "table", with a "V" representing the word "verb" on the arrow line and added a question mark beside it.

"Now, we want to change the position of the apple to be 'on the table', and we will require a verb. What is this verb?"

"Put (放 fàng)." Some of the students whispered the answer. Sarah then wrote the word 'put' under the letter 'V'.

"Under such circumstances, we will apply '把bǎ', that is,

把 — 苹果 — 放到 — 桌子 — 上 — bǎ — píng guǒ — fàng dào — zhuō zi — shàng (Put the apple on the table.)"

As Sarah read the sentence, she erased the apple on the board and redrew it so that it appeared to be on the table she had drawn earlier. With this action, her spoken word became imagery and immediately observable. Thereafter, Sarah wrote the complete sentence on the white board and prompted everyone to read together.

As the students followed Sarah to read the sentence, Peggy could tell that their tone and enunciation was less accurate as compared to when they were only reading the individual phrases. Reading a complete sentence posed some difficulties for the students, and some of them sounded more awkward than fluent. As such, Sarah guided everyone to practise reading the sentence repeatedly.

Once the students could read the sentence accurately and fluently, Sarah moved on to the next step of defining the structure of usage for "把 bǎ" in a sentence.

"Class, which part of the speech does the word 'apple' belong to?" Sarah asked the class.

"Noun".

"It is a noun. Good. What about 'put'?" Sarah asked again.

"Verb".

A SUDDEN REVELATION

> Limited vocabulary can generate unlimited expressions through grammar.

"Excellent! In this instance, 'on the table' is a place, we call it 'the desired place to be'. Using the first example, we will see the application of '把bǎ': '把_noun_verb_to_desired place to be.'" Sarah was speaking and at the same time, writing the sentence structure on the white board.

She went on to do a few more practices with the class.

During the interactive practice session, students who were interested could proceed to the podium in front of the class to share the sentences which they had constructed with '把bǎ' and were encouraged to enhance their presentation with actions.

The lecture room was designed to be in the shape of a semi-circular arc with sloped flooring, and between the podium and the front row of seats was some free space. This design enabled the teacher who stood on the podium to achieve optimal diffusion of information when communicating with the students seated. The design also facilitated student participation and was especially suitable for role play activities.

It was beyond Peggy's imagination to see such enthusiastic student participation. A young man expressed his love for his long-distance girlfriend with his sentence:

"把我的女朋友放进我心里 bǎ wǒ de nǚ péng yǒu fàng jìn wǒ xīn lǐ"
(I put my girlfriend in my heart).

It triggered a round of teasing from the class.

"This student has indeed learnt the concept of '把 bǎ' well, openly showing affection for his girlfriend though she is not around," Peggy could not help thinking.

Sarah also taught the class a few other ways to use "把 bǎ" before it was time for a break.

Among the students was an Indonesian Chinese lady named Eve, she had brought some home-made kueh lapis[11] to share with the class that day. The ever-earnest Peggy counted the layers on the kueh lapis because it is called "nine layered cake" in Mandarin; the ones made by Eve only had seven layers, but there are no strict rules of course, the colourful, and fragrant cake was rich and tempting enough for everyone and many students approached Eve for the recipe of the kueh lapis. According to Eve, kueh lapis is a mixture of rice flour and water, with sugar, coconut milk, and colouring. It is steamed, layer by layer. The different ingredients used for extracting the colourings will determine the colour and taste of each layer, for example yellow from durian, green from pandan, brown from cocoa and so on.

Interested to know more, Peggy struck up a conversation with Eve who shared that she was a Singapore-born Indonesian Chinese, doing a marketing job in the construction industry. Two months ago, she had joined a construction company from China which had a subsidiary company in Singapore, the company hoped that she would be able to help it venture into the Indonesian market.

Eve could not speak Mandarin. Her superior was a native Chinese speaker who was not good at communicating in English. Eve was therefore not able to have any in-depth communication with the superior due to their language barrier. They had to rely on sketching and gestures to get messages across to each other.

Eve was originally a user of the text messaging service "WhatsApp". In order to better adapt to the Chinese environment, she switched

---

[11] Kueh lapis means layered cake in Malay. It is also known as the "nine layered cake" in Mandarin for its nine distinctive coloured layers.

to "WeChat" to communicate with her native Chinese colleagues. She would sometimes make use of translation tools to aid her in communication, but she realised that machine translation could not accurately express her original intentions. Hence, she thought of learning Mandarin to better integrate into the company's environment. She also told Peggy that she yearned to go to China, and she was looking forward to visiting China after learning the language.

Another student Peggy spoke with was a Japanese man, suave and distinguished-looking, he was a university professor. At the institution where he taught, the students were mainly local Singaporean Chinese.

Both he and his wife liked Singapore very much and had decided to call it home. They felt that Singapore has a beautiful environment, a great public security system, rich in material resources and a democratic society. Regardless of whether one is Singaporean or a foreigner, with diligence, ability and wisdom, a safe and decent life is possible. The place where he was teaching had many local Chinese and native Chinese students, the condominium where he lived had many Chinese residents too. To better integrate into this Chinese dominated society, he decided to learn Mandarin. He was also a fan of Chinese culture; he collected Chinese landscape paintings and even played the flute. He mentioned that he believed learning Mandarin would allow him to have a better understanding of the Chinese culture.

There was also a pair of Singaporean siblings whose family background was most diversified. Their paternal grandmother had been born in China and could only speak the "Southern Min" language, which is a Sinitic language spoken in Southern Fujian and its surrounding areas in China. Their father thus learnt the "Southern Min" language as a child and subsequently picked up English and Mandarin after going to school. During the early 1980s, he went to Japan and learned the Japanese language as well. It was then that their parents met and their mother, who was Japanese, only spoke Japanese and English. Subsequently, their parents came back to Singapore and the family had a Filipino maid who only spoke English and her native Tagalog. On any day at home when everyone was gathered, their father, who had the most diverse language background, would be the only person able to speak to every family member directly, thus connecting their three-generation family.

> A family being in the same physical space but living in individual language chain, the emotional communication among family members will be affected by language.

The brother was a lawyer and the sister worked in the finance sector. Although both had received a bilingual education, their foundation in Mandarin was weak and they were already out of touch with the Chinese language years after completing their studies. They were advised by their father to relearn Mandarin well to complement their career advancement, and this led them to make time to learn the language again. Learning Mandarin was obviously easier for the siblings due to their foundation in the language.

During the second half of the lesson, Sarah provided more sentences as examples for the students and told them a little story that was culture related.

Being with people of such different ages and ethnic groups in one classroom generated a lively atmosphere and Peggy's understanding of Singapore's diversity became more vivid than ever before.

Teaching an adult to a new language is more challenging than teaching kids their mother tongue. Each language is backed by its own culture and encompasses a mode of thinking. Adults already have their way of thinking moulded, so learning a foreign language would not simply require just mimicking and modelling. Adult minds subconsciously compare and try to find equivalents between the foreign language and their mother tongue. Therefore, although the course content was simple, it could not be taught in the same way as it was to children. Instead, students had to be introduced to the thinking behind the language.

When she was an undergraduate, Peggy had given lessons to secondary level students at a private tuition centre and had experienced being a teacher in a classroom setting. After attending Sarah's interesting lesson, she gained new insights into the concepts of 'teaching' and 'classroom'. Peggy felt that Sarah's lesson was comprehensive in terms of content, delivery and form. Content refers to the course content, Sarah followed the course content closely without excessive discussion, emphasised key areas and maintained a good momentum. Delivery-wise, Sarah adopted a simple and relaxed teaching tone, she balanced speech with actions, without forgetting that her audience were adults and not young children. In terms of form, Sarah used teaching methods that were appropriate for the course content. Some of these were innovative and very successful at stimulating student participation.

When the lesson ended, an enthusiastic looking young man walked towards Peggy, greeted her with a smile and spoke in relatively fluent Mandarin, "How are you Peggy, my name is Rajan, I am from India."

"Hello Rajan. It's nice to meet you," Peggy smiled in response.

"He is the most diligent student in this class, he studies all the materials for this course thoroughly and he is good at seizing every opportunity to practise orally!" Sarah praised Rajan as she walked over to them, then she suggested to Peggy, "You should talk to him more, it will be helpful for you to get to know Singapore even better."

Coincidentally, Peggy and Rajan were headed in the same direction of the MRT station, so they bid goodbye to Sarah and left together.

"Rajan, what are you working as?" Peggy asked.

"I am working in a semiconductor company; I am an S pass[12] holder. I work the night shift from 12am to 8am the next day, I am going to go to work now."

"It must be very tough for you, to work in the night and to be here to study."

"Yes, and the course is not cheap, it costs S$550, it is almost one quarter of my salary."

"Which means that you do not have much left after deducting rental and living expenses. It is not a small expense. Why do you want to learn Mandarin?"

"China is developing fast, its economy is good, and many countries are doing business with China, many Chinese firms are already setting up factories in India. The salary I draw right now is too low, I intend to look for a better-paying job. Although I have not decided what my next job will be, seeing that China is getting stronger, I feel that it will be useful to learn Mandarin, it will aid in my search for a better job, I am taking it as a form of investment in myself," Rajan smiled happily.

> Usually, people choose to learn languages that are on the ascendant, like Mandarin, because China is now the world's second largest economy.

"How long have you studied Mandarin for?" Peggy asked again.

"Less than three months."

---

[12] The S pass allows mid-level skilled foreigners to work in Singapore. Candidates need to earn at least S$2500 a month and have relevant qualifications and work experience.

"How do you feel about it?"

"It is interesting and beautiful."

"The Chinese language is vast and profound. In China, Mandarin is the only official language."

"In India, we have more than twenty common languages. I speak Tamil and everyone can speak English. I heard this story from someone: some foreign experts went to India for a meeting and complained that the pace of the meeting was too slow because when someone speaks, it has to be translated a few times."

Peggy could not hold back her laughter, "The translators must be so busy!"

"That's right! But many languages are dying out in India. The fewer people using a language, the faster it will disappear."

"Do you know how many languages there are in the world?" Peggy asked.

"I have no idea."

"There are more than 5000 languages."

"Oh, so many?!"

> Blockchain can keep permanent records of a language and preserve its culture.

"Yes, but only about slightly over 100 are commonly used and only about 20 languages have more people speaking them. In fact, on average, every year, about 20 languages become obsolete. Every language is a unique way of viewing the world around us, once it disappears, a part of human civilisation will be lost."

Given that Peggy's interest was in languages, she could not help but feel worried when the topic about the ongoing disappearance of languages was mentioned.

On the MRT, Peggy encountered an elderly lady from China who approached her to ask for directions. The old lady was grateful to Peggy for her help and struck up a conversation with her. She told Peggy that her son and daughter-in-law were working in Singapore, her grandchild had been born in Singapore and she had relocated from China to Singapore in order to help with the care of the baby. However, she did not know English and was not able to read the English signboards on the roads, thus she did not dare to venture too far from home.

> Language requirements are fragmented and exist in various scenarios.

A few days later, Peggy attended Sarah's lesson again, this time, it was for her course on "Commercial Translation".

There were three case analyses in that class that left a deep impression on Peggy.

The first case, 'A young firefighter died'. Students translated the sentence to:

一名年轻的消防员死了。yì míng nián qīng de xiāo fáng yuán sǐ le
A young firefighter died.

Sarah explained to the class that the translation was correct but not good enough, a better translation would be:

一名年轻的消防员牺牲了。yì míng nián qīng de xiāo fáng yuán xī shēng le
A young firefighter was sacrificed.

A SUDDEN REVELATION

People from different ethnic groups and different regions view the world with different degree of fineness in certain respect, and accordingly, the degree of language granularity and fineness will also be different.

In Mandarin, there are many ways to describe death, the descriptions differ depending on the person, age, how death occurred, the death scene and so on. For example, 驾崩 jià bēng (death of an emperor), 寿终正寝 shòu zhōng zhèng qǐn (to die of old age), 英年早逝 yīng nián zǎo shì (to die in one's prime), 香消玉殒 xiāng xiāo yù yǔn (death of a beautiful lady), 夭折 yāo zhé (to die young), 牺牲 xī shēng (to sacrifice), 卒 zú (die, used in ancient times in China), 溺亡 nì wáng (drown) and many more.

The second case was about translation ambiguity. Sarah wrote three English sentences on the board and questioned how students would translate them:

I fed her cat food.

I saw him with a telescope.

She kisses her neighbour on the second floor.

These three sentences have two possible meanings each, thus leading to different translations, take the second sentence as an example, it can be translated as:

1. 我看到他拿着一个望远镜。 wǒ kàn dào tā ná zhe yí gè wàng yuǎn jìng
   I saw him holding a telescope.

2. 我在望远镜里看到他。 wǒ zài wàng yuǎn jìng lǐ kàn dào tā
   I saw him in the telescope.

Therefore, there is a need to take note of the meaning in context when doing translation.

The third case illustrated that language is a product of society. Learning a language is also about learning the way of thinking and cognition styles shared by a language community. For instance, Japan is surrounded by the ocean, so vocabulary to refer to different types of fish are especially numerous. The same kind of fish in different breeding periods also has different names. If these are translated into Chinese, due to the lack of matching expressions, they will just be differentiated by size: "big" or "small". Applying the same logic, in the Chinese language there are many expressions to describe horses, based on the breed, hair colour, size and others, examples are: 骠 piào (gallop; brave); 骊 lí (pure black horse); 驹 jū (foal); 骅 huá (fine red horse), 骝 liú (red horse with black mane and tail); 骓 zhuī (piebald horse); 骢 cōng (horse with bluish white fur) and many others. Translating all of these into English as above, means that there is not always a single corresponding expression, hence the only way is to come up with replacement terms. The diversity of a language's vocabulary is a reflection of diverse ways of thinking and cognitive styles. Different languages have differing degrees of granularity and fineness which are determined by the language community's physical and socio-environmental factors.

> Each language has its unique cultural background and rich customs.

Three weeks passed since Peggy's arrival in Singapore. During this time, she was busy adjusting to the new environment, getting used to her new job and building a new social circle. Peggy's personal public account on WeChat was thus inactive for a long time, her friends began sending messages on the platform to check on her situation in Singapore, urging her to update her public account when she had time.

The WeChat public account had always been an important platform for Peggy to record and share details of her life and thoughts. Since the setting up of her account, there were only two occasions that she was not in good form and had stopped updating for a while. This time was the third and marked the longest period of disruption.

On the way home after attending Sarah's "Commercial Translation" course, Peggy finally took some time on the MRT to record her experiences, thoughts and feelings in the past weeks, using the memo function on her mobile.

This moment, Singapore.

My apologies everyone, it has been a long time since we last "met".

I have been in Singapore for a while and I've finally found some time to reflect on my life here over the last three weeks.

Life in Singapore is as busy as I had expected. Every day, I am busy experiencing the new environment, busy familiarising and getting used to a new job, busy building up my new social circle, busy learning to improve myself…

Singapore is better than I had expected, and I am not just referring to the infrastructure. This is an energetic and charming city that is open, driven, inclusive, filled with a modern spirit but yet retaining a classic charm. I have attached some photos to share with all of you.

Adjusting to a new life can be tiring, but being in a foreign land, I am more appreciative of the warmth and kindness that the people around have showered upon me.

Living together with me is a study mama from Qingdao, Aunt Doreen and her adorable daughter. Aunt Doreen is very friendly and takes good care of me, she will keep a share of whatever she cooks for me to eat. There are many study mamas like Aunt Doreen here in Singapore, well-educated but facing difficulties getting a suitable job here. In other words, they "sacrifice" their own career prospects for the sake of their children, this shows how much emphasis is placed on their children's future and bilingual education.

I attended a clan association gathering, it was a weekend, and we were invited by the chairman of the association to have a barbecue at his house. I remember when I was studying, every province had their own clan association, but we were all students then. The clan associations here are different, members come from rich and varied backgrounds, they are of all ages and professions, there are those of our generation, our parents' generation as well as our grandparents' generation. It was interesting listening to their stories and experiences, and I was exposed to things which I had not known before.

The focus is my new job.

I am rather disheartened by the company's remote and outmoded office as well as the small-scale set up. However, the job itself is quite challenging and closely related to my field of study. Basically, I can handle my duties independently, but to adapt to the job, I must continue to learn and gain more experience before I can feel more settled in my mind…

I must talk about Sarah; she is the wife of Charles who is the chairman of the clan association. She teaches Mandarin at an adult learning institution where she conducts two courses, one is the foundation level "Introduction to Mandarin", the other is the advance level "Commercial Translation". I sat in for her lessons for both courses.

The lesson for "Introduction to Mandarin" was my first live experience of a class teaching Mandarin as a foreign language to adults. It was very interesting for me.

During lesson breaks, I interacted with some of the students, they all had their stories to tell. There was a young Indian guy who hoped to get a better job by acquiring proficiency in Mandarin, there was also a Japanese professor who was learning Mandarin to better integrate into the Chinese community in Singapore and there was another Indonesian lady who was learning Mandarin to communicate better with her superior and colleagues…

In any case, I feel their eagerness and aspirations to learn Mandarin well, whether it is out of love for the language or for the purpose of using the language as a tool for work, it makes me proud of my mother tongue! Translation is more than just a conversion of terms across two languages, it is an exchange of two cultures and thinking modes. As such, though I have already started my job, I am still making time to learn more about both Mandarin and English and one way that has been very convenient for me is by reading free newspapers on the MRT.

From the lesson on "Commercial Translation", I gained more insights into translation. It is not just a technical skill but requires an understanding of the background of the culture, ways of thinking and emotions behind the language, which explain why machines are unable to make bigger contributions in the translation field.

Attending the two courses relating to language and my two weeks of work experience have led me to think more deeply regarding my language profession, the beauty of language, the value of language, the exchange of language…it is a vast topic that requires long discussion, I shall not mention it now, but shall share further when I am more settled.

This moment, Singapore. All is well, do not worry about me.

Once she arrived home, Peggy quickly edited her words into a tweet and posted it. Messages from followers of her account began pouring in almost instantaneously.

In a language chain, everyone has the freedom to receive, create and share language related information.

"You have not updated your tweets in such a long time, I thought you were enjoying yourself so much that you had forgotten those at home!" This was the usual tone of a high school bestie.

"Looking at Senior's writing, in my mind I can imagine Singapore and your life there. Senior is outstanding and diligent; I know you will adapt fast to your new life. Please take good care of yourself," Theresa, a junior from university sent a warm greeting.

> Language is a form of common understanding, under the stimulation of a common language, similar images and models will appear in the minds of people within the same language community.

"Practice and theory are different, aren't they? As learners of language, all the more we should be exposed to the real world of languages, I look forward to more sharing from you regarding your professional experience." This was sent by her favourite teacher in her master's degree programme.

"Am I right to say that Singapore is a city suitable for working and living? Young lady, I am relieved to see that you are adjusting well and continuing to embrace learning," Zenna's words were full of comfort and encouragement.

Whilst the messages continued, one after another, Peggy had already fallen into deep sleep.

Summary:
A Sudden Revelation

The ability to master beautiful and complex languages is a biological attribute that is unique to mankind. Language enables people to reach a consensus for a common goal before embarking on large-scale collaborations. There was a legendary figure named Cangjie (倉頡) in ancient China who was an official historian for the Yellow Emperor and the inventor of Chinese text. Legend has it that when he invented text, the "deities and ghosts cried, and the sky rained millet". The creation of words was such an astounding event in the history of mankind as it relieved human of the struggle to keep records of events based on memory. We can draw inspirations from the historical civilisation made possible by languages by positioning ourselves between history and the future and connect these inspirations with the visions we have for the future. It is the magic of language ability possessed by mankind, accumulated over many generations that shaped the world today.

Changes in cultural production have always been closely linked to technological advances. Historically, printing technology has led to the emergence of book publishing, newspapers, advertising and journalism, while telecommunications technology has led to the rise of film, television, radio and recordings. Today, both the language and culture industry will see another major change brought about by information technology, and it will be more profound and radical.

We know that people within the same language community can transmit information, express thoughts, and reach a consensus quickly to collaborate and achieve a common goal. However, when people of different language groups gather, there is no way they can collaborate if they do not speak each other's languages, even if they have similar professional backgrounds.

We can deviate from the linguistic perspective to look at language from another angle.

Language is the cultural bloodline of an ethnic group. Each language is a part of human civilisation, and each embodies the basic attribute of a public blockchain.

Public blockchain means that anyone in the world can obtain the data and use the data, send a transaction and obtain a valid confirmation. It also allows participation in the network of blockchain, one that is open with no user authorisation required.

Language is expandable. It is a communal resource which can be owned and shared by everyone. Language is not restricted like natural resources such as land, forests, mines or oil, neither is it a social resource like human or subsidy which will result in losses and depletion and lead to competition among people. It is also unlike items like flowers and plants, calligraphy and painting or jewellery which will decrease in value with an increase in availability and ownership. On the contrary, when more people use the language, the accelerating diversity in nationality and ethnicity of the users, compounded with higher frequency of usage, will result in the language being more dynamic, propelling faster development and generating higher economic value.

This is an attribute similar to the openness of a public blockchain where it is open to the whole network and provides interfaces that can be called by developers without controls over them. This will in turn, encourage them to develop applications that conform to the ecosystem of the public blockchain.

There is no threshold to linguistic rights. Regardless of social status or wealth, everyone will have equal rights to learn or give up a language. This is inherently autonomous, and no permission is required. The

SUMMARY

language that people master from young is influenced by the family environment — it is the choice of our parents. When we grow up, learning a foreign language is a choice typically influenced by social environmental factors. Everyone has the liberty to master any language in the world.

This is in line with the feature of a "no user authorisation" mechanism of a public blockchain where individual node does not require any permission or authorisation to enter or exit a network.

Users in a language community are not just participants in the consensus process; in fact, they are also the creators of the language. Everyone is a user, a witness and a participant in the process of language development. Users will reach a consensus on the meaning of new expressions, initiate the usage and disseminate the use of these expressions. Some of these examples are "佛系 fó xì (to be indifferent)", "锦理 jǐn lǐ (a symbol of luck)", "杠精 gàng jīng (be obsessive about dissenting)", "躺枪 tǎng qiāng (to get unjustly ridiculed)". In our life journey, we will continuously witness new words appearing and old words becoming obsolete, and we can be on an equal footing being part of this language creation process.

This is consistent with the public blockchain's process of participation in the execution of a consensus protocol. Every node on the public blockchain can be part of this execution process and similarly in a language group, each person is a node of the group.

Language not only has the same attribute as a public blockchain but also has similar forms of expression. There are more than five thousand types of languages in this world. The languages with the most users are Mandarin, English, French, Russian, Arabic and Spanish, which are spoken by about 50% of the world population. In the last two years, all kinds of public chain sprung up in large numbers but with limited ones widely in use.

Different languages bear different perspectives. The people from oriental nations place importance on ethics and holistic thinking and that makes Mandarin a paratactic language emphasising meaning. Westerners focus on rational and logical thinking, hence making English a hypotactic language emphasising form.

Mandarin as a paratactic language can be observed in the following Chinese practices and beliefs. China's small-scale agricultural economy made people realise that good harvest cannot be separated from good weather and therefore, thinking modes linked to nature are formed. In all-natural phenomena that involve heaven and earth, sun and moon as well as yin and yang, to integrate all things on earth with man being an integral part of nature, the pursuit is to achieve universal harmony between human, nature, and the almighty.

Traditional Chinese medicine gives a comprehensive diagnosis of the state of illness by observing, listening, asking and feeling the pulse. The popular Beijing Opera Art integrates singing, dialogue, acting and acrobatic. The quintessence of traditional Chinese paintings comprises painting, poem, calligraphy and seal cutting, all of which are essential. The Mandarin-speaking community, therefore, perceives the world through a holistic analysis of context.

The English language was developed in the marine geographical environment and has contributed to people's strong interest in astronomy and geography, which resulted in cognitive styles of exploring mysteries of nature and finding a solution from nature. In addition, western philosophy stress on giving attention to even the smallest details and pursuing clear and accurate concepts. This is evident in the advancement of science and technology, as well as rational and logical thinking in the western society.

Language is the best reflection of human nature. Every language is a blockchain. Every language represents an emotional world — a way to perceive the world. Different language users live in their own language blockchain. Language is like an intangible net, segregating people from all over the world into their native language world.

SUMMARY

The world that we see is a translated world, and similarly, we are perceived by the world through translation. The global circulation of materials has become so easy that it appears that the world is flat. However, on a spiritual level, the world is not flat with the erection of information barriers due to language diversity.

With the development of material conditions, human interactions around the world have grown deeper and become more extensive. The interconnection and interdependence among countries are more frequent and intense than before.

Translation being the medium for effective conversion of information between different languages, is like the cross-chain technology in blockchain. How to break through the bottleneck to switch freely between languages for effective communication to share and promote different cultures is an important mission for people from all nations.

Note

———— Chapter 3 ————

A Perpetual Deadlock

The Language-Based Translation Services Industry
Retains a Workshop-Style Existence

P eggy received a complaint about the quality of translation for one of her projects. Subsequently, she attended a gathering of local translators to better understand the working conditions and demands of this community. She also helped Doreen with interpretation at a parent-teacher meeting. As she worked, Peggy was able to further observe and reflect upon the current developments and existing problem areas of the translation services industry and she gained clearer insight of the overall situation.

The rapid development of the internet has contributed to a tremendous increase in the volume of information. However, the translation profession, which performs the function of making accessible information across languages, has not seen many changes in the way it operates over the years; translation services companies are still operating in the form of workshops. The world as experienced by human beings is in fact a translated world, the boundaries of language set limits to our cognition. Due to language barriers, a large portion of human civilisation cannot be shared and cannot be re-created collaboratively.

1   Clients lack easily accessible language services.
2   Translators' high-quality output do not equate to high returns.
3   Significant statistical data in the industry cannot be gathered effectively.
4   Lack of capacity restricts industrial development.

***

Not too long after she started the job, Peggy received a complaint from a client. It was regarding a legal letter of defence for which the translation had been managed by Peggy.

The client spoke angrily over the phone, "It was so close, the letter was so close to being sent out, I simply cannot imagine the consequences if the letter had been sent! The terrible translation service you rendered has already impacted negatively on my superior's appraisal of me. This is a serious problem, a very serious one! What kind of professionalism and attitude is this!"

At the receiving end of this tongue lashing from the client, Peggy felt dismayed, but she controlled her emotions and replied as mildly and politely as she could, "Sir, I am very sorry that our translation service did not meet your expectations. Please let me know exactly where the problem with the translated text is. May I request that you send us the details via email. We will investigate and get back to you and we will ensure you receive a satisfactory response to the problem. My sincere apologies."

Peggy's colleagues looked over at her when they heard her apologising over the phone. Peggy signalled with hands that she was able to handle the matter, though from her expression, one could tell it was not a small issue.

A PERPETUAL DEADLOCK

77

Within thirty minutes, Peggy received the email from the client.

> The client could not determine the quality of the translation; one of the main functions of a translation services company is to check for quality.

In the email, the client listed out the key lapses in translation. These mistakes had been spotted by the client's friend who had legal knowledge and was also fluent enough in both English and Mandarin. The client himself did not know English, otherwise, he would not have approached a translation services company.

'"独头掘进 dú tóu jué jìn' was translated as 'separately', it should be 'blind heading'. It is an entirely different meaning and our grounds for appeal would not be able to be established.

'稳车 wěn chē' was translated to 'steady vehicle', it is definitely a mistake, it should be 'winch'.

> Translation is an all-rounded job of creativity, a translator not only needs to know the language but also to know the nuances in meaning that similar terms offer.

The concept of 'safety' was not clearly understood, where production is concerned, '安全 ān quán' should be translated into 'safety' and not 'security', 'security' is about public order.

There was a big issue with tenses, many of the expressions should have been in past tense but the content was mostly translated into present tense, this completely misrepresented our desire to express all that we had done. We have no intention to talk about what is being done at this moment.

There are three or four missing translations. For example, after an accident happened, after a training session where assessments and evaluations were required, many of these are missing in the translation.

> It is inevitable that humans make silly mistakes, but machines will not. Fundamental tasks can be handed to the machine while human beings focus on jobs of creativity.

There are mistakes on the basics too! Inappropriate use of words, wrong usage of singular or plural nouns, spelling errors, 'each' became 'reach', resulting in the wrong meaning reflected. This is not a technical error but a problem with attitude!

Due to time constraints, I will not list everything out in detail!"

Upon verification, all the points in the client's feedback were valid. Although she was not the direct target of the complaint, as a newcomer, it was the first time Peggy was handling a client's complaint. Even with the screen as a barrier, she could still feel the wrath of the client and panic-stricken. Therefore, she approached the boss for help.

The client did not claim damages from the company after further discussion, taking into consideration that no substantial harm had been done since the defence letter had not been sent out. The boss apologised sincerely to the client on behalf of the company and appointed another translator to do the translation all over again. At the same time, he promised the client that significant discounts would be given with no strings attached if the client wished to work with their company again.

The crisis was resolved but traces of the turbulence remained. The next morning, David called for an urgent meeting.

"We had a complaint from an angry client yesterday about our translated text. Thankfully the matter has been resolved. As a newcomer, this is the first time Peggy has received a complaint, let's have a short meeting to discuss this. First of all, I hope everyone will understand that in our profession, receiving complaints is inevitable. However, we should learn from the situation to review and refine our performance. Peggy, can you analyse the problems in this complaint?" Peggy was thrown the first question.

"I think the chosen translator was not suitable. She was not conscientious enough nor responsible in her work attitude. We gave her ample time to complete the job. I saw her sample translation and thought it was not bad," Peggy looked down in guilt.

"You saw her sample translation, but did you look through her final translated text?" The boss probed.

"Um…I had other things to handle and the client was chasing for it; I merely glanced through but did not do any textual research on the commonly used professional terms for the translation…" Peggy felt embarrassed.

> Quality control has been a problem faced by translation services companies. In any of these companies, no single quality control specialist will be able to cover all language types and specialisations.

"Generally, large-scale translation services companies will have designated personnel to do quality checks in accordance with standards or based on the client's requirements. The initial stage serves to control the quality and subsequently, another check is done to examine the quality of the final translation. The purpose of the initial check is to analyse the degree of difficulty of the source text and extract the terminologies for verification. We are small in scale, so project managers usually have to take on these two tasks and give suggestions directly for amendments on the translation," Lily added.

"Our company has a compilation of complaint cases with clients' feedback. Lily, can you send the document to Peggy after you add this case into the file? As the saying goes 'a fall into the pit, a gain in your wit (经一事，长一智 jīng yī shì zhǎng yī zhì)'." The boss continued and his words became more direct, "Peggy, you cited the chosen translator being unsuitable as a reason. Did you decided on the translator solely based on her resume? If you stay long enough in this industry, you will realise that the resume is not completely reliable, some people will include specific fields which are not within their area of specialisation just to get more jobs."

"What!" Peggy had always placed importance on honesty and trustworthiness, she was therefore taken aback by this revelation.

"Some translators may exaggerate certain aspects of their resumes. If they indicate areas which they do not specialise in but yet are not completely unfamiliar with, it will be more tedious and time consuming for them to do the translation, but ultimately, they will also receive more jobs. Therefore, before deciding on a translator, besides looking at their resume, you should also conduct an interview or look into their previous translation profiles." There were significant implications in the boss's expression, "In this profession, it takes time to settle in."

The boss then concluded, "Overall, the problem lies with us and our choice of translator, we have to evaluate our own work performance and reflect on this issue. On the other hand, this client is not faultless. He was only prepared to pay a standard price for a piece of work that required translation of technical terms."

"Do not be discouraged, the translation profession has its prospects. I have on hand, a paid copy of the latest data from CSA research, it shows that the outsourcing of the global language services industry had a market capitalisation of US$46.5 billion the year before. Year on year growth was at 6.62% up to the amount of US$49.6 billion. In the past eleven years, our industry had compounded growth of up to 7.76%. Therefore, our profession

> Societal demand for translation has been increasing.

has vast prospects, we should be confident and continue to work hard," David seized the opportunity to encourage everyone.

"I have read the book *The World is Flat* by the American author, Thomas Friedman. The author posited in his book that rapid advancement of technology and communication is allowing people from all over the world to be closer to one another, which means that the world is gradually being flattened by technology. However, I beg to differ. I feel that the world is yet to be flattened. The proximity between the eyes and the screen is the distance between an individual and the world. Although the internet at present facilitates access to huge volume of information, a lot of this information can be seen but cannot be understood," Peggy replied, with a tone of helplessness.

"That is true. And lack of understanding will easily create misunderstandings. Language barriers block direct access to local news in foreign countries, we can only see the world through the eyes of media, blended with misunderstanding and bias," Lily said.

> The world as seen by people is a translated world, the boundary of language sets limits to our cognition.

"Lily is correct. By the way, do not think of our company as being small with only a few employees, we are in fact doing just fine based on industry standards. There are many setups that comprise of husband and wife or father and son teams, operating without a business space. In fact, most of the time they work from home, much like the setup of a workshop," David continued with confidence.

He highlighted that even for the biggest translation services company, business volume was only about 2 to 3% of the local market, there was no way for any one company to become a monopoly, unlike in other industries. Translation

> Translation services companies are widely dispersed and operate like workshops.

services companies were basically small setups operating in a perfectly competitive market where there was no scale, no brands, no production chains and with 80% of the businesses outsourced to part-time translators, blurring the operation boundaries.

"Why doesn't everyone collaborate?" Peggy was eager to keep asking questions as soon as they popped into her head.

"On collaboration, my belief is that 'one's ability falls short of one's wishes (心有余而力不足 xīn yǒu yú ér lì bù zú)'. If there is a platform or channel that allows everyone to collaborate spontaneously, that would be perfect. The problem is, currently there are no suitable platforms to allow for such a large-scale collaboration. Although companies with good relations will recommend businesses to each other, generally, all of them still prefer to keep their clients and translators to themselves. Holding on to data of clients and translators is only rightful..." The boss continued after a pause, his words had profound implications, "sharing is a virtue but it may not always be possible to do so, for survival..."

As the discussion continued, everyone became eager to get a word in, whether regarding the current status of the company, review of their experiences and lessons learned from daily work, or their observations and thoughts on the translation services profession. And thus the meeting continued.

The exchange of information during the meeting and the sharing by the boss on the industry research report encouraged Peggy to think further and more deeply.

Given her engineering background, she quickly thought of the possible application of technology to the translation services field. With the development of artificial intelligence, she already knew machine translation was becoming more popular, and that translation software was emerging in an endless stream, but these did not reduce the market share of the translation services providers, instead, business volume continued to increase consistently. On one hand, development in globalisation had increased the demand for language services; on the other hand, it also seemed to Peggy that relying solely on artificial intelligence would not be able to revolutionise the translation services industry.

This prompted Peggy to recall an experience during her days at the university. She had been a student volunteer at a forum held at school where the invited guests were mostly Chinese scholars, but occasionally she would encounter foreign guests who could only speak English.

At that time, the content of every lecture had to be recorded, and it was difficult to record the lecture content of an English-speaking foreign guest. The whole lecture would be recorded via a recording software before a translation software was used to translate the content. The translation software could only rigidly translate the lecture content word by word and it was impossible to achieve the Triple Principle of Translation: "Faithfulness", "Expressiveness" and "Elegance". If the guest lecturer spoke with an accent, even the accuracy of the translation could not be guaranteed.

> Machine translation will not replace human translation. Instead, it helps to expand the market and increase the demand for human translation.

Machine translation is akin to possessing weak vision, it allows people to access information which were once out of reach, however, this is far from adequate. The use of machine translation can assist in finding the general location of required information, but people will still seek the help of human translators to achieve accuracy in the translation.

All these thoughts made Peggy more doubtful, "How much do I really understand about the translation profession?"

Henceforth, as she worked, she would utilise her spare time progressively for further research and also to carefully analyse the materials gathered, in order to find the answers to her questions.

When she started her job, David had given Peggy a name list of all the translators she could work with and told her that under normal circumstances, the company's reserves and maintenance volume for translators had to reach ten times the company's actual business volume. As such, expanding and maintaining the pool of translators was very important.

Peggy was particularly attentive to this point since she was sensitive to smooth operation of the business. She made sure she kept abreast of the work that the translators were doing. Besides being in touch with the selected translator for each project, Peggy also initiated communication with other translators in the name list, so that she could get recommendations on qualified and reliable peers.

Incidentally, through one of the translators, Peggy established connections with a translators group. Operating as self-employed freelancers, they had formed the group to gather strength from one another, and support one another emotionally and professionally. If there was any job that one translator was not able to take up, it would be recommended to another who was on close terms and also skilled in that domain.

This group of translators would also organise physical gatherings to share professional information and recent developments in one another's lives, and of course, to have fun together. Since Peggy was keen to enlist more potential translators for her company and also curious about hearing more from translators, she happily accepted an invitation to attend one of their gatherings at Tekka Centre.

Tekka Centre is a groceries market. A wide variety of Indian cuisines is available on the first level and the second level houses many apparel and accessory shops, catering especially to the Indian community in Singapore. There are many Indian temples and shrines in the vicinity of Tekka Centre. These places are gorgeously decorated in gold and a kaleidoscope of colours during festivals like Deepavali and Thaipusam.

There were about thirty people in the translators group, but only slightly more than ten people were in attendance, with ladies being in the majority. Translators are mostly busy with reading and translating texts, some do not talk much in a day. Thus it was a rare chance for them to gather and chat, clearly, everyone treasured the opportunity to engage with one another in conversation.

Although Peggy was a project manager, given her major, she was certainly competent in translation work. While this was not part of her work scope, she was keen to get to know more about translators and their work, since they were so closely linked to hers.

The gathering led her to realise that every profession has its difficulties and obstacles. Everyone had grievances and feelings of haplessness at work.

"What is everyone working on lately?" One of the older female translators kicked off the conversation.

> There is a limit to the companies that translators can get in touch with. In general, they are passively waiting for job assignments.

"The translation services company that I usually work with has not been able to assign more projects to me recently, I can only wait and at the same time also try to establish contact with new companies. As you know, it is better to cooperate with the usual company, working with new companies requires time to adapt and the rates quoted will generally be lower," a lady translator began to pour her grouses immediately.

"Why is it that new companies will quote lower rates?" Peggy blurted out.

Everyone turned to look at Peggy.

Another younger looking translator replied, "Are you a new translator? I have not seen you before. There is a process for a translator and translation services company to build up trust in each other. In the beginning, it is usual for any translation services company to quote a rate lower than the usual standard of any translator. We will not quote too high a rate either; gradually, when both sides become familiar and the working relationship is stable, the rates will increase over time till it matches with individual ability."

> Translators will have to adapt to individual translation services company to be identified.

"This process of trust building is established at the expense of time and pricing. The level of trust that a translator can establish with the translation services company is limited because it involves a long process before translators reached the level of familiarity and trust for translation services companies to remunerate rates according to translator's professional ability. With an extensive listing of translators in each company's database, the chances of receiving assignments that match individual capability are limited." The translator who initiated the conversation explained.

"There is not much that can be done about this. In this line, blowing one's own trumpet will not work, a glorified resume will also not work as well as a piece of work that is well translated." A male translator who looked slightly older than Peggy responded.

Peggy replied, "Thank you for explaining. I have just joined this group. I am trained in translation but currently I am working as a project manager, so expanding our translator base and safeguarding the interests of translators are part of my responsibilities. I feel that I do not know much about this community and I may venture into translation work in the future, that is why I am here to join today's activity. In the days to come, I hope all the seniors present today will give me your guidance and support."

> Translation service companies are typical intermediaries.

"Translation services companies have all the advantages. You just link up and communicate with the client and the translator, then make profit without having to do much else. Unlike translators, who can only be passive and are dependent on translation services companies to assign jobs," a young translator grumbled.

There were all kinds of problems that Peggy and her colleagues faced in the course of their daily work, but it seemed the translator had reduced these to "work that paid easy money", Peggy wanted to defend herself but before she could do so, other translators also began pouring out their grievances.

"The assignments from the translation services companies are quite limited as it is and not all projects can be accepted. Our livelihoods are really constrained by circumstances."

"On occasions where an assignment is in an area that we are not well-acquainted with, we will still bite the bullet and accept it. As a result, the quality of the translation may not be as good as if the work was within our specialisation. The client and the translation services company are not bothered, all they want is the output. But we definitely do our best for the translation."

"I do not really want to accept any job that is not within my specialised domain, but I have housing loans to service and the kids need to go to school, I must support my family. If there are enough assignments which match my skilled areas, that would be perfect, but such a perfect scenario does not always happen."

"Indeed, with the development of Artificial Intelligence growing rapidly, machines are replacing part of the job. To save costs, some clients will just use machine translation and we are not needed anymore. It is tougher and more stressful to survive in this profession."

"That is not always the case. I have a client who had some data written in a foreign language, he tried using AI to do the translation and realised that those were valuable data that could be compromised by using technology. He then approached me to do the translation for part of the data."

"Translation is a process of re-creation, but how many can understand our work of creativity?"

When people of the same trade meet, there is so much to talk about. Peggy was glad that she had made effort to attend the gathering. Many of the translators who were present had not worked with Peggy's company before, but expressed their interests to join the company's pool of translators.

It was fruitful being able to expand her translation resource list through such a gathering but for Peggy, the list was not the most rewarding. Instead, it was the better understanding that she had acquired: of the difficulties that translators faced, as well as their reflections and thoughts about their profession.

Translators mainly rely passively on a few translation services companies to assign them jobs. They can explore their own client base, but the volume is limited. The building of trust is a process, it requires cooperation over time before a translation services company believes in the ability of a translator. This approach is reasonable and conforms with the norm, but it is also not fair to a translator. The crux of the problem lies with "an inability to recognise and showcase each translator's ability on a

> It is no easy task to distinguish between translators, even if they manage to establish a personal reputation, it is difficult for them to be recognised on a large-scale basis.

larger-scale basis", it is therefore difficult for translators to procure projects that match their professional ability.

There are numerous occasions in life that one may require translation and/or interpretations but only a small number of these requires extensive and comprehensive service in large volumes, whether executed through translation services companies or through self-search for translators. The remaining ones are small in volume and fragmented in form. For example, when one is analysing an issue and looking up information in a foreign language publication, translation is required. When communicating with a foreigner speaking a different language at a meeting, interpretation is required. When reading a user manual that is not in one's native language, translation is required. In the case of Peggy's personal experience when travelling in the MRT, the elderly Chinese woman needed help because she couldn't read or speak English. For all of the above situations, most people will just try to avoid them, if possible, otherwise, the alternative is to adapt to the situation or compromise as best as they can. Approaching a translation services company or translators is usually the last resort or may not even be considered.

After working for some time, Peggy eventually managed to establish a pace for work and develop a regular routine.

On a usual day, Peggy would basically start and finish work on time. Occasionally, she would work extra hours. In any case, Peggy kept up with her habit of reading daily. This habit had been cultivated during her university days and had become an integral part of her life.

Singapore is a country that places great emphasis on reading. The government has made concerted effort to encourage reading, library services are convenient and easily accessible. The library is always packed with people, and it is common to see people reading in public and on public transport. This aspect of Singapore made Peggy feel very comfortable; on the weekends, she could often be found at the National Library Building.

The National Library Building is sixteen-storeys high and has three basements. It has a collection of more than 600,000 books and more than a hundred computers and over 6000 types of media resources are available to library members, providing a wide and diversified range of services.

With a glass panelled facade, a huge rooftop canopy and a wind tunnel, designed to enhance the effects of natural ventilation and daylight, the building is an imposing sight. The lighting and temperature of the building's interior spaces can be adjusted according to the change in temperature of the external atmosphere. Sky terraces and roof gardens are utilised to lower local ambient temperature as well as beautify the surroundings. On the top floor is an event space known as "The Pod" which provides a panoramic view of the central district.

The design of the National Library Building in Singapore thus allows it to stand out as a public building in the city. A large part of the ground level is public space, occupied by an atrium which provides space for various events. The other spaces in the building also host exhibitions, conferences and other activities.

Peggy had always been interested in attending seminars as she felt that hearing speakers present the results of their research or thoughts accumulated over a period of time was not only convenient and informative but also helpful in broadening her horizons and thinking.

On one occasion, Peggy was at the library as usual when a seminar poster titled "Nobel Prize and Collaborative Co-Creation" caught her eye. On the poster were portraits of Madame Curie, Einstein, Bohr and others pictured with their inventions, accompanied by a few eye-catching questions:

Do you know the facts of collaborative co-creation for the various categories of the Nobel Prize Awards?

Do you know which are the specific fields that need collaborative co-creation?

Do you know the trends and obstacles for collaborative co-creation?

The guest speaker was an expert in Information Sciences from Hong Kong.

He began the seminar with a few warm-up questions:

"Which year was the Nobel Prize established?"

"What are the specific categories of the Nobel Prize?"

"When were the various categories of Nobel Prizes first awarded?"

"It was established in 1895."

"The categories are Physics, Chemistry, Physiology or Medicine, Economics Sciences, Literature and Peace."

"Apart from the Nobel Prize for Economics Sciences which was first awarded in 1969, the rest of the five Prize categories were first awarded in 1901."

Clearly, many members of the audience were familiar with the Nobel Prize as answers to the questions could be heard in soft murmurs around the room.

"Earlier on, everyone answered that there are six categories for the Nobel Prize. Today's topic is 'The Nobel Prize and Collaborative

Co-Creation', before I go on, do you think collaborative co-creation is essential and possible for all these categories?" Before the audience could respond, the speaker continued, "The Literature Prize is naturally characterised by individual creation, this is not difficult to comprehend. A novel jointly written by two persons is quite unthinkable, is it not? Writing is a very personal endeavour which requires individual decision and courage, if jointly created by two persons, any disagreements may lead to fights."

The speaker's humour triggered laughter from the audience.

"Our focus today will be to analyse the other four prize categories. However, to analyse only the conditions for collaborative co-creation is insufficient. Today's sharing will be divided into three parts: The first part being the details of presented prizes and the introduction of exceptional prize winners; the second part will cover nationality, the organisations which the winners belong to, age, doctorate achieved, research domain and other characteristics; the third part will reveal the collaborative facts on prize winners, development trends and cause analysis. Finally, we will leave some time for interactive exchange."

Peggy found the sharing on the facts of presented prizes and the introduction of exceptional prize winners an interesting exposition. From the speaker's lively narration, Peggy learnt that the Nobel Prize was meant to be awarded only to the living but there were three exceptions, namely, the Nobel Literature Prize in 1931, the Nobel Peace Prize in 1961 and the Nobel Physiology or Medicine Prize in 2011. The youngest Nobel Prize winner to date is Malala Yousafzai from Pakistan, she was awarded the Nobel Peace Prize in 2014 for her advocacy of human rights, "to fight against exploitation of children and young people and for all children to have the right to education". The Curies were the Nobel Prize's "celebrity family", Madame Curie and her husband were awarded the Nobel Prize in Physics, and subsequently, Madame Curie was again awarded the Nobel Prize in Chemistry. Twenty years later, their eldest daughter, who had discovered artificial radioactivity together with her husband Joliot were also awarded the Nobel Prize in Chemistry.

In the second part of his presentation, the speaker did an analysis of tabulated data for the various prize categories. Peggy felt strongly about the tabulated results, they reflected the reality that academic innovations were closely linked to a country's economic strength, attributes of citizens, technological policies, social stability and other factors.

The third part was the main body of the conference, the speaker revealed the facts of collaborative co-creation for the Nobel Prize.

The speaker divided the facts and figures of the Nobel Prize in Economic Studies awarded from 1969 to 2004 into six stages. The other three prizes awarded from 1901 to 2001 were divided into five stages and the specific data were filled into the relevant spaces. The timeline taken was from 1901, with 1950 as the dividing line, till 2001. For these four prizes, the number of collaborated works that were awarded the prize for the latter 50 years were about 5.3 times more that the initial 48 years.

> Collaboration is a trend. Before that can be done, to be effectively identified is the key.

Noting the trend for collaborative prize winnings, at the ninetieth anniversary celebration of the Nobel Prize ceremony, a professor from the University of California, Berkeley, had actually suggested that The Royal Swedish Academy of Sciences review and explain the terms in Alfred Nobel's will and amend the original restriction of awarding to works produced by a maximum of three persons to a research team instead.

"Let us look at the Nobel Prize in Physics specifically. In the earlier years, the more well-known prizes in Physics were mostly individual achievements by scientists such as Albert Einstein, for his achievements in Theoretical Physics, and especially for his discovery of the law of photoelectric effect. The Nobel Prize in Physics was awarded to him in 1921. The 1922 Nobel Prize in Physics was awarded to Niels Bohr for his services in the investigation of the structure of atoms and of the radiation emanating from them. However, the table also showed the trend of prizes being awarded to collaborated works by multiple parties. These include collaborations from scientists of the same country as well as from different countries."

Specifically, if we split the 100 years period from 1901 to 2001 into two phases, before 1950, the achievements of most scientists were completed individually, and that added up to forty times, and accounted for 90.9% compared to 9.1% which were done through collaborations; whereas after 1950, achievements from collaborations added up to 27 times, which was about 50.9%. These numbers showed research studies on Physics, in particular, were slowly moving from individuals to teams.

"Why is this so?" asked the speaker.

"There are three main reasons:

Firstly, the capacity for information sharing from various fields is increasing rapidly, there is also more cross referencing across the different disciplines. The limited time and energy levels of individuals will clearly not be able to cope with such a situation. This can also explain why it is now not possible to have an all-rounded scholar.

Secondly, it is very costly to engage in scientific research, it easily involves tens of millions or even hundreds of millions in US dollars. Besides heavy sponsorships from government and social organisations, international collaborations and joint investments are also good choices. An example would be the European Centre for Nuclear Research.

Thirdly, as scientific research progresses, more research instruments are being invented, some of these include the

Electronuclear Machine, Hubble Space Telescope, Large Hadron Collider, Supercomputers and so on. All of which require more than one person to operate. Therefore, one research project will involve many professionally trained research personnel."

During the interactive session, everyone gave their opinion on the topics discussed.

A manager from a multinational company (MNC) based in Singapore shared about his work experience, "If the Nobel Prize is a positive representation of collaborations, then the current operations of MNCs will show that collaboration is still not the mainstream. MNCs look internationalised, but in reality, being multinational is only in form. We set up small centres in different countries, based on operation requirements, the communications and connections are handled by the management who are a bilingual minority. The management is either appointed by the head office or locally hired bilingual professionals. Most of the branch employees can only speak one language, so the MNC is like an independent community made up of small centres around the world."

Existing multinational companies are not cross-border collaborations.

Peggy also had a question, "Hi, you mentioned in your speech that collaborative co-creation will be the trend for the Nobel Prize. This leads me to think of my profession, I am a project manager in a translation services company. I realised that for elites like top-notch research personnel, the proportion that engaged in collaborations is not significant. I feel that the main obstruction is the language. For everyone else, the language barrier will be even greater and that includes the gentleman who mentioned that language is also a problem faced by MNCs. Civilisation and knowledge know no boundaries, but judging from the current situation, this is only a theoretic ideal. What are your thoughts on this?"

"This lady's thoughts are spot on. Although I did not mention in my speech that language is an issue, as she mentioned, language is indeed the biggest obstacle for multinational collaborations now. Exactly how it can be resolved, I do not have an answer. I hope anyone here with insights can contribute their wisdom to resolve this issue. Lastly, I would like to conclude today's session in two sentences. Firstly, the boundary of language sets limits to our cognition. Huge aspects of human civilisation could not be shared due to the language barrier which makes it more difficult to co-create. Secondly, the co-creation of human civilisation is an inevitable trend, but if there is no auxiliary to help with translation between different languages, there is no way to put the best team together to accomplish an objective."

> Co-creation is an inevitable trend, but language is a barrier for collaborative co-creation.

Weekends were not only spent at the library. Occasionally, Peggy would go for activities organised by the clan associations or update her WeChat public account to record recent life details and reflections.

For Peggy, writing had many advantages. First and foremost, it was for the purpose of recording her experiences. Memories can never keep up with time, people and events flash past us daily, if we do not make a note of them, the majority of these memories will fade over time. In addition, the process of converting thoughts into words helps in reflection. Anything that can be written clearly and systematically would have gone through a process of contemplation. These were the main reasons Peggy tried to update her WeChat public account whenever possible.

Sometimes, there were unexpected appointments on weekends too. One night while Peggy was reading, Doreen knocked on her door.

"Please come in," Peggy put down the book she was holding.

Doreen came in with a plate of cut fruits and asked, "Peggy, are you reading?"

"Yes, Aunt Doreen, I see you are feeding me something nice again!" Peggy was grateful.

"Peggy, will you be free this coming Saturday? I would like to seek your help."

"I have no arrangements for now. Aunt Doreen, don't be shy, please go ahead to ask me for anything."

"There will be a parent-teacher meeting at Candice's school this coming Saturday. As you know, Candice will complete Primary Three soon, it will take her a step closer to the Primary School Leaving Examination (PSLE). This examination is very important for children in Singapore, it is a milestone that determines if a child will be able to get into a reputable secondary school and ultimately to a good university. Thus, I would like to have a detailed discussion with her teachers."

"Is this the first time you are meeting her teachers, Aunt Doreen?"

"No, I have been to previous meetings. The administrative office for schools in Singapore are usually staffed by Singaporeans from the various ethnic groups. They speak both English and their mother tongues, so communication between parents and the school is not a problem. However, not all teachers can speak Mandarin."

"How did you manage for previous meetings?" Peggy was puzzled.

"I asked the bilingual parents of her classmates for help to translate. But then again, it is quite embarrassing to trouble them. There are many issues that I would like to discuss which cannot be explained in detail. I have been in Singapore for a few years now, I can speak a bit of English, but I am still not able to have detailed discussions. Since you are here, I hope you can kindly help me out as an interpreter for this meeting."

Lack of language services that is easily accessible and complies with the required scenarios.

"Aunt Doreen, you don't have to be so formal, I am very thankful to you for taking good care of me since I came to Singapore. Anyway, I do not have any engagement, so I am happy to accompany you."

Candice was studying at a neighbourhood school, though the school compound was not big, the surrounding environment was beautiful. It was Peggy's first visit to a primary school in Singapore, she was curious, so she asked Doreen to show her around the school.

On the left side of the main entrance was the car park, and behind it was a two-storey office block. The upper floor housed the teachers' offices while the offices of the principal and other administrative staff were on the ground floor. Behind the office block were the classrooms sited in long colourful three-storey buildings, with railings along the corridors for safety.

On the ground level, there was a canteen and also an open space that was adjacent to the sheltered sports complex where activities such as the flag raising ceremony, school events or physical education lessons, were held. On non-rainy days, the physical education lessons would be conducted at the open space. The school also had a small playground, a small but lush garden with green vines and a small fountain beside it.

The school compound was surrounded by tall coconut trees, all standing upright like security personnel for the school grounds. The exterior of the compound was surrounded by green wire netting, beyond that were HDB flats and mango trees, Peggy felt invigorated at the pleasant aroma of the mango trees in the air as she walked past.

But what surprised Peggy most was a cage of chickens in the garden; there were also eggs laid by the chickens. Some children were crowding around the cage, watching the birds and chattering away. Peggy took out her mobile phone to snap a few pictures, "Aunt Doreen, why do they rear chickens in school?"

"This is because Singapore is a city state, most children have never seen a chicken, duck or other farm animals up close, some schools will keep these animals so their students can observe them and also learn to care for them and about them."

Peggy and Doreen continued chatting as they followed the signs and directions from volunteers to the hall, the venue of the parent-teacher meeting.

"What is Candice's form teacher like? Can he or she speak Mandarin?"

"She is Miss Kate, a young female teacher who was transferred to the school when Candice started Primary Three. Candice said that the teacher grew up in Australia, she came to Singapore not too long ago so she can only communicate in simple Mandarin. She is very conscientious and responsible. I remember the last time I came to the school and met her along the corridors outside the general office, she told me Candice's results for the recent examinations and praised Candice for being hardworking. She was not referring to the result slip, but she could remember Candice's results. This incident left a deep impression on me and Candice has also mentioned time and again that she likes this teacher."

"Candice is lucky indeed, good teachers really make a difference to the school experience."

Peggy had no trouble interpreting for Doreen. The parent-teacher meeting started off as a group meeting for all parents of children in the class and then continued as individual interactions with the teachers for parents who had enquiries.

> Translation is a long-tailed market. None of these companies will provide language services for all segments without guaranteed returns. Not in the past, not now and not in the future, there will only be a large ecosystem.

It was the first time that Doreen would be able to have such a smooth and thorough communication with Candice's form teacher, so she was full of anticipation. From a general overview of how well her daughter was learning and her weaker subjects, to her behaviour in school and relationships with her classmates, Doreen could not wait to get to the bottom of it all. The teacher was, as described, friendly and responsible. Besides giving comprehensive answers to questions on all matters brought up by the parents, she also knew the results and characteristics of every child at the back of her palm.

Work had become busy for Peggy as well. Jason, who was responsible for website operation and market development had made some modifications to the keyword search and that had increased the company's business volume. Peggy and her colleagues had their hands full as a result.

After her unpleasant experience of receiving the complaint, Peggy became even more self-disciplined and strict with herself in terms of work. She made sure to exercise stringent control over the quality of work for her projects, and soon she encountered a case that gave her "food for thought". The translator in this case was a Malaysian Chinese, strong in English and slightly weaker in Mandarin, she was assigned a Chinese-English translation job.

Peggy wasted no time in contacting the translator, "Miss Helen, I saw your submission for the final translation, it is just passable because there are many areas that can be better translated, but you used only the most basic and common translation."

When Helen did not respond, Peggy continued, "Take for example the phrase '胸有成竹 xiōng yǒu chéng zhú'. There are better ways to translate this, such as 'have a well-thought-out plan', 'have a card up one's sleeve' or 'have an ace up one's sleeve'. But you have chosen 'have faith in', this does not quite capture the meaning of the phrase, does it? Another example, the phrase '釜底抽薪 fǔ dǐ chōu xīn', your translation is 'take away the firewood under the cooking pot', this is a literal translation. Fundamentally, this is not wrong, but why not translate it to 'take a drastic measure to deal with a situation', which expresses the idiom's original meaning more clearly…?"

> On a daily basis, people are spending time and energy to do repetitive translations. A better version of the same content that may have been translated could not be retrieved for sharing.

Having heard Peggy's explanation, Helen responded, "Why should I bother making effort to translate to this extent? As a project manager, you know full well that the job is paid based on the number of words in the original text. No matter how well the translation is done, it will not impact on my income level. Without going against my conscience, it is sensible for me to just meet the basic requirements."

> A translator's high-quality output does not equate to high returns.

Peggy was taken aback by Helen's response. Indeed, it had been "composed, certain, and resolute" and Peggy could not find anything to refute. Given that Helen was abiding by the bottom line, Peggy did not have the right to criticise her on moral grounds. Feeling disgruntled, she hung up the phone shortly.

From this incident, Peggy realised that under the existing industry system, a translator's conscientious effort did not necessarily equate to the same level of returns, hence there was no doubt that this had an effect on the level of quality work produced.

One of the reasons had been indirectly highlighted by the translator: the flexibility of language use. Language flexibility allows for multiple possibilities in translation. Helen's translations were not wrong, but Peggy's suggested versions were better. Another reason was the diversity and richness in culture where there may not be a matching common term in both languages. A "sofa", for instance, was once viewed as a foreign item in China and there were no corresponding words to describe it. It was not acceptable to translate it as "a chair wrapped with cloth". After several corrections, it was subsequently transliterated as "沙发 shā fā" and has become the widely accepted translation since. This process of wide acceptance however only took place over time.

These attributes of language and culture create a problem not only for individual translators but also for the profession. A well-translated piece of work requires extra effort, but translators are not usually rewarded for such extra effort, translators are therefore not willing to make the effort to achieve "faithfulness, expressiveness and elegance" in their translated output. At the professional level, the application of artificial intelligence to translation is also hindered as software is not able to standardise usage for mass production, given that good translation requires understanding of context.

As Peggy pondered on this issue, memories of herself reading Chinese translated text when she was learning English began to float into her mind, there were both pleasant and unpleasant ones. She recalled the occasions when the same foreign language book had two translated versions in Chinese, but with a world of difference in the contents of both; one that was too difficult and the other too easy to understand.

In particular, Peggy had a deep impression of a book on linguistic studies that had been translated into Chinese. The author had been an American scholar. The translator, understanding that the translated text was mainly targeted at young learners and those

> Essentially, a good translation is rewriting, it is a high-level mental work that is irreplaceable by machines.

who were not well-versed in English as a foreign language, omitted some of the technical terms which did not affect the overall understanding of the original text. There were areas where literal translation could not express the original intention of the author, so they were replaced by a word or a Chinese idiom. In addition, some of the American examples quoted in the book were either omitted or replaced with examples from China. Peggy vividly recalled being highly impressed by the professionalism and consideration of the translator.

Before she knew it, the end of the month arrived. At the company's monthly meeting, Peggy took the initiative to share with everyone her recent research findings. At the same time, however, she accidentally discovered a 'trivial matter'. She realised that there was a big gap in the figures for total sales from all the project managers versus the total monthly sales of the company. Curious about this discrepancy, Peggy asked Lily about it, Lily revealed that the boss had a few big clients whom he managed personally, in short, the rest of the employees would never have a chance to be connected to these clients.

> Translation services companies are natural competitors that resemble isolated islands of information — data are widely dispersed and there is no avenue nor incentive to share.

Seeing the look of dismay on Peggy's face, Lily consoled her, "It is alright, it is the same in all other translation services companies. We do not need to take offence."

"I understand. We are just employees, we should just do our jobs well," Peggy smiled. It was time to knock off for the day, Peggy left the office after saying goodbye to Lily.

Summary:
A Perpetual Deadlock

Translation is a process to convert information among different languages. Despite several industrial revolutions, the operating nature of the translation services profession has not changed. The typical mode of processing information supplied by the clients remains the same. These companies have low threshold, are small in scale and continue to operate in the form of workshops.

Translation services companies are typical intermediaries, linking client's requirements to a translator. They will source for suitable translators to complete a translation job and package the completed job according to client's requirements before exporting them.

The rapid development of the internet has contributed to the tremendous increase in the volume of information. However, being the profession that does the conversion of information, the speed of development for the translation field could not keep up with the changes over time. This is due to the peculiarity of the industry, or more accurately, it is determined by the peculiarity of languages. As a result of language flexibility and cultural richness, language conversion could not be done on a standardised and large-scale basis. The three parties in the translation industry namely the client, the translator, and the translation services company, are in a painful state of a deadlock.

From the client's position, they seek help with translation as they do not understand the language and they are unable to assess the quality of the translation. Language services are generally required as part of our daily routine such as learning, working, living and other scenarios. It is seldom required as an independent piece of work. Under normal circumstances, the outsourcing service model requires the user to extract the specific content from a scenario to hand over for translation which is of great inconvenience.

Under a centralised system, none of the companies in the translation field will be guaranteed revenue by providing convenient and efficient language services for all the different scenarios.

In the blockchain era, tokens can be the driving force and act as the incentive mechanism to connect and distribute resources to expand the coverage to meet the requirements of different scenarios. This joint establishment of a large ecosystem for language services facilitates sharing of values.

From the translator's perspective, the lack of a standardised, open and reliable evaluation system restricts identification of translation talents. Most of the time, these talents could only receive low value jobs like those of an average translator with the same returns. Due to the lack of capacity and channel for disseminating information, language talents could not receive any recognition for the valuable data translated by them.

The vast amount of linguistic data in the language industry are largely distributed among the computers of translation agencies and those of the numerous bilingual professionals. These valuable linguistic data are largely idle, lying in the respective computers like an isolated island of information. Under a centralised system, there is a natural distrust and subconscious competition that exist among different language services companies. As a result, information could not be shared, and this hinders the setup of an integrated system for open and reliable evaluations.

In the era of blockchain, the rights to digital assets ensure records are not tampered with. Also, the mechanism of token allows value exchange and information sharing. These enable the sharing of the credentials of language talents among translation services companies and the identification and recognition of talented linguists. The use of tokens facilitates sharing of value in exchange for a channel to unleash greater values for an individual.

For translation services companies, there is a natural distrust among language service providers and individuals under a centralised system. There is also a situation of dispersion in the language service sector. Crucial statistical data relating to languages are isolated from industry players. As a result, artificial intelligence, which relies highly on these crucial data could not play its role, limiting the use of advance production models in the language service sector. Out of the total expenses incurred for a project, the language service provider would only receive 40–50% of the amount, a significant amount will be exhausted by traditional and outdated production models.

In the blockchain era, the ability to connect and share big language data with guaranteed attribution and revenue allows faster development and deeper application of artificial intelligence technology and a new model of collaboration in the language services sector.

The original centralised business processes, which were built based on information asymmetry will be transformed by blockchain into a decentralised business system and a disintermediated business process. This will enable established economic or social systems to achieve greater efficiency. It will also redistribute profits previously held by the central nodes and intermediaries in the business process. The translation industry that has not changed fundamentally despite several industrial revolutions, is well suited for blockchain transformation. The traditional business models of translation service providers will disappear, and the resources exhausted in the process will be freed for the benefit of both clients and translators.

The translation profession could not mass produce translations due to the natural attributes of language. However, the common characteristics of language and blockchain could transform the translation industry to

SUMMARY

107

give this traditional profession a new lease of life. Translation services companies, which have always existed in an intermediary mode, will disappear and the industry will be revamped, while creating a so-called blue ocean market.

The business volume of the top global 100 translation services companies is < 15% of the total market volume.

70% of the translation services companies have less than 10 employees.

Note

———— Chapter 4 ————

Unrecognised Gifts

The Lack of a Suitable Model for Bilingual Talents to Actualise Potential

Peggy joined her countrymen for a half day tour around Singapore. They viewed residential properties, had a meal at a Hunan restaurant and toured the Henderson Wave, the highest pedestrian bridge in Singapore. Everyone had an enjoyable time. Peggy was able to chat freely with her fellow native Chinese participants about language and translation. She expressed deep admiration for the talents of her new acquaintances, particularly when she realised that many of them were well established in their professions and also effectively bilingual or even multilingual. However, she also realised that their comprehensive skill sets were like scattered pearls, not accorded the value they deserved or given opportunity for display and development.

Diversity in language expressions due to the richness of national cultures constitutes a natural attribute of language which causes difficulties in assessing the quality of any translation. The reality is, on one hand, there is insufficient production capacity for translation and on the other hand, bilingual talents with capacity are dispersed across different trades and professions. The lack of an open, transparent and credible model creates an obstacle for the value of these talents to be identified, incentivised and priced in the market.

1   The natural attributes of language cause difficulties for assessment of the quality of translation.
2   The value that translators provide is not easily distinguished nor acknowledged extensively.
3   Language ability of bilingual talents is reflected as instrumental value, a tool to aid in achieving a goal.
4   Bilingual talents with comprehensive professional and linguistic skills cannot be remunerated for their value add without a proper model.

***

In the midst of adapting to life in Singapore, Peggy was introduced to another social group of native Chinese people that was aptly named "flavours of home".

More than just a chat group, it was a community that shared practical information for daily life in Singapore. Whenever someone came across any useful information, such as a particular dance class that offered good value for money, a newly opened Chinese restaurant or sale of second-hand furniture, it would be shared in the group. Those who had businesses could also post ads in the group, this did not make anyone uncomfortable and in fact, everyone was very supportive because they wished to help their fellow countrymen.

Occasionally, their group members would also organise in-person activities and meetups. One of these that Peggy attended was a "half day Singapore tour" on a Saturday. It was suggested by Frank, a real estate agent because some members of the group were considering buying a condominium. The plan was to view some units that were for sale first and then having dinner and a walk along the Henderson Wave bridge. Interested participants could just pay a small fee and assemble at the designated location at the specified time. Although Peggy was not looking to invest in a condominium, she was keen to know more about the property market in Singapore and to take this opportunity to unwind, so she signed up for the tour.

Peggy did not usually pay much attention to her dressing and make-up but since it was her first meeting with people whom she had only previously conversed with online, she made an effort to look presentable. After applying some light make-up, she put on new ear studs and tied a nifty bun on her head. Clad in a beige-coloured dress and a pair of brown moccasins, she said goodbye to Doreen and left for the activity.

Singapore is divided into twenty-eight districts. The housing projects that were being marketed at the sales office where Frank worked were in the prime areas.

Facing the southern part of the construction site was a busy traffic junction but it was surrounded by a lush forest which helped block out the noise to a certain extent. Not too far away was the entrance to the MRT station, the area was surrounded by tall buildings and public amenities such as a hospital, and even a school and a shopping mall.

Frank led the group into the sales office.

At the lobby of the sales office, a framed cartoon hung prominently on the wall caught Peggy's eye. It was titled "The ladder of success". There were eight stick figures showing different actions, starting from the left bottom corner to the right top corner, representing eight states of mind: "I will not do it", "I cannot do it", "I want to do it", "How will I do it", "I will try to do it", "I can do it", "I will do it now", and finally the last figure with a smile and in high spirits, "I did it!"

On the right bottom of the cartoon was the line of words: "Which stage are you at?"

"This is such an interesting cartoon," Peggy thought to herself.

"I believe everyone knows that Singapore has three types of housing, namely, HDB flats, private condominiums and landed property. The purchase terms of condominiums are relatively more liberal, foreigners of any identity can make a direct purchase. It can be a single buyer or joint buyers," Frank continued talking, "Our company mainly takes charge of sales for private condominiums and this includes projects under construction as well as existing housing units, in short, both new launch projects and resale units. We have different units in a wide price range. My colleague and I will show you around, you may ask questions at any time."

"Can we look at the existing units first?" An elderly couple inquired.

"Of course, please follow me this way," Frank's colleague, a female property agent replied. "The existing units we have are mainly new, but there are some resale units too."

"Is it more cost-effective to buy a new unit or a resale unit?" A middle-aged lady asked.

"There is no absolute good or bad, it depends mainly on individual requirements and affordability. For projects under construction, there is an issue of price increase. In Singapore, new housing projects take about two or three years to complete. When new condominium units are ready for occupancy, generally there will be an increase of about 10% of the original purchase price to these new units. Under normal circumstances, the increase in price will clearly be higher than the rental paid for the two to three years of waiting time, therefore, it is good to wait if you can."

This explanation sparked fervent discussion.

"Housing prices in Singapore increase fast!"

"It is worthwhile to buy early and the ones who can afford should try to buy new units, it does feel different."

"We are here to view on behalf of my son and daughter-in-law, we definitely hope that they can live in a new house."

"I think that there is nothing wrong with buying a resale unit, as long as it is worth the price." A middle-aged lady dressed in floral short sleeve blouse responded, she seemed to be there alone. "I would like to buy a condominium unit, it has to be near the central district, it is alright for it to be smaller in size. I am only concerned if there were any unpleasant happenings in the house before."

With blockchain, historical information of any house or flat can be added as a block onto the chain and be viewed clearly at a glance with absolute authenticity and credibility.

The lady sales agent replied immediately, "Yes, Madam, if you have interest to purchase any unit after viewing, this information can be obtained after registering with the Housing and Development Board."

"We do not need a big unit either since it will just be the two of us for now. However, we would prefer to buy a new unit." This comment was from a young couple dressed in matching couple outfits. Seeing that they were holding hands and smiling broadly, Peggy guessed that they were probably newlyweds or soon to be married.

Frank and his colleagues thus proceeded to show the group a few units.

The different units had already been renovated, with built in cabinets and wardrobes and different types of floorings for the rooms, the walls had also been painted and had well-equipped kitchens and bathrooms, even the air-conditioning system had been installed. The new owner would just need to decide on lights, curtains and purchase some furniture and they would be ready to move into the house.

The real estate developer that Frank worked for was generous. Every buyer would be gifted with a washing machine, a dryer and an oven for his/her new home.

One of the condominium units that the group viewed was particularly well-received because of its three-metre-high ceiling. In Singapore, the ceiling of HDB flats is about 2.5 to 2.6 metres, and for condominiums it would be about 2.8 to 3.1 metres high, some going even as high as 3.5 meters. The unit with the high ceiling had an atmospheric and beautiful loft layout, the bed was set up on the upper deck with abundant space below that could be well utilised. The reddish-brown wood flooring, combined with the neutral colours of the home appliances and wallpaper added to the novelty and style of the unit.

There were many facilities in this particular condominium, which were often common in condominiums in general; swimming pool, private car park, barbecue area, basketball court, garden, outdoor fitness corner and indoor gym. The female agent also mentioned that many developers try to be innovative in developing new condominium projects by having creative themes for all facilities in the estate. It was the same for the units in their sales office.

"We have a question here. If we are already owners of a HDB flat, can we buy a condominium?" A couple with two daughters in tow raised this question.

"If one of your family members is a Singaporean, you may go ahead to buy a condominium. Otherwise, you will be required to sell the HDB flat within six months after the handover of the condominium unit," the sales agent replied immediately.

> With blockchain, authentication can be done quickly and accurately.

Having viewed the different layouts of the units, some important questions about home purchase were raised.

"We have heard that there are three types of real estate ownership in Singapore, would it be a better choice to buy a ninety-nine-year leasehold property or a freehold property?" The elderly couple was the oldest among the group and were naturally more concerned about issues relating to property rights.

"Sir and Madam, your question is tough. The real estate property market comprises mainly of ninety-nine-year leasehold units. Generally, for the same area, a freehold title deed will cost about 20% more than a ninety-nine-year leasehold title deed. I feel that it depends on your budget, if there is a limit, it will be better to invest in a ninety-nine-year leasehold unit. If budget is not an issue, then it is your preference."

"Which one will give a better rate of return?" The elderly couple asked.

Frank responded to that question, "It depends on individual situation, but according to internet statistics, in a comparison of a ninety-nine-year leasehold title versus a freehold title at the same area, the former tends to have a better return."

"Indeed, buying property is also an investment. Considerations must be given to more than just one or two factors, there are other factors such as government planning, entry level prices, sites for development and other related issues," the female agent remarked, showing her professionalism.

The young couple had another question, "What happens if we buy a new housing unit and there is an issue with quality?"

"You do not have to worry about that because the Singapore government has a set of regulations to control the real estate property market. All new housing units will have a one-year warranty period for repair and maintenance. Within a year of handover, if there is any quality issue with the house, you can feedback to the developer and they will arrange for their maintenance team to resolve the issue."

Well, it is usual that people will want to compare different offers before committing to a purchase. Seeing that no one was prepared to make a decision on the spot, Frank concluded enthusiastically, "Buying a house is not a trivial matter, it is wise to view and compare. However, should any one of you decide on any of the units here, please feel free to come anytime to this sales office, just quote my name and you will be given preferential rates. As fellow countrymen, I will definitely help everyone secure the best discount!"

With that, the group proceeded with the next part of their itinerary: dinner. Dinner had been arranged at a Hunan restaurant under the recommendation of another member, Ken and his wife Rose, who were originally from Hunan province. They had been in Singapore for more than thirty years.

"The Hunan cuisine from this restaurant is good, it serves the most authentic Hunan dishes that we have had in Singapore. We come here regularly and sometimes my son, daughter-in-law and granddaughter will join us. There is something magical about these authentic foods, just one taste is sufficient to bring us back to our familiar hometown in a flash," Ken told everyone.

"We will leave it to the both of you to decide on the menu then!" Frank exclaimed.

Ken replied with a smile, "We will gladly oblige. Dishes like mala chicken, steamed fish head with chopped pepper, xiang-style stuffed beancurd, family portrait (a traditional starter dish where about twelve food items are cooked together and served in a big pot) and stir-fry shredded tripe are classic Hunan specialties. We will have them all. The signature dish of this restaurant is the braised pork."

UNRECOGNISED GIFTS

"Hangzhou has braised pork too, known as Dongpo pork (东坡肉 dōng pō róu — The dish is named after Su Dongpo (苏东坡), the famed Song dynasty poet who was considered the inventor of the dish). What is the difference between Hunan braised pork and Hangzhou Dongpo pork?" Peggy was curious to find out.

"Young lady, we have not personally tried Dongpo pork. But Hunan braised pork lives up to its reputation, try it later and you will know. We will have these few signature dishes for now, please feel free to add on other dishes you would like to try," Ken responded.

While waiting for the food to be served, everyone began chatting, it did not take long for the group to become familiar with one another.

"Maggie, you are a translator! I am a project manager with a translation services company. What a coincidence!" Peggy's excited voice rang out above the others. She was thrilled to meet Maggie who like her, had attended the activity alone. Maggie was working freelance as a translator.

"Then we are partly in the same trade. Peggy, you studied language?" Maggie replied, equally happy.

"Yes, I did! I studied translation. Maggie, do you want to join our company's pool of translators?"

> A large number of bilingual talents are not full-time translators but are dispersed across different professions and have varying linguistic abilities to meet language needs in different situations and at different levels.

"Of course! My area of studies was not language but literature. I love languages and I can do some translation. However, I have not been accepting too many translation jobs, I do more writing of articles and at present, I am preparing to write a novel."

"Wow Maggie! You are not only self-studying translation; you have a love for literature and writing too," Peggy was delighted to find a kindred spirit and they quickly exchanged contact details.

"I see this young lady have made a new friend who appreciates your talents. Look at how excited she is," another member of the group known as Wooly teased, "You mentioned translation. In fact, my job has a little to do with translation too. I am an accountant and I work for a few companies on a part-time basis. Occasionally, I will translate some simple accounting materials."

"I do not understand the translation profession, but all of you have made me feel that there is translation everywhere, is this a tough job?" Frank blurted out, keen to participate in their conversation.

Peggy recalled her time of intense reflection on the language services industry and answered earnestly, "Translation itself is difficult but interesting. There are some problems in the industry, these issues ultimately have impact on individuals. The supply and demand do not match. On one hand, many translation professionals do not have enough work that fits their abilities. I attended a gathering with a group of translators and heard about their grievances. On the other hand, there are a myriad of minor needs for translation in our daily lives that are not fulfilled. I met an elderly lady from China on the MRT who could not read English signboards and needed help for directions. I also accompanied my co-tenant Doreen to her daughter's parent-teacher meeting as she needed help with interpretation."

> The quantity of both supply and demand is high, but there is a lack of appropriate platforms to establish links between them.

"You are so right, Peggy. I am glad we are now proficient enough to read documents and materials in English," Joan joined the conversation, she and her husband were the newlyweds who were looking to buy a new house. "We studied biology and we hope to continue in this field, so being able to read in English is an essential skill. When we started reading documents in English, we had to copy and paste paragraphs of text into the translation software and decide from the output which sections were really useful before we read them in detail."

"My wife and I were the first batch of exam candidates after the college entrance examination was reinstated back home in China. There were no machines and without any conditions to facilitate simultaneous learning in listening, speaking, reading and writing, people had to learn English in a very unnatural and awkward manner. We had to study the dictionary and memorise the content in the dictionary without regard to whether we could speak or understand what we heard. Actually, reading and understanding is a priority," Ken also chipped in and shared his unpleasant past experience.

"Well, learning a new language is difficult, maybe even a pain! The pre-requisites are firstly, patience and secondly, hard work! I cannot remember who it was who came up with this viewpoint through a joke, 'one who is too intelligent cannot learn a language well'," Jerome remarked with a grin on his face.

"Why?" Peggy took it literally.

"The process of learning a language is very slow, intelligent people would rather use the same amount of time and energy to work on other tasks and see instant results. Learning a language has no guarantee of results or quality improvement even after a month or two," Jerome continued.

"But intelligent people have excellent willpower," Peggy replied.

"That is why this is just a joke," Jerome shot back.

Everyone burst out laughing.

Amidst the chatting and laughter, the food was served. The plate of Hunan braised pork was placed in the centre of the table. It was sliced neatly into squares, with the skin layer facing up, carefully arranged on a layer of vegetables. The amber red of the braised pork set off the emerald green of the vegetables perfectly.

"Try this everyone."

"The meat is so soft, and the texture is so good."

"The gravy is rich and fragrant."

"The pork is fat but not greasy."

For a moment, there was silence while everyone at the table savoured the pork. "How is this braised pork made? Aunt Rose, can you tell us the secret to this dish, we would like to learn how to do it," Joan piped up.

"To cook braised pork, patience is key. It takes at least an hour of work, alternating between strong and low fire during cooking. After rinsing the pork with water, blanch it in hot boiling water. Drain the water and cut into cubes of 2.5cm," Rose briefed.

"2.5cm? So precise?" asked Peggy.

"This is just a guideline of course, no one is expected to measure before cutting, experienced chefs can do it instinctively. It tastes best with the meat cut into cubes of this size," Ken explained.

"It is fresh and sweet. I suppose sugar was added?" Another member of the group named Michael asked.

"That is right, after the meat is blanched, it will be fried and coated with sugar for colour," Rose replied.

"White sugar?" Joan asked.

"We have to be particular about the type of sugar used, the best sugar is granulated sugar as it can withstand high temperature. Pour chicken stock and stir continuously till the white sugar becomes a reddish wine colour. The sugar is then mixed with oil and further melted into a bright and moist syrup. The meat is then added and pan fried, with the syrup scooped over it continuously to create a coating. The next step will be to add cooking wine, salt, monosodium glutamate, soya sauce, fermented bean curd, scallions, ginger, dried chilli and cinnamon, continue to stir fry for about 30 minutes before lowering the fire to stew and finally when the gravy thickens, the meat is ready to be served," Rose rattled the steps off the top of her head, clearly she was an expert.

"This sounds easy but I'm sure it will be difficult to actually do it. The ingredients already make me confused," Jerome sighed.

"Youngsters like you are busy with work and I suppose you seldom cook. Well, eating at restaurants is convenient too," Wooly remarked.

"It is even easier to order food delivery," Jerome said with a laugh.

"Ken, you are from Hunan, I have seen the Hunan Tanci (弹词),[13] on TV, can you do that too?" Frank mentioned the Chinese folk art out of the blue.

"Don't be surprised that he does know a little, but he has not done it in a long time, I am not sure if he is willing to embarrass himself today," Rose smiled and looked at her husband.

"Ken, do it please!" everyone cheered.

"Ken, let us hear your voice."

---

[13] The literal translation of "弹词 tán cí" is "plucking rhymes". It is a form of storytelling with accompanied stringed instruments.

"Yes, I will but I think it is necessary to do an introduction to the Hunan Tanci. As you may know, Tanci is one type of traditional opera, Changsha (长沙), Yiyang (益阳), Xiangtan (湘潭) and other places have their own local versions, it has a history of more than 200 years. During the revolution of 1911, some of the progressive intellectuals had made use of this traditional art to spread the ideology of the democratic revolution. To perform Tanci, one must be dressed in a traditional long gown and play the lute (a plucked string instrument with an oval shaped sound box). I do not have these now but since everyone is interested, I will sing a few verses without the instrument."

Ken cleared his throat and began to sing the "Ode to the Ancient City《古城颂 gǔ chéng sòng》".

A bright moon shine over nine states

一轮明月照九州 yì lún míng yuè zhào jiǔ zhōu

Xiangjiang river water flows leisurely to the north

湘江北去水悠悠 xiāng jiāng běi qù shuǐ yōu yōu

The ancient city of Changsha has a long history

古城长沙历史久 gǔ chéng cháng shā lì shǐ jiǔ

Hear my rhymes to know the origin

且听我弹词说来由 qiě tīng wǒ tán cí shuō lái yóu

Poems from the Chu and Han dynasties sing praises of elegance

楚辞汉赋颂风雅 chǔ cí hàn fù sòng fēng yǎ

The homeland of Qu Jia sings about the country's worries

屈贾之乡唱国忧 qū jiǎ zhī xiāng chàng guó yōu

To spread filial piety from the Dingwangtai towers

定王台上刘发传孝道 dìng wáng tái shàng líu fā chuán xiào dào

The tribe of King Ma fights in the palace to eliminate enmity

马王堆里宫斗泯恩仇 mǎ wáng duī li gōng dòu mín ēn chóu

The Four-goat square vessel filled with wine

四羊方尊盛美酒 sì yáng fāng zūn shèng měi jiǔ

Wu state of The Three Kingdoms abbreviated the spring and autumn period

三国吴简写春秋 sān guó wū jiǎn xiě chūn qiū

The melodious ode sung by Ken filled the dining room. Everyone listened with bated breath. Even the two young girls were entranced, though they very likely did not understand the profound meaning of the verses. At the end of his short performance, Ken received a warm round of applause and cheers. He smiled and bowed slightly but also remarked sadly, "Tanci is a precious part of Hunan folk art…but fewer and fewer people know about and can appreciate this traditional art with each passing year."

The rest of the group looked at each other, but no one seemed to know what to say, they all nodded quietly in agreement and resumed eating.

"Peggy, how is business at the translation services company you work at?" Maggie decided to change the subject and resume her conversation on translation with Peggy.

"It is not bad; I have to put in overtime occasionally. I was a little disappointed on my first day, I thought this company has such a beautiful website, why is the office environment so small and humble? The staff strength is small too. But the boss said that at least our company has a shopfront, it is one of the better ones in this industry."

"What is the scope of business?"

"It is pretty extensive, translation, interpretations, licence translation, all of these are included. You can indicate your area of specialisation, language pairs, rates and any other information, as well as samples of your translated work, I will add you into the database."

Joan joined the conversation, "Peggy, does the company accept all types of assignments?"

"What do you mean by 'all types of assignments'? Well, remuneration is the primary driving force for our work but of course, we do not accept anything that violates the law and discipline…!"

"What I meant is, will you also accept a small assignment?"

"Yes, we may, on a case-by-case basis. But frankly, if it is a small problem, generally, we will not mobilise resources to get a translation."

Joan nodded in acknowledgment, she seemed lost in thought. After a while, she continued, "I am just thinking aloud, for people like us living in a foreign land, there are some common small issues that every one of us encounters, or maybe it is a requirement that is common for a group of people. For example, when I was driven crazy trying to read the English documents, I had this idea, many people must have read this

> Bilingual talent is fully capable of discovering the latest industry information and translating it into another language, but this potential is not being utilised because of the lack of a delivery model.

document before, why is it that no one, especially those who are able to, has been kind enough to translate and share it?"

"Are there any benefits to translating and sharing?" Maggie was amused, "but you do have a point, well, you can always organise a group of people to work on such a project."

"Oh no…I am not being serious. When I was able to read the English materials fluently, I did not become one of those kind-hearted people either…! By the way, Peggy, does your company accept translation of books?" asked Joan again.

"Yes, we do, but not usually. Novels account for the majority of book projects, not so much for professional books. I am thinking that this is probably due to the stricter professional threshold for these books, so most of such translations are done by experts within the community themselves," Peggy was thinking as she responded.

"I have a good friend from university who is a high school teacher now. Based on my understanding of what she shared, high school teachers are not willing to translate books but more interested to publish books because translation reaps a lower return. The more qualified the scholar, the less willing he or she will be to do translation work. Experts can easily conduct a lecture and earn a good income, why go through such effort to painstakingly translate a book?" Joan said.

Wooly was drawn to their conversation, "But translation is important. I was working for a company and almost got into a lawsuit due to a mistake. Thereafter, I am very careful with translations and will always check repeatedly. Afterall, I have not been professionally trained in translation."

"Regarding damages caused by translation blunders, I have read of a severe case. It was about a fire in a factory in France that resulted in losses of several million Euros. Investigations after the fire showed that there was a problem with the translation of the instruction manual, the workers followed the instruction manual and set too high a temperature for the operations," Maggie explained.

"On the importance of translation, I was impressed by what the former Secretary-General of the United Nations Javier Pérez de Cuéllar said: The fate of mankind is decided first by politicians and then by translations…!" Peggy laughed.

> Translation is important, it can (re)create reality.

"Translation blunders not only result in economic losses; they may result in separation of a couple too. Let me share a story, a guy fell in love with a gorgeous female classmate at the university. One day, she finally sent him a message, 'Wenn du mich nicht verlässt, werde ich an deiner Seite bis zum Ende der Welt sein.' He knew it was German but could not understand, so he quickly sent the message to a friend who was studying German. His friend looked at the message and replied, it says 'if you don't leave me, we will perish together'. This guy was devastated and he stopped all contact with her. Subsequently when he studied the German language more, he realised that the phrase had actually meant 'if you stand by me always, I will stick to you in life and death'," Joan said, a wide grin on her face. The ladies burst into peals of laughter.

The main course of the meal was almost done, and the waitress began serving the fruits.

"What are you ladies talking about that made you laughed so happily? Share it with all of us and let us join in the fun," Ken said.

"We are talking about jokes made out of translation blunders," Maggie was clearly well-read and eager to share, she quoted another example, "I will share another case of a political translation blunder, this is not just funny but it had serious consequence. In 1956, Nikita Khrushchev gave a speech at a reception at the

Polish embassy in Moscow. In the course of the speech he said, 'We will bury you', the translator translated this to 'We will have all of you buried'. The sentence promptly became the headline for numerous magazine covers and newspapers, it also further chilled the relations between the Soviet Union and the West (Europe and America). Was that the intended meaning of Nikita Khrushchev? In fact, his exact words were closer to 'We will dig you in', which meant 'We will dig a grave for you'. The two sentences sound similar, but according to other sources, his intent was to say that communism would 'dig a grave' for capitalism, it was not directed specifically at any country."

"My goodness! There is so much to learn about translation."

"This is interesting!"

Everyone was astonished.

"Although I did not study language and translation, I would like to share a case which I had encountered. This case tells us how beautiful a good translation can be," Joan who specialised in biology continued, "I came across a great translation, the gene that is known as 'timeless' was translated as '永恒 yǒng héng', which we all know means eternal and always constant, something that has achieved faithfulness in its elegance and expressiveness. This translation is so much better than the term 'no time' which I saw in previous science articles. With this translation, the four main terms to describe the biological clock of the drosophilid fly is wonderfully complete and thematically accurate: they are 'period', 'timeless', 'clock' and 'cycle'."

"Ah, this I understand perfectly. My wife often receives praise that she looks like she is in her thirties, clearly, she has 'timeless' beauty!" With this public display of affection from Michael for his wife, all the singles at the gathering looked around at one another with mixed feelings and clapped.

"Can you use machines to do translation?" Jerome had majored in Artificial Intelligence (AI), he was smiling, clearly enjoying the chat and laughter.

> Machines convey information. Human imparts expressiveness.

"Yes, we can, but machines can only perform basic translation. It is impossible to rely on machines to achieve 'elegance' in translation. Do you all remember the song which I shared in our chat before? It's 'Someone like you' by Adele. A netizen created classical translation of it and named it 'In search of another deep blue sea《另寻沧海 lìng xún cāng hǎi》'."

"Yes, I do, and I remember the first few lines of the song," Jerome started humming the tune and Joan recited the corresponding classical version:

"I heard, that you are settled.

已闻君，诸事安康。yǐ wén jūn, zhū shì ān kāng

That you found a girl and you're married now

遇佳人，不久婚嫁。yù jiā rén, bù jiǔ hūn jià

I heard, that your dreams came true

已闻君，得偿所想。yǐ wén jūn, dé cháng suǒ xiǎng

Guess she gave you things, I didn't give to you."

料得是，卿识君望。" liào dé shì, qīng shí jūn wàng

"It is so sweet to see this couple echoing each other," someone quipped, as everyone else burst into laughter.

The last activity for the half day Singapore tour was a walk along the Henderson Wave bridge.

The Henderson Wave bridge is the highest pedestrian bridge in Singapore. It is twelve storeys high and 275 metres long. Henderson Wave bridge is part of the nine-kilometre chain of hills of the Southern Ridges in Singapore. It connects Mount Faber to Telok Blangah Hill.

The bridge has a unique wave-like structure with four wave crests and three wave troughs. The designs of the waves give it a dynamic feel. Before they stepped onto the bridge, Peggy and the group took in the view from the side and were amazed by the visual impact. The sun had not set, the evening sky was pastel blue but still bright, it was almost like seeing a painted blue canvas fighting to shine through the layers of white clouds.

The group entered from the west side and moved slowly along an extended but gentle slope. Quiet during the visit of the show flats and dinner, Michael's two daughters were clearly interested to explore the bridge. In particular, his younger daughter was full of energy, running back and forth and finally to her mother. She tugged on her mother's hand and expressed her impatience, "Why are you adults walking so slowly!"

Rose was amused and asked Michael, "How old are your daughters?"

"One is in Primary Three and the other in Secondary One."

"Both girls are so pretty, they look like you."

"It is right for them to look like me! There is a saying that daughters will look like their fathers, sons will look like their mothers!" Michael replied, looking pleased with himself.

"Do you send them for any enrichment classes?" Rose continued asking.

"Yes, both are learning to play traditional musical instruments, one is learning the flute and the other is learning the zither. It is good for them to know music. The younger one is also learning calligraphy and the older one is learning tae kwon do. Girls should learn a bit of martial arts to protect themselves. The older one is also a member of her school's drama club. We often see her memorising long paragraphs of English lines and practising her acting. Zoe, can you perform something for us?" Wooly asked her daughter.

Zoe did not hesitate and immediately obliged with a short monologue.

Listening to young girl speaking perfect English and performing with such confidence, Peggy was full of admiration and remarked, "Children these days are amazing, they can speak a foreign language so well at such a tender age."

"That is because the environment is different. They have received a bilingual education from birth! My husband and I are also bilingual and we make it a point to speak both languages at home so as to train them to be effectively bilingual. It was different for us, wasn't it? Learning a foreign language was so tough for us," Wooly sighed.

"It was hard work, but we managed to do it. We found good jobs and have fewer problems nurturing our children, we ought to be content," Michael consoled his wife cheerfully.

"What do you work as Michael?" Maggie asked.

> For many bilingual talents, their language ability is a useful tool.

"I am a colorectal surgeon at a public hospital. Being a doctor has been my aspiration since I was young and I have achieved my goal."

Just then, Joan and Jerome walked over hand in hand, "It is true, people of our generation are very lucky, although our parents were not highly educated, they were determined to support us in our studies. We worked hard and both of us were successful in our applications for doctoral scholarship in Singapore. We have been working in Singapore since we graduated," Jerome shared.

"Some of our classmates were not so lucky. When I was doing my master's, I had a classmate who was very keen to do his doctorate, and he actually did very well for his specialisation. However, he did not pass the English test for the doctorate entrance examination. Because his family did not want him to spend another year "fighting a second battle", he gave up this hope and is now working in China. As you know, in our domain of biology, the higher one's academic credentials, the more valuable," Joan added.

"This reminds me of a friend I had when I was doing my master's degree too. His experience was kind of interesting. He studied Chinese as an undergraduate and he did well. Due to exceptional circumstances, he was recommended for postgraduate studies at the university's school of public administration. At the end of his first year, he realised that he was indeed very interested in political studies and thus keen to apply for an overseas doctorate programme. He managed to get recommendation letters from the most reputable teachers at the university. Guess what happened after that? He was not able to pass the Test of English as a Foreign Language (TOEFL) nor the International English Language Testing System (IELTS). He was so frustrated…" Michael lamented.

> Due to a lack of proficiency in English, many professionals from non-English backgrounds cannot find a suitable global platform that adequately reflects the value they possess and can add.

"These students who are impeded by language difficulties remind me of something, I am not sure if any of you have had the same experience," said Maggie, "At times, I would have classmates

> The demand for language services exists widely in our daily lives and they are not adequately fulfilled.

from China who would approach me out of the blue to help them search for some foreign language materials relating to their trade or domain. Some of these materials were truly unavailable in China, some of them simply could not handle this matter due to their low level of language proficiency, but they genuinely needed the materials. To be frank, I was not always willing to help because a great deal of time and energy is needed particularly for areas which I am not familiar with. Some of them mentioned that they would pay me for the work done but since we were classmates, it would be uncomfortable for me to accept payment from them."

"I have this same experience. Helping to check on a book is a small matter, but there were also requests like yours to help with searching for a whole lot of materials. At times, I was so busy myself and so I had to be hard-hearted and turn them down. I felt sorry though, I am probably too sensitive…"

Peggy suddenly asked, "Have all of you already become permanent residents (PR) in Singapore?"

"Ken's family of three generations and Michael's family are PR. We are not but we intend to, this is why we are considering buying a condominium," Joan replied.

"I see…" Up until that moment, Peggy had treated Singapore as a training ground and had no intention to live permanently in Singapore, she loved her home country and was sentimentally attached to China.

Knowing that everyone had emigrated to Singapore or will be doing so, an unexplainable feeling well up in her.

Michael seemed to have noticed Peggy's reaction, he took the opportunity to bring up another matter, "I recently had the chance to browse through the 2014 issue of *The International Talent Blue*

Book on China's Overseas Chinese Professionals Report. Can you make a guess on the number of Chinese that are overseas?"

"Tens of millions?" Peggy guessed.

"About fifty million people, close to ten million of these people are new emigrants after China's reform and opening up to the outside world. Can you make another guess on how many professionals are amongst these emigrants?"

"This is not easy. How many are there?" Joan asked.

> Just this group of overseas bilingual Chinese talents alone is a huge community.

"Actually, there is no accurate data on the number of overseas Chinese professionals. This blue book that I am looking at combines the statistics of research data from various organisations and research personnel, they think that there almost four million overseas Chinese professionals."

"Well, I believe most are in the US," Ken added.

"Yes, there are about 2.4 million in the USA. Followed by 800,000 in Europe and 260,000 in Canada. There are quite a number in Singapore too, about 100,000, which is the fourth position. Those in Japan, Australia and New Zealand are quite significant too, but I cannot recall the exact numbers."

"What is the distribution like for these professionals, in terms of specialisations and job positions?" Peggy posed another question.

"On this issue, the blue book has a detailed classification, from 'three knives (choppers, scissors and razors)' to 'three professions' to 'three expertise'."

Wooly asked, "what do they refer to?"

"In the olden days, the images of the overseas Chinese were mostly chefs, tailors and barbers. In modern times, the professional images are now engineers, doctors, and accountants, as well as scientists, entrepreneurs and inventors."

"This is an interesting classification," Joan was intrigued.

"In short, this group of people generally possess a wealth of knowledge and high-level skillsets, they are financially well-off and have understanding and appreciation for their cultural heritage. Because they are exposed to the world outside, they are familiar and comfortable with foreign culture too. Besides working in educational institutions, and the finance and information technology sectors, they are also scattered across industries such as advanced biology and medicine, arts creation, new energy, energy conservation and environmental protection, advanced material science and many others."

> There are bilingual talents everywhere and they are highly mobile and possess good knowledge of the local cultures within which they live.

"Globalisation has facilitated and normalised talent mobility. However, it is still a requirement to learn a foreign language like English well. The pharmaceutical and biotechnology firm that I work for has employees from Korea, Japan and Russia. All of them know at least two languages, working and communicating in English is not a problem at all."

Ken and Rose decided to join in the conversation as well. "We graduated from the university a long time ago and did not received any formal training in foreign languages as students, but we have been overseas for more than thirty years and we have picked up new languages well. I am not exaggerating but I think students during our time had a good knowledge base."

Rose continued, "Although we have both retired, we are still hale and hearty, we would like to take on some interesting work, but there have not been any good options. We are not keen to join other senior citizens in the service sector, so we mostly stay home to read and watch the news and to care for my granddaughter."

"'One is never too old to learn' is a perfect description for Uncle Ken and Auntie Rose!" remarked Maggie.

> The value of the information discovered by bilingual talents has not been fully tapped into.

"Indeed, that has helped us to keep our minds sharp. I specialised in mechanical engineering and my wife in biology, we are still reading from books, newspapers and the internet on the latest developments in these two areas. But we have not been able to apply what we know and therefore, we just read for leisure," Ken said.

"Uncle Ken and Auntie Rose, you are such diligent students!" Peggy exclaimed, triggering laughter all around.

"Of course!" Ken made no show of modesty, "We have observed that regardless of one's specialisation, English is the most powerful and universal language. It is basically impossible for books in other languages to be circulated widely if they are not translated into English."

Just as Peggy was about to probe further into this interesting discovery, Michael's younger daughter cried out, "Come and see, there are monkeys!"

"Where?" The whole group walked towards the girl and looked in the direction she was pointing. Not too far from them was a tree with two monkeys on it, one big and one small, hanging and swinging on the branches while looking towards the bridge.

"This is such a great ecological environment; I even saw squirrels just now," said Peggy.

"Many have said that Singapore is a typical man-made city, but I feel that it has done well in creating a balance between human and nature in a largely urban environment. The Henderson Wave Bridge is a good example, look towards the south of the bridge," said Maggie.

"I can see the ridge line," Joan said.

"It is surrounded by hilly slopes, trees and the sea," Peggy replied.

"This bridge adopts barrier-free access, the surface of the bridge is anti-slip, and it is installed with handrails. In 2009, it received 'The President's Design' award," Maggie said.

At that moment, the sky had already turned dark, this transition from twilight to dusk seemed to have happened in a flash, without any of them noticing.

The bridge provided a panoramic view of the beautiful night scenery of Singapore. The Henderson Wave bridge was connected to two parks, filled with trees of different species. These trees rose high above the ground, but at that moment on the bridge, the crowns of the trees all felt like they were within reach.

Peggy looked down from the bridge, the traffic below looked like two thin pieces of ribbons moving at high speed, someone with a fear of heights may have felt afraid, but Peggy only felt invigorated.

Some of the other members in the group had grown tired however and were resting on the benches. Everyone else gathered around them.

It was then that Peggy heard Jerome talking to a guy in a black coloured short sleeved shirt, she knew that his name was Willsher from his self-introduction at the showroom that afternoon, but she had not spoken to him nor heard him say much.

"Willsher, you have not told us much about yourself. What do you work as?" asked Jerome.

"I work at Science Park on blockchain technology," Willsher replied.

"What is blockchain?" Lately, I have heard this term more and more frequently," Peggy asked.

"To put it simply, blockchain is a new technology, bitcoin is a type of cryptocurrency and it is an application of blockchain," said Willsher.

"I still do not quite understand, haha. That's how the saying 'A world apart in different trades' must have come about," Jerome shook his head in embarrassment.

Peggy too did not quite understand, but she was always keen to probe into new things and very interested to know more about this term that she had encountered a few times. She moved closer to the guys, "I studied translation for my master's programme, but I majored in mechanical engineering for my bachelor's degree. What exactly is this blockchain that you are talking about? I have heard this term a few times."

"It is quite complex to explain this. Have you heard of bitcoin?" Willsher asked.

"Yes," Peggy and Jerome answered in unison.

> Blockchain is a technology, bitcoin is a successful application of blockchain in the financial sector.

"Bitcoin is a virtual currency. Take this as an example: if blockchain is a big flowerpot, then bitcoin is a flower in this pot. There are many other flowers but right now, bitcoin is the biggest flower in the pot."

"I get it now but what are bitcoins used for?" Peggy inquired further.

"This is another good question, and it is equally complex. All I can say is that I made some money out of bitcoins."

"What is the connection between bitcoins and the existing currencies we have? Do you make profit from selling bitcoins or are there other methods? Is there a limit to the number of bitcoins…?" Willsher briefly answered Peggy's series of questions one by one, but Peggy still did not feel that she really understood. Just as she was about to probe further, she heard Frank gathering everyone to bid goodbye.

Willsher evidently had a favourable impression of Peggy, seeing that she was so interested in blockchain and bitcoin, he took the chance to ask her for her contact details and even offered to send her home.

"Peggy, do you live far from here?"

"Not too far, the MRT will get me home quickly."

"Shall I send you back?"

"There's no need! Public order in Singapore is excellent, it is safe for me to go home on my own. Besides, it will be too late for you by the time you reach home," Peggy declined his gesture with a smile.

"In that case, there will be a public holiday a few days from now, would you be interested to have lunch together?"

"Yes, of course!" Peggy accepted the invitation readily without much thought because she was curious to ask him more questions about blockchain. The group bid one another farewell and dispersed for the night.

Summary:
Unrecognised Gifts

The translation profession continues to operate in the form of workshops, and it is falling behind times. The capacity of translation comes from bilingual talents, but they have not been able to showcase their values adequately.

Language expressions are rich and varied; something that is common will have different forms of expressions under different cultural environment. This is accepted through common practice; it is not a standard issued by any authority. For instance, traditional Chinese musical instruments such as the dizi (bamboo flute), xiao (end-blown flute), guzheng (Chinese plucked zither), pipa (pear-shaped lute) and erhu (two-stringed fiddle) have long history and are widely known as instruments used in Chinese Orchestra. In mainland China, they are known as "minyue (民乐)", in Hong Kong as "zhongyue (中乐)", in Taiwan as "guoyue (国乐)" and in Singapore as "huayue (华乐)". Although they are all in Mandarin, to cater to the readers of different regions, translation must take into consideration the local culture and the expression must be localised. In mainland China, even the word "screwdriver" is expressed differently in different districts, it can be known as "qizi (起子)", "luosidao (螺丝刀)" or "gaizhui (改锥)".

The same expression, in different context will have different implications. To quote an example from the stage play "Thunderstorm《雷雨》", there were six scenes with the "Oh (哦)" expression. Under different scenes in the play, the expression denoted "unconcerned", "surprised", "reply", "pain", "panic" and "embarrassment". This requires thorough understanding of the context to appreciate the differences to achieve conciseness and vividness in the translation. The thoughts and emotions reflected through work of creativity are unattainable by machines.

While these natural linguistic attributes allow appreciation of the language uniqueness, it could also create baffling problems for clients on their choice of translators. Clients need translation because they do not know the language. They can compare the time frame required and the price, but they are not able to determine the merits and drawbacks of the translation. Therefore, they entrust the job to a professional translation services company. However, these translation services providers are not all-powerful. While they can be the credible endorser who will proofread the final output as the utmost step to their quality control, they will unlikely be able to give accurate assessment for all languages and all specialisations.

Translators are important resources for translation services companies. It is necessary for translators to establish long-term cooperation with these companies to gain trust, be assigned more jobs and be given higher rates of remuneration (the rates given to a translator is a distinction of their quality). It takes a long time before both parties get familiarised, keeping in mind that each translator can only work with a limited number of translation services companies. It is impossible for translators to gain wide-ranging trust for their professional ability and language standards to secure adequate and matching job assignments on a global scale. In addition, a translator's hard work does not always equate to high returns and as a result they are not motivated to devote more time into creative work, which would have maximised their value.

Besides translators, there is a significant number of bilingual talents found in all trades and professions. Not only do they possess strong bilingual ability, but they are also skilled professionally. Language ability sharpens their acumen, and they get access to information quickly and comprehensively, and be active in their key positions to emerge as an elite in their professions.

SUMMARY

Bilingual talents put in tremendous time and effort to learn a foreign language and they are also well-established in their professional domains. With their language ability, they can browse websites and access information quickly, communicate freely with foreigners, express their viewpoints at international conferences, demonstrate their products at international exhibitions and be at the forefront of their profession. However, the value of their language ability is mainly reflected only as a tool for access to information and communication.

Bilingual talents possessed the combined value of their language ability and professional knowledge. Based on their knowledge and experience, they can take the lead to identify information and convert them into another language to benefit more people. This will help to fill the gap for other professionals who lack language ability and create opportunities for comprehensive language services such as information collection, professional consultation, overseas business negotiation and others. However, there are no channels to fulfill this potential of identifying information and providing language services due to the absence of an open, transparent, and credible model.

Concurrently, huge volume of valuable language data could not be shared due to isolation of information in the language service industry. Around the world, a great deal of repetitive work takes place in the translation field, day after day, year after year. The internet of information has given us the convenience of information dissemination, but it cannot resolve the problem of the inability to share and exchange isolated language data. On one hand, translation engines need a large amount of language data to support rapid and high-quality information conversion, and on the other hand, a large amount of valuable language data is lying dormant and hardly ever of value. The fundamental reason is the lack of an effective mechanism to enable these data to be shared and rewarded accordingly.

Bilingual talents are like scattered pearls, dispersed all over the world in all trades and professions. Their ability needs to be recognised and their potential unleashed, so as to benefit more people.

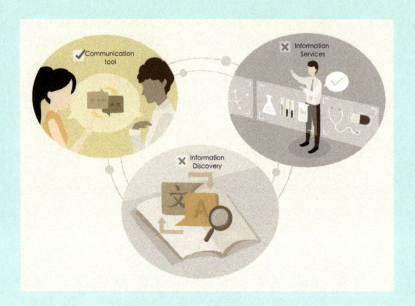

Wide Recognition

Blockchain Reveals the Value of Bilingual Talent

Peggy was recommended to be a live interpreter at an international conference on Blockchain. She did not realise that the keynote speaker, an expert on blockchain and tokens, was in fact, her childhood playmate, Henry. Peggy and Henry were able to spend time catching up and they shared with each other candidly about their respective careers. Peggy confessed about the confusion and disconnection that she encountered in her translation work, while Henry became convinced that the token could be of value in the field of translation and was determined to explore this possibility further.

Blockchain provides the technical support necessary for bilingual talents to actualise their value. Blockchain's characteristics of trust and being tamper-proof enable the comprehensive capabilities of bilingual talents to become credit assets; the terminologies and language data created in the process of translation are accumulated as language assets. It not only reflects the value of the dispersed translators but also boosts the growth of Artificial Intelligence (AI) as a result of the availability of Big Data. With machines to convey information, human beings to impart expressiveness, production capacity for translation will increase substantially.

1   Establish credit assets for translators.
2   Establish language assets for translators.
3   Develop mutual reinforcements between machines and humans.
4   The value of bilingual talents to be made tangible with price, through tagging on blockchain.

***

After they agreed to meet again, Willsher took pains to look for a suitable venue. Taking into consideration that ladies are usually health conscious and concerned about their diet and figure, Willsher finally decided on a place.

"I made a reservation at a Taiwanese vegetarian restaurant that serves Italian food, this restaurant was recommended by a friend of mine. I came twice and thought it was good." Willsher introduced the restaurant to Peggy as they walked towards it, "I did not seek your opinion on this but I hope you will like the food here."

"Haha, there's nothing to worry about! I am a foodie and always ready to try new restaurants and dishes."

The restaurant was quite spacious and tastefully decorated. There were options for al fresco dining or a private dining space partitioned by semi-open cylindrical wall panels. With a neutral colour theme and soothing music, the atmosphere put Peggy at ease immediately.

Willsher chose a table at a quiet corner. With a smile, the waiter handed them the menu and served pre-dinner drinks.

"Peggy, please place the order, take a look at what you would like to eat."

"No, you know this restaurant well, you should decide, I am not a picky eater."

"Alright, if you say so. Shall we have the set meal? We can also add anything else you like, there are the main courses, soup, salad and snack items."

"Let's have some salad."

"This is a 'Eat Clean' restaurant, and the prices are reasonable for the food served," Willsher gave their order to the waiter and turned back to Peggy.

"Eat clean, does it mean that the food is so good that all will be eaten up?" Peggy joked.

"This is part of the meaning, I'm sure! It also means to 'eat healthily' and to feel cleansed after eating. There is increasing awareness that we can cleanse the body through food, by reducing consumption of processed food and chemical condiments and including only natural ingredients as much as possible in our diets."

"This is an interesting concept…"

"Peggy, how are your cooking skills? I'm guessing you must be a great cook!"

"Hah! How would you know? I won't say that I am great at it, but I do know some basic home cooking. However, I have been quite busy since I came to Singapore and have not been cooking much."

"Do you live alone?"

"No, I live with a mother and daughter who are from Qingdao. Aunt Doreen is a study mama, and the little girl is studying in Primary Three. Aunt Doreen takes good care of me, she will cook for me at times too, it is a blessing to have warm food after work."

"It looks like your landlord is kind, it seems to me that many people in Singapore do not cook at home, they will either dine out or takeaway the food to eat at home. This is one reason many Singaporeans are not willing to rent their property to tenants who want to cook at home, they are afraid the tenants will dirty the house."

"Well, my landlord is from China and knows us Chinese are particular about food having the 'aroma of smoke and fire'!" Peggy winked as she replied.

"Ah yes! Have you by any chance seen the documentary 'A Bite of China'?"

> Each country has its own unique food culture. Due to language barriers, these unique details are often not able to be showcased comprehensively.

"Yes, I have but only one episode of it. Recently, I am reading the essay collection of 'The Greatest Taste on Earth' by the documentary director, Chen Xiaoqing."

"What is it about?" Willsher's curiosity was piqued.

"It is about food and the feelings of people contained in the food. After reading, I started to miss home. I was thinking that a person who is able to write about the thousand flavours on earth and relate them to life must be someone who has a keen descriptive mind and a profound love for life and the world."

Willsher nodded in agreement, "By the way, where are you from Peggy?"

"I am from Suzhou, the Jiangnan region of rivers and lakes."

"Suzhou is a great place. I am from Wuhan."

"Such a coincidence, I did my bachelor's and master's degrees at Wuhan."

"Oh, that shows we do have a special connection!" Willsher stood up to help Peggy with her napkin as he spoke, "How do you feel about Wuhan?"

"It's okay, thank you, I can help myself," Peggy politely declined Willsher's gentlemanly gesture with a smile. Willsher nodded and returned to his seat.

"I feel that Wuhan is great. Although many people have mocked Wuhan as the biggest construction site in the central region, with digging works everywhere, I've always felt that it was exaggerated. I was not too impressed with the traffic though. Maybe I loved my school too much, so I love everything associated with it!"

"Did you learn to speak the Wuhan dialect when you were studying there?" Willsher grinned.

> Each region has a language that reflects local characteristics.

"I know the phrase '卯起搞 mǎo qǐ gǎo' which means to start working between 5am to 7am."

"There is another phrase from Wuhan '清爽流了 qīng shuǎng liú liǎo' (a spill over of beauty)."

"What does this mean?"

"Generally, it describes a fresh-faced lady who is not only beautiful '清爽 qīng shuǎng' but also straightforward. '流了 liú liǎo' connotes a spilling over, a spilling over of beauty, which creates a more vivid image than words like pretty and beautiful."

"I see! What a descriptive phrase!"

"As you know, Wuhan is a city with lots of water, so it features prominently in the way we speak."

The food was served and they continued chatting over the meal.

"The last time we met, I heard you mention that you are a project manager with a translation services company. What exactly do you do as a project manager?"

"To put it simply, the project manager is a middleman between the client and the translator. The complexities involved cannot be explained in a few words. My boss has said that in this field our skills need to be honed, the more I work on the job, the more I understand what he means."

"Is the project manager involved in translation too?"

"The project manager mainly communicates with the client and the translator to facilitate the completion of the job, but we do need to have bilingual ability and some knowledge of translation, it would be tough to work in this job otherwise."

"Why didn't you consider being a professional translator, after all, you studied translation, didn't you?"

"How should I explain this? A project manager requires more comprehensive skills and I like challenging jobs. Besides, I am also keen to know more about the industry. I like to do translations, but I think that if my work was only to look at words and documents all day, every day, it would become uninteresting after a while."

"Is translation only in the written form?"

"Translation are in the written form, then there are interpretations too, which are oral. I did interpretations with my lecturer at some international conferences when I was studying translation."

"Which area of translation do you specialise in?"

> Translation requires both language and professional abilities. It is a form of works creation that has high requirements for comprehensive capabilities.

"Culture, business and mechanical engineering. I am stronger in the first two areas. For mechanical engineering, I can translate some basic content which I learned when I did my bachelor's degree, but I have lost touch with the cutting-edge stuff. Translation requires not just the language ability but also to be at the forefront of the profession. Ultimately, the translated content that clients want are generally about the latest developments in any industry. As for culture, I have always had a keen interest in it. I do not limit myself to a specific area for translation, if I am confident about my ability to learn, I will accept jobs in unfamiliar areas too."

"I can feel that your learning ability is quite strong," Willsher complimented.

"Hah, well I should not say so myself, it is not humble. But I was given good evaluations by a few teachers when I was studying, so it depends on whether you are willing to trust their evaluations…"

"Of course! Here's why I raised this topic. Lately, there have been quite a few meetings on blockchain held in Singapore. Three weeks later, there will be a high-profile international conference on blockchain, it will be held at the Marina Bay Sands Expo and Convention Centre. Are you willing to be the interpreter? It requires simultaneous interpretation. There are currently many meetings on blockchain, but as it is something new, there are not many suitable translators. The translator is expected to have strong language and learning abilities," Willsher asked eagerly.

"I have indeed done interpretations a few times but other than the information that you shared with me previously, I have no knowledge on blockchain at all. You mentioned that this is a high-profile meeting, I am afraid…"

"Do not worry, it is just interpretation for a section of the meeting, it will not be for too long. Do you want to challenge yourself to do it?" Willsher looked at Peggy keenly.

> Translator must have good understanding of the source language, at the same time, must be able to express accurately in target language.

"But in our translation profession, generally the target language should be the translator's mother tongue. Will I not be doing the opposite?"

"You've already said that this is the general case. Since you have mastered the foreign language as well as the Chinese language, does it matter what the target language is? Besides, blockchain is new, so the translator also needs an in-depth knowledge of the source language to translate well. However, do not feel pressured, this is just a casual request."

Peggy felt apprehensive, but she was brave and liked challenges. She hesitated for a moment before agreeing.

"Great! I will add you into the conference preparation group chat, the event organiser will send you some materials. I think it will be enough for you to do your preparation work based on the materials given. Do feel free to ask me if you need anything else or you may seek advice from the organiser in the group."

"Thank you for this opportunity! At our last outing, my curiosity was aroused by your brief introduction of blockchain. In particular, the analogy of the flowerpot and the flower, blockchain being the flowerpot and bitcoin as a flower in the pot. I understood right away. Can you share with me more on blockchain?" Said Peggy.

"Well, to talk about blockchain, we have to start from the core characteristic, which is 'decentralisation'."

"Decentralisation?" Peggy was puzzled.

"Yes, human society has experienced the process of being non-centralised to becoming centralised and subsequently highly centralised. Blockchain attempts to take human society to the next level, which is decentralisation."

"What do you mean?"

"Our ancient ancestors lived apart from one another, it was very inconvenient to get in touch with each other, this is an example of non-centralised society. When villages and towns were formed, they became central points for people to come together. But that was still not highly centralised. In her whole life, my granny had never stepped out of the town she lived in. With cities, human society became more and more physically centralised and with the internet, it has become highly virtually centralised as well. For instance, the big internet companies are the central points. We have to make use of their platforms and software to exchange information on the internet."

"Why is blockchain decentralised?"

"In a nutshell, blockchain is a new application model driven by information technology in the process of digitalisation of human society. Under the current situation where the big internet companies dominate, we have contributed a lot of data, but we are practically not receiving anything in return for these data. What blockchain will do is remove these central points and provide transparency and accessibility to these open data. It will allow people to gain from contributing data and at the same time, others can also pay to use any publicly available data."

"How can this be done?" asked Peggy, again.

"This will involve complex technology, and it is this complex and rigorous technology that supports blockchain's characteristics of decentralisation, distributed ledger, non-tamperability, traceability, openness, consensus and more. With the use of blockchain technology, within a very short time and with very low transaction costs, more than 7 billion people around the world can be brought together to contribute their value to a common objective and be rewarded with appropriate incentives. This will enable the optimal allocation of assets on a global scale," Willsher explained patiently.

"Wow, you used so many words and phrases to describe the characteristics of blockchain, that is so professional, I am still having difficulties processing them."

"Hah! It looks like I am still not good at explanation. How can I explain this better? The nature of blockchain is a reconstruction of organisational structure, that is, a collaboration mechanism to change how society is organised. Let me ask you, what do you think of when 'asset' is mentioned?"

"Money, houses, cars, stocks and shares and other things that can be financially counted."

"These are definitely assets. In fact, our everyday behaviour, our body mass index, the words we use, points of interest and many other aspects of ourselves, these are our digital assets. All of them have value. But most of these have not been utilised and some are being taken away from us without us receiving anything in return."

"What?"

"Blockchain technology can record the digital assets of individuals, transmit them on the blockchain, and assign them value through the issuance and execution of smart contracts, thus changing the collaboration mechanism of society. In future, if our digital assets are used by others, we will have a share of the profits."

"I briefly understand now. That means we will have a new source of income in future."

"Take this as an example, are we not talking about being 'big on medical care' and 'big on health' in China's healthcare system? With the help of blockchain, elderly people doing daily recordings of their vital health data at home can also create value for this behaviour, such as by contributing the data in exchange for a reduction in medical fees."

"Oh…that will quickly mobilise everyone to participate actively!" Peggy understood this simple example and was very happy.

The next day, as promised, Willsher added Peggy into the preparatory group of the blockchain conference.

Peggy immediately sent a private message to the chief administrator Rita who was overall in-charge of the event. From her experience, Peggy knew it was common practice to request for all the relevant information, including the title of the conference in Chinese and English, agenda of the conference, list of speakers, overview of activities, introduction of the organisers and participants, text of the speeches to be made, as well as other related information.

Rita replied that the organiser had only received the presentation slides in softcopy from the guest speakers, and that information on the speakers' backgrounds and other details were not available.

"How many speakers will I be responsible for?"

"Just one or two, each guest speaker will be allocated one hour to speak, and twenty minutes will be given for question-and-answer session (Q&A)."

"Can you introduce my working partner to me? If we could discuss the division of work in advance, it will be more efficient for the pre-conference preparation.

"No problem."

> Every translator will have their own list of accumulated terminology and language data. These data are scattered and stored in the translator's personal computers.

Fortunately for Peggy, her working partner for this project had already attended many meetings relating to blockchain. He was quick and enthusiastic to share with Peggy the glossary he had compiled from the previous meetings, it contained a detailed list of terminology and common industry expressions arranged in an orderly manner.

"Bernard, thank you so much! This glossary will save me a lot of work!" Peggy was overwhelmed with gratitude.

"Don't mention it, Peggy. Do you think it will be alright to do it in this way? Since I am more familiar in this area, I will take care of the first half hour's speech and the Q&A session by the first guest speaker, you will take care of his speech in the second half hour. We will switch for the second speaker. In addition, I will also do the interpretation for the brief opening and closing."

"Okay, what we have now are the presentation slides and not the text for the speech, I guess we will just roughly split it into two parts?"

"I will share a small trick with you. With these slides, we can have a rough sense of the order of the presentation. The slides in themselves will give us an idea of the speaker's thoughts and intent, so we can actually prepare a sight interpretation of the slides from the perspective of the speaker. Feel free to ask me any questions anytime."

Over the next three weeks, Peggy used her spare time to familiarise herself with the data repeatedly. She printed the materials and marked out with coloured pens all the professional terminologies, incomprehensible points, speaker's viewpoints and other information. She also wrote the translated text beside the markings. She even tried sight interpretations in front of the mirror by translating orally the content of the written materials complied.

As the day of the conference approached, Peggy and Bernard stepped up their preparation work. Over a video call, they practised sight interpretations and exchanged suggestions for improvement. Since it was not a domain that she was familiar with and also a high-profile event, Peggy was more diligent than ever so that she could do her best for the conference.

On the day itself, Peggy carefully dressed in professional attire and doublechecked that she had brought along her materials, jotted notes and conference documents before leaving the flat. She arrived an hour earlier at the Marina Bay Sands Expo and Convention Centre. After collecting the meeting schedules and other information, she made her way to the interpreter's booth to check on the equipment and get ready.

It was her first time at the convention centre and the sight of the luxurious and expansive venue made her heart skip faster. When she saw that the listed guests in the conference brochure were leading experts in the global blockchain industry, entrepreneurs, university scholars, investment professionals and renowned media professionals, she realised that the conference was indeed of great significance and began to feel a little nervous.

Bernard noticed and handed her a piece of chocolate with a wink, "I heard chocolate helps to relieve stress."

"Thank you," Peggy could not help but laugh and afterwards felt more relaxed.

"The theme of this conference is 'Blockchain Reshapes the Economy and the World', the guest registration and the opening ceremony already took place yesterday in the afternoon. This morning there will be the opening keynote address."

While Bernard was interpreting for the first guest speaker, Peggy put on her headset to listen and learn at the same time. Soon, it was her turn to take over; before she knew it, she had also completed the interpretation for the second half of the speech, to her great relief.

During the interval, Peggy glanced at the name of the next keynote speaker — Henry Zou. She immediately recalled the close playmate in her childhood who had this exact same name, they had not met in many years and seeing a similar name, Peggy was momentarily dazed.

Just then, there was a round of applause to welcome the speaker who had taken the podium. It was too far for Peggy to see the face clearly but somehow the figure felt familiar. Anyhow, Peggy had no time to think further and she started the interpretation.

Henry's presentation topic was "The Token Economy as the New Collaborative Organisation on the Internet of Value".

At the beginning of the presentation, he explained that production relationship is a sum of the relationships formed in the process of production, exchange, distribution and consumption. In existing production relationships, not all value-creating inputs are duly rewarded, and not all values are shared fairly. Hence, there is a need to change the production relationship, and that blockchain is a technology that can effect such a change.

He then introduced the topic of the presentation — the token.

Henry spoke clearly and simply, without using unnecessarily long and complex sentences. This was a great convenience for simultaneous interpretation, a thought flashed across Peggy's mind as she was interpreting, "this person is a good presenter indeed!"

In the first part after his introduction, Henry first explained why tokens are translated as '通证 tōng zhèng' rather than '代币 dài bì'.

The word 'token' was originally used in computing as a directive, in layman terms, it was a code, a password to authorise a subsequent operation. Before any data is transferred, a password check is performed, and different passwords are required for different data operations.

> An accurate translation of a new term requires an in-depth understanding of its function and meaning in order to be both figurative and evocative.

"It is quite interesting when we unpack the translation of 'token' into Mandarin. It was first translated as '代币 dài bì', which means 'monetary representation'. Is that a correct translation? My answer is, yes and no. I say yes because it does embody the value function of the token on the blockchain; I say no because it does not fully embody the inherent function of the token, and sometimes gives way to misunderstandings. In contrast, the translation of 'token' as '通证 tōng zhèng' is brilliant, it reflects not only the function of the token, but also conjures an accurate image. We can understand it in three ways."

As he spoke, Henry simultaneously displayed a diagram on the big screen, "通 tōng (pass)" "证 zhèng (certificate)" "值 zhí (value)", three points forming a circle.

> The token is the soul of blockchain.

The token "通证 tōng zhèng" as the term suggests, is a certificate for circulation. On blockchain in particular, it is an *encrypted digital* certificate that can be circulated.

There are four types of tokens: the first is a value-based token, which acts as a carrier of value and can be directly converted into value, such as stored value cards, exchange certificates, bankers' acceptances, etc. The second type is a rights-based token, which allows the bearer to receive rights and interests in the application scenario, this will include discount cards, VIP cards, etc. The third type is an income-based token, which gives one a right to receive proceeds and can generate income over time, such as bonds, shares etc. The fourth type is an identity-based token, it does not carry any value features by itself, but it is an identification of an asset with value or an objective fact, such as a senior citizen pass, a property ownership certificate, etc.

The word "通 tōng (pass)" in Mandarin means that the token can be widely circulated, which also means that it can be validated and used quickly, it can then be quickly converted into other tokens. It can be used, transferred and converted.

As for "证 zhèng (certificate)", it means that the token represents some form of rights and with the help of blockchain technology, it can be actualised, distinguished and tamper proofed.

Last but not least, "值 zhí (value)" means that it is a carrier of value with social consensus.

Henry then moved on to talk about the relationship between blockchain and the token. He first highlighted that by definition alone, a token can have no connection with blockchain. Q Coin, which had already been popular for many years in China, is a token that does not require blockchain technology. He then used a vivid analogy to reveal the relationship between the two: the blockchain is like an expanse of earth with many buildings on it, each building is a node, and tokens are like many trolleys on earth carrying a lot of glittering gold. The trolleys come and go constantly on earth, sending gold to different buildings according to the transaction status between buildings.

Henry's vivid analogy won him a big round of applause. This coincided with the switch over of duty with Bernard, but Peggy was so captivated by Henry's presentation that she continued to listen to the rest of the presentation without thinking to stop for a break.

For the last part of the presentation, Henry spoke about the functionality of tokens. In simple terms, a token is a symbol in network propagation that can replace existing third parties to build new trust, thus enabling humans to quickly establish large-scale, ad hoc collaboration in networks where they do not know each other.

Evolution theory purports that 70,000 years ago, humans acquired the ability to speak due to a genetic mutation, they were thus enabled to communicate and collaborate on a large scale to triumph over other species on earth. In the same vein, tokens could make it possible for people around the world who do not know each other, to build trust and have large-scale collaborations without the need for a third party.

After the presentation, Henry put on his headset to get ready for the Q&A session. He heard a gentle, sweet female voice translating melodiously between the audience's questions in English and his replies in Mandarin, without missing a beat.

"This person has such a nice voice!" Henry was instantly drawn to Peggy's voice.

He was not able to ascertain the accuracy of the translation but the attentive eyes of the audience and the thunderous applause from time to time indicated that both the presentation and the interpretation had been well-received.

In a presentation that requires interpretation, the effectiveness of the presentation not only depends on the standard of the presenter, but also that of the interpreter. An interpreter who is not up to standard may ruin a good presentation and a good interpreter is definitely an amplifier. Henry was well aware of this fact since he had participated in other large events like this one before, so he was keen to express his thanks to the interpreters.

After the Q&A, the emcee concluded the session, Henry immediately turned to the conference staff, "Hi, the interpreters worked hard, I wonder if you can take me to them so I can thank them in person?"

"Sure, let's go, this way please."

"Finally, it is over!" Peggy switched off the machine, leaned back in her chair and heaved a long sigh of relief. Bernard gave her a tired grin and the thumbs up sign, they were both glad that they had completed the job successfully.

"Bernard, you are very professional."

"You too, Peggy."

"I am very sincere in my praise of you."

"Yes, so am I." Bernard replied with a solemn nod, his eyes twinkling.

"Haha! From the initial stage when I began communicating with you and sought your help, I knew I was fortunate to be able to work with you. After listening to your live interpretations today, I can see that you are well-versed in this domain," Peggy was grateful.

"If you had not mentioned it when we first met, I would never have imagined that this is your first time interpreting for a blockchain conference. You have amazing learning ability! Mainland Chinese are really smart."

"Well…thank you for the compliment and I thank you on behalf of my countrymen too!"

"In future, if there are any blockchain-related events that require interpretation, I can refer them to you if you are keen," Bernard clearly thought highly of Peggy.

"Thank you so much, Bernard. An old Chinese saying just came to mind."

Bernand looked at her quizzically.

"在家靠父母，出门靠朋友　zài jiā kào fù mǔ, chū mén kào péng yǒu we depend on our parents when we are at home, and on our friends when away from home."

"You're right, my friend!" Bernand replied with a smile, he was about to say more but was interrupted by someone knocking on the door and entering the booth.

"Hi, you must be Peggy and Bernard? A guest speaker would like to thank both of you in person. He is just outside."

"Oh, there's really no need, this is our job after all," Peggy was surprised by the message of appreciation. The familiar name that she had seen in the conference programme came to her mind again.

"We are happy as long as the speakers and audiences were satisfied, it is not necessary to come by specially…" Once again, he was interrupted by a brief knock on the door, it opened and in walked Henry.

Peggy was instantly dumbfounded, "Henry! Henry! It's really you!"

Meanwhile, Henry was completely caught off guard, "Peggy?"

Nevertheless, Henry regained his composure quickly and earnestly thanked the two interpreters in his capacity as the guest speaker.

Upon hearing that Peggy and Henry were long-time friends, Bernard left quickly after packing up.

"Earlier on, I saw your name in the conference programme and your figure from afar, I wondered if it was you, but I did not expect such a coincidence," Peggy was delighted to see her old friend.

"Oh, so you saw my name, I had no idea at all! This is such a small world; I can't believe that we are actually meeting again here. The little girl I used to play with has grown up!"

Peggy's cheeks reddened at being called a little girl by the older brother figure she had admired in childhood.

"It is not just me. Henry, you are all grown up too!"

Henry cut a dashing figure in his smart black suit over a slim-fit white shirt. Although he still retained some boyish features from childhood, his overall appearance was that of a confident young man. Peggy recalled him speaking eloquently in front of so many people earlier and mentally noted that this made him very attractive indeed.

"Yes, in the twinkling of an eye, we have all grown up. I still remember the last time I saw you. I was in Primary Five, my parents were going to start a new business back in their hometown, so our family was moving away. You had just completed Primary Three then. On the day of my departure, you held onto me and cried so badly, you simply refused to let me go!"

Peggy blushed when Henry recalled the embarrassing crying incident and retorted, "Did you forget that you also cried? You're talking like you didn't!"

"Yeah, you were crying so hard, it would have been so mean if I didn't. Just kidding, of course…I could not bear to part with you either."

"Well, in those days, mobile phones were not widely available yet, and calls had to be made by landlines at home, not to mention QQ[14] and WeChat. I felt like I was going to lose my very good friend and thought we would never see each other again, I was terribly sad," Peggy replied, a tad embarrassed.

"You were alright after that, weren't you? We both made new friends and now we are grownups."

"But even now I am still not good at bidding farewell. It's embarrassing to say so, but as long as I have to say goodbye, I usually end up in tears. The summer vacation after my undergraduate degree, I went to Dazhu in Sichuan with my friends to teach. I was the only one who did not stop crying when it was time to leave and to think I was the oldest in the team."

"It is not embarrassing; this is your true nature, you have the same sensitive temperament as when you were a kid."

"Indeed, that's what everyone says…!" Peggy acknowledged it somewhat ruefully and they both burst into laughter.

"By the way, Peggy, are you interested in blockchain too? Why are you here as an interpreter?"

"I am just a novice when it comes to blockchain."

"Tell me more."

"I was at a gathering with some of our countrymen and one of them who works at Science Park mentioned blockchain. I was interested to know more, so he explained the basics to me and also recommended me as an interpreter for this conference."

"So, you have only just started to learn about blockchain?"

---

[14] QQ is an instant messaging software service.

"That's right."

"Wow, and yet you did so well for a first-timer, I see our Peggy is as smart as ever."

"Not as smart as compared to you, someone who was always first in exams."

"Ah...I could hardly reach the top position after entering high school, there were too many bright students. I'm sorry Peggy, I must attend to some matters relating to this conference now and cannot invite you for lunch even though I wish to, shall we exchange contact details and talk more again later?"

"Of course, I am feeling very drained right now, I was planning to go straight home to rest anyway."

They exchanged contact details and bid each other goodbye. Henry watched as Peggy's slim, graceful figure gradually faded into the distance, all kinds of memories and feelings began to flood his mind.

An image of Peggy as a child appeared immediately. She always had her long hair tied in two braids. She loved to wear dresses and was a cry baby. When she lost something precious to her, she would cry; when she could not complete her homework, she would cry; when she could not get what she wanted, she would also cry... Of course, crying did not solve her problems, but it did make her the centre of attention. Apart from the crying, she was a good-natured and well-behaved child. She especially loved to stick to Henry and kept calling him "Big Brother Henry, Big Brother Henry". They would play together after school till the sun went down and would part only when their parents yelled for them to go home for dinner. As the Chinese saying goes "a young lady is very different from the little girl she once was (女大十八变 nǔ dà shí bā biàn)". In the blink of an eye, the little girl he had known was now a graceful and intelligent young lady who was clearly very competent in her work.

Peggy also had much to reminisce about on her way home. When they were young, Peggy and Henry had attended the same kindergarten and primary school. Both their families lived in a big compound of the Academy of Sciences and they often travelled to and from school together. Whenever Peggy complained that her school bag was heavy, Henry would carry it for her on top of his own. He took very good care of her but was at times playful and would play pranks on Peggy. He was very smart and had always emerged as the top student in examinations. Peggy had not imagined that they would meet again, but was not surprised that he had achieved enough success to be invited as a keynote speaker for a high profile conference.

That evening, as Peggy was reading quietly, the WeChat notification sounded on her phone.

"Cry baby Peggy, are you there?"

"Hey, Henry, how long has it been? You are still making fun of me!"

"Just kidding, you are now a fine young lady!"

"Where are you now? Resting at your hotel?"

"Yes, I'm staying at the Marina Bay Sands hotel."

"What luxury!"

"This is not luxury; this is the principle of proximity."

"You came to Singapore specially to attend this international conference?"

"Yes, our team is doing a roadshow around the world and Singapore is the first stop."

"When are you leaving?"

"Our flight is at noon tomorrow."

"Oh, time is tight…"

"Staying for too long at the Sands hotel, now that would be considered luxury." Henry paused for a moment and said, "if you don't mind, can we do audio chat, it is quite troublesome to type."

"That's exactly my intention."

"Peggy, you studied translation?"

"Yes, as a matter of fact, I did, but translation is a side line, my main job is project manager in a translation services company."

"How long have you worked there?"

"It has been just over six months."

"Is everything going smoothly? Did you encounter any difficulties?"

"It is better now, there were a number of minor issues initially. When I attended one of the staff meeting as a newcomer, the boss told me that we need to hone our skills in this industry. The more I experience on the job, the more I find that the boss has a point. One of the more troubling matters at the moment is that I have problem finding people for a project."

"Huh?" Henry's single word reply prompted Peggy to explain further.

Many translation projects require the collaboration of several suitable translators and require consistency in terminology and style.

"The company took on a big project and my boss assigned it to me, but I am having trouble finding the right number of translators to work on it right now," Peggy replied with a sigh.

"Did you approach your colleagues for help?"

"I did, two other project managers also provided some leads to look for translators, but it is not working out. I am going to have to rely on existing translators to recommend other translators. At the same time, I will see if the boss can help."

"Are smaller jobs easier to handle?"

"Not necessarily so. Smaller jobs have their problems too. If it involves highly technical fields like petrochemicals or advanced manufacturing, it will not be easy to find someone who understands the language, have professional knowledge in the field and is available at the exact time you need him or her."

"Can AI and big data come in handy?" asked Henry.

"Hah, people with engineering background will always ask if AI can be applied. Unfortunately, it is not very helpful."

"How can that be true? Although I am not an expert in this field, I do pay attention to it, for instance, I know Google has launched an amazing tool for translation, the annual Boao Summit uses a robot for simultaneous interpretation. According to reports, the user experiences were quite good, and many agree that machine translation is more efficient and sometimes uses more varied vocabulary than human translation."

"Yes, humans will definitely not be able to compete with the efficiency of machines. However, machine translations are not accurate enough, for there is complexity in thought and culture behind each translation." As Henry did not respond, Peggy continued, "let me tell you a story."

"In 1954, Premier Zhou Enlai attended the Geneva conference. He instructed the conference staff to show participants a coloured

Shaoxing opera[15] film titled 'Liang Shanbo and Zhu Yingtai' who were the characters in the Chinese legend 'The Butterfly Lovers'. The staff-in-charge was a meticulous person and was concerned that foreigners would not understand a Chinese opera film. Therefore, he hurriedly asked someone to write a fifteen-page synopsis for the opera and brought it to Premier Zhou for review. After reading it, Premier Zhou said, 'target audience disregarded, asking the audience to read this is akin to casting pearls before swine'! The staff was bold, he retorted, 'Showing foreigners a film of this genre, that would be truly casting pearls before swine.' Premier Zhou was not offended, he smiled and said, 'Let me show you a different way to cast the pearls. You just have to put this sentence on the invitation: Please enjoy a coloured opera film, the Chinese version of 'Romeo and Juliet'.' As a result, the audience was mesmerised by the opera film and the venue resounded with applause from time to time," Peggy preached.

> Translation is not a simple language conversion but requires in-depth understanding of the cultures behind two different languages.

"I get it, translation is not a mechanical conversion of words, it is a form of cross-cultural communication and exchange. Just like the example that you have quoted, machines will not be able to translate as well as humans, meaning it can only be communicated by someone with an in-depth understanding of the two country's cultures."

"The culture behind the language is a very important reason but of course there are other reasons that prevent machines from being used and useful in translation. Let me give you another example."

"Okay." Henry was curious.

---

[15] Shaoxing opera is the second most popular Chinese opera genre. Peking opera is more popular nationwide in China.

"For languages with a similar structure, where the meaning of words can be fully corresponded, or where there are certain patterns for conversion, such as between European languages, machine translation is not difficult and fairly accurate. However, for languages where the conceptual correspondence is not so neat and there are differences in language structure, there is a lot of room for improvement in machine translation."

"Such as Chinese and English?" asked Henry.

"You are smart!"

"That is true, when I was learning English, I was so sick of the grammatical structures, to me, Chinese is so concise and rhythmic."

"On one hand, the structure of English clauses requires the translator to think over and over while translating, to break up the whole into parts and to convert complex structures into simple ones. On the other hand, a single word in English can often have many meanings corresponding to it in Chinese, exactly which one is suitable will depend on the context. The machine will not be able to do that, it will usually just auto-select the most common one."

"Then what about big data? Can it be useful?"

"AI can still play some part in translation. Afterall, machine translation is more and more common these days. But big data is almost of no use at the moment."

"Really? Why?"

"One very important reason is that the translator's data and the client's data are treasured assets of individual companies, others have no access to them." Peggy continued her explanation, "Take for example, the interpretation which my partner and I did for you this time, if he had not sorted out in advance the list of

> Quality linguistic data sleeps like droplets in the computers of bilingual talent, without a model for actualisation, and AI is in dire need of such quality data.

blockchain-related terminology and sent it to a novice like me, for reference, our work would definitely not have gone so smoothly. What he has with him are extremely valuable data which I believe other translators also have, however, these are all stored in their individual personal computers, there is no way nor incentive to share. While search engines have quality data like these, the data volume is too small to generate interest. Thus, the data remains protected but also isolated."

"You are right, translators compete with one another for work. It is the same for many other industries."

> Translation services companies have low thresholds and are small scale. The information of clients and translators are important assets, and there is a serious problem of homogeneity and competition.

"After working for a while, I realised that our boss manages a few big clients himself, I suppose it is a safeguard for him, in case anyone of us ever thinks of setting up our own business and poaching them from him. Our industry at its best, is a small circle of well-connected bosses collaborating on a small-scale basis."

"Tell me more."

"A second point I want to make is that individual translators are actually also creators. Some of their translations actually provide great value and are then used repeatedly, becoming part of the lingua franca. Let me give you another example."

"Sure! It is so interesting to listen to your translation stories and I am beginning to feel amazed by the wonders of language."

> Blockchain can be used to explicitly attribute these good expressions in the form of linguistic assets and embody value in circulation, through the affirmation of rights.

"For instance, in China, we usually refer to elderly people as '老人 lǎo rén', but in Singapore, the term 'senior citizen' is used; it is translated as '乐龄人士 lè líng rén shì (people in their golden years)'. Another example, in Singapore a 'foreign worker' is called '客工 kè gōng (guest worker)'. Don't you think that the person or people who translated these terms into such apt expressions did well? To me, they reflect a certain aspiration and expectation and encourage people to reflect on societal groups. Yet, I don't believe the translator(s) received any reward or even thanks for this good work."

"I see what you are trying to say. Yes, it is understandable that one will not share when it is clear that there is no reward for sharing."

"There is no proper platform for sharing even if there is an intention to share! By the way, do you know the development process of machine translation technology?" asked Peggy.

"Of course…I don't know. I am waiting for you, the professional to educate me!" Henry joked.

"To put it simply, the first generation was the rule-based translation system, the second generation was the statistical translation model. We are now in the midst of developing the third-generation neural machine translation system and the new bottleneck facing neural machine translation is the lack of timely and effective big data."

"What if everyone's direction and abilities are tier labelled and made public, readily available and accessible to those who need it. Wouldn't that solve the problem?"

"Many translators work hard to promote themselves publicly. However, the scope of exposure is limited, and the root cause of the problem is still not resolved."

"Apart from the limited exposure, there is a very important reason and that is, it takes more than just self-promotion for others to believe in one's ability," said Henry.

"Exactly. Some of the translators I work with are in fact, very skilled professionally but there is no way for accurate assessment of their capabilities. For each project, we can only trust that the translator will do a good enough job, based on his/her previous work and our experience in working together.

> Recognition is the basis for cooperation, and the better the recognition, the stronger the basis for cooperation.

"Am I right to say that the core issue is how to effectively recognise each translator's abilities and make it public? The party in need of translation can then find a suitable translator quickly and the translator will be able to do work that fits his scope and ability. In such a transaction, friction will naturally be reduced considerably."

"Big brother Henry, you are so smart; a hint is all it took for you to understand! Alas, there is no solution…"

"The problem is not insurmountable."

"Oh, what solution do you have?" asked Peggy.

"It is not me who can provide the solution, it is blockchain."

"What do you mean?"

"Do you remember the theme and main points of my presentation at the blockchain conference this morning?"

"Yes, I do, the theme was 'Blockchain Reshapes the Economy and the World'. There were three main points: 1. Why the word 'token' is translated as a certificate for circulation (通证 tōng zhèng) and the types of tokens, 2. The relation between blockchain and tokens and 3. Functionalities of tokens."

"Exactly! What I am saying is that the incentive mechanism of blockchain can be leveraged to reflect the value of the interpreter in a comprehensive and dynamic manner and thus help to build unhindered trust between user and interpreter."

"How can this be done specifically?"

"Okay, I want you to try to recall what I said this morning and at the same time listen to my analysis."

"Okay, I'm ready for a lesson from my big brother Henry, let's begin!" Peggy stretched out on her bed and waited in anticipation for Henry to continue.

"A very important characteristic of blockchain is decentralisation, do you know this?"

"I know, in modern times, for example, marriage is endorsed by the Bureau of Civil Affairs, whereas in ancient times it was only necessary to be witnessed by a group of relatives and neighbours."

"This is correct. I will quote another example. When you shop online, why are you willing to make payment before the seller sends the goods? This is because the money will first enter the account of a third party, after you have verified that you have received the goods, the money will then be credited into the seller's account. Is this right?"

"Yes." Peggy nodded her head.

"Do you agree that a translation services company like yours is equivalent to a third party between the translator and the client?"

"Yes, our company is a typical intermediary."

> An important function of a translation company is to act as an endorser between the client and the translator.

"Well, for various reasons, your role as an intermediary is not working out in an optimal manner, but without you as the intermediary, the situation would be worse: interpreters and clients would be looking for one another like needles in a haystack, the establishment of contact and trust between both sides would be more difficult."

"Yes, we are very important in that respect."

"Blockchain is decentralised, any translator can make use of it to publicise and renew their information, including personal information, professional qualifications, as well as project and transaction information etc. It is equivalent to setting up an increasingly comprehensive personal profile, and providing unconditional access for those who need it. This eliminates the need for a translation services company as a head-hunter, the system itself is the head-hunter."

> The holographic digital identity of the translator can be continuously, dynamically, securely, completely and faithfully recorded on the blockchain.

"But this will just mean that translators can make themselves more visible, but visibility is not the same as credibility."

> Bringing together a large number of trusted, highly recognisable translators and making this information available to the language services industry.

"This will involve another characteristic of blockchain that is traceable and non-tamperable."

"How?" asked Peggy.

"Earlier on I mentioned that it is possible to update transactions on the blockchain, right?"

"Yes."

"Well, it is not only the translator who can update a transaction, the client who paid for the service can update too, other related parties can also update. This is equivalent to a complex new ecosystem that requires the participation of multiple parties in the industry and no single person can call all the shots. Blockchain connections are stringent, both to enhance credibility through human testimony and to filter the hodgepodge of practitioners through a network of connections."

"Will the data be safe on the platform?"

"Blockchain is non-tamperable and completely transparent, once there is a record on the blockchain, there is no way to get rid of the trace, and any process of tampering will be traceable. There is a high cost to pay for fabrication and cheating."

"It involves therefore, the building of trust through technology, not a third party."

"A brilliant summary! In a nutshell, trust in blockchain is trust in something common and that is cryptology. This is quite complicated to explain, you do not need to understand it at this point."

"The information that is made public on the blockchain equates to a new kind of big data."

"That's right, these big data can be used to quantify the competency and creditability of translators. It is like having an invisible ruler. The translations of '乐龄人士 lè líng rén shì (people in their golden years)' and '客工 kè gōng (guest workers)' that you just cited are also good quality big data. If this contribution can be validated, those who need it can use it directly at a very low cost, and the data providers can be rewarded accordingly, then everyone will

> Bilingual talents can establish their language assets on the blockchain.

> Quantifying translator's capabilities and credit through big data.

have incentive to actively contribute and focus on creating meaningful and apt translations, thus forming their own language assets."

"The inability to perform works of creation is a weakness of the machine."

"Yes, human and machine can work together to translate. The machine is an assistant to the human, and will work in coordination with the human in translation."

"Are there any other requirements?" Peggy pursued.

"This will be free-form, with this platform, it is all about creativity."

"Can a few translators work together?" Peggy asked again.

> Building credit assets on the blockchain for bilingual talents so that they can be identified and trusted to collaborate reliably. Building language assets gives them a model to actualise their values that they could not otherwise deliver, while also providing timely, high-quality big data for machine translation.

"Of course. The descriptions we defined just now are exactly how we can set up credit assets and language assets. With capabilities of translators being clear and reliable, whenever there is a need to collaborate, it will be easy to form a team that matches the project requirements and communicate the work content and distribution of benefits. When the project is done, a smart contract will be activated that can, according to the agreement, distribute benefits according to the work done, there will not be issues of chasing for payment or arrears."

"What else is important to know?"

> A circle is both a gathering point where translators can provide content, contacts and interests, and a space where translators can create additional value and income on their own initiative.

"It is possible to form small circles and create value together based on individual contributions. Let's imagine that you are a digital data controller who is proficient in English, you can gather people with the same interest and ability, find the provider of the latest digital product evaluation information from abroad and translate their work into Chinese. Locals who need the information can pay to get them. By doing so, you not only gain monetary benefit, but also promote the exchange of information."

"Wow, you're right, a translator's value can be fully utilised and remunerated."

> Every bilingual talent and even every individual can contribute to language proficiency.

"Each node on the blockchain is characterised by a high degree of autonomy. Nodes can be freely connected to each other to form new connecting units. The impact between nodes will form non-linear casualty relations through the network. This is an open, flat and equal structure which enables each community member to be a small and independent contributor to the development of blockchain projects."

"This is amazing!" Peggy was amazed and excited by the blueprint that Henry had outlined, but in the next moment, she yawned involuntarily. "Don't get me wrong, Henry, I am not bored..." Peggy hastened to explain.

"You must be very tired Peggy. It's time for you to rest."

"It is almost 11pm. But we only talked mainly about me and my work, you haven't told me much about your life yet..." Peggy protested.

"Do you have any plans for tomorrow?" Henry had a new idea.

"No, why?"

"I intend to change my flight and return to Beijing in another day or two."

"Oh? Will it disrupt your work in Beijing?"

"I should have taken a few days to relax after this meeting and besides, this is my first trip to Singapore, I would like to tour this legendary 'garden city'. Before Peggy could reply, Henry continued, "Actually, the main reason is that I want to talk to you more and take a good look at you, I was in a rush today and did not take a closer look at you."

Peggy's heart skipped a beat at his words, in the next instant, she could almost feel bubbles of joy welling up within her as she pictured Henry's tall figure in her mind. However, she replied in as neutral a tone she could manage, "Well, that sounds good, let's talk more tomorrow."

"You should rest. I will look up places to go and send the meeting time and place to you tomorrow morning. Or shall I pick you up? Where do you live?"

"No, don't worry, the MRT is just at my doorstep, it is very convenient."

Peggy set her alarm for 7am and with her pillow, she fell asleep.

Henry did some research on the internet and left a message for Peggy on WeChat, "Young lady, I will be sending my juniors off in the morning, let's meet at Sentosa at 11am." When Peggy did not reply after a while, he guessed that she must have fallen asleep, and he sent another message, "Sending my good morning greetings in advance, be there or be square!"

Summary:
Wide Recognition

Blockchain provides the technical support to realise the values of bilingual talents. Blockchain is immutable. It can be the way to build credit assets for translators.

Language is viewed as a window to human nature. This is because language is a product of the human cognitive mechanisms. The universal laws of language largely reflect the laws of human cognition, and the diversity of language reflects the diversity of the human society and the natural environment in which human lives.

The development of linguistic intelligence is tied to the characteristics of language. Human language is personal, contextual, chronological and regional and these resulted in rich and varied forms of language expressions. Even human is prone to ambiguity, not to mention machines. Language is evolving and the thinking modes of human are also constantly changing. Jobs that are standardised, repetitive, and quantifiable can be replaced by machine intelligence. However, works of creation such as translation requires comprehensive understanding of text to express and embody emotion, knowledge, culture, and others — aspects which machines will never be able to surpass human. In other words, the works of creation which reflect human thoughts and intelligence are irreplaceable by machines.

Using big data, blockchain acts as a ruler to quantify translator's professional ability and creditability, just like a profile, to record the translator's holographic digital identity in a continuous, dynamic, secured, complete and faithful manner. It is a comprehensive description of the translator's professional background, abilities, client's evaluation, peer recognition, professional development etc., to form the translator's credit assets. It is also possible to establish translator's linguistic assets through authentication on blockchain.

Machine translation has undergone the first generation of rule-based translation system, the second generation of the statistical translation model and now the third generation of neural machine translation system. After a breakthrough in natural language processing through neural network translation techniques, there have been new bottlenecks due to lack of high-quality language data and slow progress in quality improvements.

High-quality language data are dispersed across the computers of translators and bilingual talents around the world. These professionals generate new language data continuously as they engage in their daily language conversion work. These highly valuable language data are essentially in an idle state.

Looking back at the changes in the basic resources of mankind, surface resources in the agricultural societies such as land, forests, livestock, plants, and water were fundamental for which people depended on for survival. Due to the development of science and technology, underground resources such as oil, mineral deposits, and geothermal heat have also become basic resources in the industrial societies. However, after thousands of years of development, the surface resources as well as the underground resources have already been fully exploited. The data resources of the internet era, on the other hand, mark the beginning of the march from the natural world to the artificial world. This has enabled human knowledge and wisdom to become the raw materials, and provided an impetus for the in-depth development of human's intellectual capital.

Language, embodying history and culture, is the fruit of human wisdom. People learn about a society through language, and at the same time, express wisdom through language. Therefore, language data resource

SUMMARY

is important as it can fully reflect human thoughts and wisdom. It is the raw material and driving force for building an era of intelligent systems. The internet has changed the way we shop, travel, etc., but these are merely our behavioural data. It is language that reflects the human mind, and these are the actual data of intelligence.

The human society is entering a new era of digital economy. In this era, machine intelligence will be closely aligned with human intelligence, and machine intelligence will participate in large-scale collaborations that previously involved only humans. The basis of large-scale collaboration is trust. Building the credit assets of translators on blockchain allows translators to be recognised. Recognition is the foundation of collaboration, and the higher the level of recognition, the stronger the collaboration and the better the effects of the collaboration.

The concept of asset has evolved. Petroleum has always been available, but it is only in the last two years or so that petroleum has been classified as an asset. Technological developments have led to changes in the categorisation of assets, and only resources that simultaneously meet the criteria of being controllable and recognisable by the system to generate economic benefits can be classified as assets.

Language is not just a tool; it is also a resource. For a long time, language-based creative work has not been able to take the form of a product to generate a return. The reason is that creative work like language is not controllable once it is separated from its creator. At this stage, there is no system in place to provide recognition, and therefore, creative language work has not been able to be classified into an asset.

China has defined data as a factor of production at the national level. It is now trying to bring individual language creation into the realm of assets by using technology to make language data controllable, protectable, identifiable, and exchangeable, so that language creation is socially recognised and rewarded.

Mandarin is a valuable resource that carries thousands of years of global Chinese wisdom. The classification of language data as an asset will certainly lead to more accurate and flourishing creation of language and cultural products, thereby unlocking a phenomenal new asset class.

Bilingual talents engaged in creativity work can integrate their linguistic and professional abilities and showcase their abilities through personal credibility and language assets built on blockchain. Their sense of social identity, self-satisfaction and accomplishment can be adequately fulfilled in the blockchain era. This will unleash the human potential for creative work and machine translation will also be made better by a constant supply of timely, high-quality big data.

Machine conveys information and human imparts expressiveness. Machine and man will form a mutual reinforcement model for development. Machines will become more intelligent because of the big data provided by human, and human can focus on creative work with the help of machines to provide high-quality translations. Ultimately, the translation capacity will increase substantially by attaining the speed of machines and deriving high-quality output from human.

———— Chapter 6 ————

A Perfect Match

The Wonderful Union of Language and Blockchain

Henry and Peggy began exploring the characteristics of the industries that could best bring out the value of blockchain. They were pleasantly surprised to discover that the language services industry and blockchain were a perfect fit for each other.

The entire business process of language services can be done online, the client-oriented ecosystem is diverse, the product is a result of intellectual labour and the industry is fragmented. These characteristics fully align with the industrial characteristics which are appropriate for blockchain applications.

Blockchain and language are mutually necessary, exemplify two-way empowerment, and amplify each other's value. Blockchain needs to overcome language barriers, to enable barrier-free language communication and flexible collaboration on a global scale and ultimately leverage the power of value transfer. Language needs blockchain to identify bilingual talents and enable recognition and remuneration for the value they provide, thereby incentivising bilingual talents to create and share value and making language data and information attractive for global distribution.

1. In the era of blockchain, breaking down language barriers is a priority.
2. Blockchain requires languages to fulfil the potential of global collaboration.
3. Languages need blockchain to demonstrate the appeal of global communication.
4. Blockchain is a natural fit with language.

***

The next morning, Henry and his junior colleagues gathered at the hotel lobby with their luggage.

"I made a decision late last night and could not inform all of you earlier. I will only go back to Beijing a few days later, I have changed my flight booking."

"What? Is there an emergency?" "He doesn't look anxious." "What's fascinating enough to keep you here?" …

In reply to his "twittering" colleagues, Henry's simple response was: "I met an old friend in this distant land."

"Oh…" everyone seemed to understand readily and began giving him knowing smiles.

"What's this nonsense about an old friend in a distant land, more like love at first sight!" Roche, who was closest with Henry, nudged his shoulder and flashed him a cheeky grin.

"Cut it out, I'm speaking the truth, she's a childhood neighbour who's like a younger sister to me, we grew up together," Henry retorted.

"Oh, it's a lady indeed! Tell me quickly, how did you meet?" Roche probed.

"She's the lady who did the interpretation for me at the presentation yesterday." Henry's colleagues began to chatter among themselves once more, everyone agreed that Peggy had done a good job, and a few even lamented not having the chance to see her face. Henry felt embarrassed, "Come on, stop it. Let's go now. We already planned to go to Orchard Road, if we leave any later, you will miss your flight!"

"You are coming with us to Orchard Road too?" Roche asked, puzzled that Henry was not rushing off to meet Peggy.

"Yes, I will go with you to Orchard Road and I will buy a few things there. After that, you all should go directly to the airport, I will check into another hotel," Henry replied.

Located in the heart of Singapore, Orchard Road is regarded as the most famous tourist shopping street in Asia. This is where branded fashion boutiques and specialty shops are found. It caters to all levels of consumers regardless of spending capacity and it is popular with tourists from all around the world.

The architecture on Orchard Road is distinctive, with the road itself flanked by clean and spacious pedestrian walkways on both sides and rows of tall trees providing shade in the tropical heat. Amidst the gleaming modern buildings, elderly ice cream hawkers with their humble carts and brightly coloured rainbow umbrellas dot the landscape, for a dollar or two, one can enjoy a cheap cold treat.

After a short stroll, the humid weather became unbearable, so Henry and his colleagues decided to visit the ION SKY observation deck located in the ION shopping mall.

The elevator was dark, and the flaming starry sky on the electronic screens in it created anticipation in everyone's minds; within a minute or so, they arrived at the fifty-sixth-storey observation deck.

The observation deck was 218 metres high, with floor-to-ceiling windows all around. The 360-degree view from the observation deck gave one the feeling of being in the clouds, the sights on the ground became very small, providing a panoramic view of the beautiful city of Singapore. Looking further into the distance, Henry thought he could even see Malaysia and Indonesia.

The entire observation deck had striped wooden floors and soft benches had been strategically placed all around for visitors to relax comfortably and enjoy a brief respite from shopping. While taking a rest, visitors could also watch a multimedia watercolour animation, which covered the developmental history of Orchard Road from the eighteenth century to the present.

Once the shops opened, Henry and his colleagues headed off for some souvenir shopping. Some people bought tonics from an established brand, others bought Merlion chocolates, and one lady bought a classic gold-plated orchid flower pendant necklace. She told everyone about the story behind the flower, Vanda Miss Joaquim and another romantic story behind the gold-plated orchid: a young scientist, in order to please his wife, conducted countless experiments and finally achieved a way to frame the beauty of natural orchids with the purest gold.

"When a scholar expresses his love, it's really a big deal," a junior colleague joked, everyone laughed.

Henry purchased some health products for his parents and carefully selected an exquisite hand-painted tulip silk scarf for Peggy.

"Don't indulge too much in Singapore and forget your home and work. Come back soon, there is a lot of work to do in the company." Roche teased Henry again as they bid farewell.

"Don't be cheeky, go now or you will miss your flight!"

Amidst such good-natured teasing and banter, everyone bid goodbye to Henry and headed for the airport. With his luggage in tow and the elaborately wrapped silk scarf, Henry took the MRT to Sentosa, he would drop his luggage at the hotel before meeting Peggy.

When they met, he saw that Peggy was wearing a sleeved floral dress in pastel yellow with white shoes. She looked refreshingly pretty.

"Peggy, you look very good today."

"Well, I'm afraid you do not look as good as you did yesterday!" Peggy replied jokingly. Henry had dressed casually in a grey short sleeved shirt and dark pants.

"Hah! Okay, if you say so. Here, a present for you." He opened his backpack and took out his gift for her.

"What is this?" Peggy felt like she had just signed for a delivered parcel and could hardly resist the urge to open it.

"Save the surprise for later when you open it. Are you hungry? Shall we have lunch?"

"There's a Malaysian Food Street here, shall we try some local fare?" Peggy suggested.

Peggy ordered a plate of char kway teow — a local delicacy of stir-fried noodles with fresh clams, bean sprouts and prawns. Henry had a bowl of laksa, also a noodle dish but with soup that is flaming orange and spicy, containing coconut milk and dried shrimps, and topped with fresh clams, prawns, deep fried fish cake.

"You came to work in Singapore alone, aren't your parents worried? How did you convince them?" Henry asked.

"Actually, it did not take much effort to convince them. As you know, my family has always been quite democratic, my parents were satisfied with the reason I gave them for wanting to work here. Besides, I have a teacher who did her master's and doctorate degrees here, she returned to China to teach eventually but I received a lot of information about Singapore from her, so I did not feel worried."

"Where did you do your bachelor and master's degrees?"

"In Wuhan. Let me test you, my school is known as 'Guanshankou (关山口) Vocational and Technical College for Boys',[16] make a guess which school is that?" Peggy smiled.

"That's easy! Our schools have names that are quite similar actually. I studied at 'Wudaokou (五道口) Science and Engineering College'[17] in Beijing."

"I know it!" Peggy replied with a grin. They easily guessed each other's schools. "What did you major in?" Peggy continued.

"Bachelor's degree in finance, master's degree in computer science."

"I did mechanical engineering for my bachelor's and then realised that I enjoy learning languages so I went on to study translation for my master's."

---

[16] Guanshankou (关山口) Vocational and Technical College for Boys is the layman's name for Huazhong University of Science and Technology (华中科技大学). There is a bus stop in front of the south gate of the main university campus called Guanshankou Station. The predominance of male students in the university is the reason that it is called a college for boys.

[17] Wudaokou (五道口) is the district where Tsinghua University (清华大学) is located in Beijing, the respective faculties all use Wudaokou in their layman names, e.g., Wudaokou Engineering and Technology University.

"I remember that when you were a child, you were very conscientious, you rewrote your homework if it were not neat enough by your standards and sometimes you would tear the pages in the workbook as a result of too much erasing. That was when I thought, no matter what you do in your life later, you would definitely do well," said Henry.

"Yes, when I do what I like, I will do it well; I tend to follow my intuitions."

"I am pretty much the same, whatever I learn or work on depends a lot on my preference, although it is not always possible to do what I like."

Peggy was savouring the sweet and delicious char kway teow when a thought suddenly struck her, she changed the topic and asked, "Did you ever go back to Hangzhou after moving away?"

"I did, twice, in fact, once to attend an academic conference while I was still studying, and another time to attend an event in Hangzhou after I had started work."

"Did you not think of visiting us?" asked Peggy.

Henry was caught off guard, "Well…I did not know if you were still in Hangzhou and it has been so many years since I contacted your parents, I didn't think that it was a good idea to disturb them unnecessarily, so…"

When she saw that Henry had choked a little on her question, Peggy regretted asking it, after all, she too had only thought of Henry occasionally, and never actually stayed in touch or thought of looking for him. Quickly, she changed the topic, "Do you remember Brenda and Fanny?"

"I definitely do! We were in different levels at school, but we were a 'gang of four', weren't we? Well, after I moved, I also lost touch with them."

"Hah! Try to guess what each of them is doing now."

"I have no idea. All I remember is that all three of you were lively and outgoing."

"When Brenda was in high school, she was deeply inspired by the books and programmes of some famous media personalities, so she studied journalism and entered the media industry. She is now a reporter for a technology newspaper in Beijing."

"A technology reporter? You studied mechanical engineering and Brenda is a science and technology reporter, wow, you ladies are so powerful."

"Hah, are you trying to say that women are naturally inferior to men in science, technology and engineering?"

Henry raised both hands in mock surrender, "No way, of course not!" He quickly continued, "What about Fanny?"

"Fanny studied business and joined a foreign trade company which specialises in cross-border e-commerce. Her company's headquarters are in Beijing."

"Such a coincidence, my company is based in Beijing too."

"You should arrange to meet them when you go back," said Peggy.

"Without your presence, it will not be the same."

"No problem, we can do a video call and I will 'cloud' your historic meeting," they both burst out in laughter at Peggy's witty pun.

"Time passes really fast. We have all grown up and are living our lives at our own pace and according to our own preferences," Peggy sank back into memory.

"Indeed, the years I spent in Hangzhou as a child were some of the happiest and most important years of my life. All I remember of those days is that the sky was blue, the lake was clear, and in summer, parents and children would stroll and relax in the compound of the academy," Henry reminisced.

"Oh yes, I remember those days too. Remember the kite you made that flew so high? The three of us girls were so eager to play with it you ended up not getting a turn when we played together."

"I guess the compound must look different now."

"It has been demolished. The academy has been moved to the suburbs. The land we used to live on has become a park," Peggy said.

"When will we have the chance to go back together? I'm beginning to miss my hometown," Henry sighed.

"Never mind, let's not get into such a depressing topic, eat up!" Peggy replied.

"The noodle in this laksa dish is really special, springy and smooth," Henry gulped down the little soup that was left in the bowl.

After the both of them had finished eating, they decided to buy some teh tarik (literally "pulled tea" in Malay) and take a walk along the beach. Teh tarik has a similar colour to milk coffee, so Peggy was curious and asked the stallholder more about it. The latter patiently demonstrated his skill of "tea pulling" by swiftly pouring the condensed milk-sweetened tea back and forth from one cup to another. He explained that this helps to cool down the tea.

"Henry, since we are here, do you happen to know the meaning of 'Sentosa' in the Malay language?"

"Sunny beach?"

"Nope. It means peace and tranquillity," Peggy replied.

"Since you asked, you obviously want to tell me the story behind it."

"Yes! Let me tell you the story of Sentosa."

Henry grinned and gestured for her to go ahead. The salty sea breeze swept across his face and although it was sunny and humid, he felt relaxed and comfortable.

"In the beginning, Sentosa was just an ordinary island, where the inhabitants fished for a living and led a simple, rustic life. With the outbreak of the Second World War, this small fishing village was transformed into a British military base because of its geographical location, destroying the original tranquil atmosphere. After independence, control of the island was returned to the new government, and Sentosa was transformed into a leisure resort. With the hope that the island would never be subjected to war again, it was given the elegant and atmospheric name of 'Sentosa'," said Peggy.

> There is a memorable historical story behind the names of many places.

"I see...it is a small island with a rich history."

"Let's sit here, Henry."

The pair sat down under a coconut tree and gazed out at the sea, the sand was warm, soft and fine, the sun cast mottled shadows on the beach through the gaps between the leaves. In quiet companionship, they observed the seabirds screeching and flapping their wings in the air. The birds swooped down into the waves from time to time, as if diving into the water, but very quickly they flew up again, with fish clasped tightly in their beaks.

From a distance, a flock of seagulls flew onto the beach together. Peggy and Henry noticed that one of them suddenly started behaving strangely. It began flapping its wings hard, and flew higher and higher into the air, way above all the other birds, before circling the flock.

"Is it trying to attract the attention of tourists…" Peggy muttered.

Before she even finished her sentence, the gull dived into the flock like a bomb, and then shot right out again. It appeared to have grabbed a bit of food from another gull's beak, an act that provoked angry screeching from the flock. "Ah!" Peggy exclaimed, stunned by the sudden turn of events.

"Wow, I did not expect that to happen…such strife and cruelty among the seagulls. To think I had believed they were a team, flying together in order to share and collaborate," Henry sighed.

"Ah, what you just said makes me think of wild geese. The V-shaped flying formations are said to allow the whole flock to fly 71% faster than if each goose were to fly alone. According to the researchers, if any of the geese fall out of formation because of fatigue or illness, a few other geese in the flock will follow suit to keep it company and care for it," said Peggy.

"Yes, and did you know that the leader rotates? The bird flying at the V point is subjected to maximum air resistance, so when it gets tired, it drops back down and another bird moves forward, such rotation enables the whole flock to fly continuously over long distances."

"A flock of geese is a true representation of collaboration."

"Collaboration can create a great deal of new capacities," Henry replied as he scrolled through the photo album on his phone before showing some to Peggy. "This is the European starling, look at these pictures in succession, they fly in flocks, at one moment the flock looks like an exploding mushroom cloud, in the next, it is a huge ceremonial flower blooming in the air, but no matter how the shape changes, they stay firmly close to one another."

> Many species are naturally capable of collaboration, but humans are limited in their ability to collaborate flexibly and intensively on a global scale because of language barriers.

Peggy was blown away by the spectacular sight of the starlings in the photos. Henry showed her another picture: a landscape of the ocean floor, a large school of fish gathered in a spiral shape, trying to resist the attack of some dolphins.

Henry explained, "There are many big and powerful creatures in the ocean, on their own, sardines are vulnerable, they have neither the ability to defend themselves nor the ability to hide. Thus, they gather together to form a 'swarm effect' so as to defend themselves against predators. When large predators approach, the sardines gather in a shoal, and the rule is simple, each sardine will keep an eye on the fish around it, staying at the same distance from and moving in the same direction as the others. In this way, the rapid but concerted movement of the shoal provides safety in numbers."

"I have seen clusters of geese and other animals like ants before, but nothing was as stunning as the pictures of the starlings and sardines you just showed me," Peggy replied, nodding in amazement.

"Yes, the beauty and power of collaboration in nature is really beyond our imagination."

"Henry, tell me about your university life."

"What's there to say? It was just the ordinary life of a male engineering student, albeit at a prestigious engineering school."

"Let me guess, checkered shirt, backpack, an umbrella in the left outer pocket and a water bottle in the right," Peggy teased.

"What?!"

"That's the typical image of a male science or engineering college student."

"Hah! You're quite right, but not completely. Well, although my school is more well known for science and technology, it also places great importance on providing a quality humanities education. Therefore, I am both technically and artistically inclined." Henry was amused.

"There was a philosophy professor at your campus whom I particularly adored. I even entertained the thought of pursuing my master's degree at your university so I could learn from him."

"It looks like you had a real love for this teacher. Sadly, I have never taken a humanities class in college…It's a loss."

"It's not just any loss, you have suffered heavy losses," Peggy said.

"Well…At least I did not waste my time at university, I took my studies very seriously, participated in some professional workshops and competitions, achieved decent results, and even had a few solid internship experiences."

"Our similarities, then, should be that neither of us wasted our time. I think what we did makes a difference though, I participated in competitions and workshops too, but I probably spent more time reading, thinking, attending lectures and writing."

"Yes, thinking is important. I once saw this quote: 'a person who engages in deep thinking spends 20% of the time reading and 80% of the time thinking, so as to find out the nature of an issue.' Although I find that this proportion is exaggerated, it does have some truth," said Henry.

"The professor I was talking about once said that life is about contemplation; I was very much influenced by him."

"When you are talking about this person you adore, your eyes glow brightly."

Peggy looked slightly bashful, "I am already restraining myself from gushing…I actually have immense power when it comes to describing how good this teacher is."

A thought suddenly entered Henry's mind, "Was Peggy courted by many boys at university?"

Peggy raised her eyebrows, as if to ask "What do you think?"

"I bet there were many. I just wondered what sort of a man would be able to finally capture your heart, that's all."

"Well, I dated someone but we broke up eventually. 'All great things on earth do not last', Teacher Yang Jiang (杨绛), the renowned Chinese playwright, author and translator, quote this when speaking of her husband Qian Zhongshu (钱锺书) and her daughter," Peggy said.

"Don't be pessimistic, since you describe it as a great thing now, it shows that you were both sincere and happy at the time, so it was all worth it."

"Hah, no, I am not pessimistic, I consider myself an optimistic pessimist!"

Henry did not want Peggy to get upset and decided that it would be safer to talk about himself, "I had a relationship in university too, but it did not last either. I am awaiting the next one and I hope it will be 'the one'."

"Ah…I see. I suppose you know the love story of Yang Jiang and Qian Zhongshu? When Qian Zhongshu told Yang Jiang that he wanted to write a novel, Yang Jiang not only suggested to Qian Zhongshu to reduce his teaching load, she also personally handled all the housework after the maid resigned. She gave tremendous support both in words and in action. However, she has never compromised her self-identity in love, she was a truly graceful woman who lived her life to the fullest, and I thought that was wonderful," said Peggy.

"Historically, there are no lack of such love stories. The kind of love I have in mind is where both parties are evenly matched in terms of values and personal strength, able to accompany and support each other, as well as progress and grow together," Henry said.

"I feel that it is important to have agreement on three fundamentals: firstly, one's worldview, secondly, values of worth and lastly, outlook on life. It is also equally important to have spiritual compatibility. In any case, women cannot be expected to give up their careers for love and marriage, no matter who they marry."

Coincidentally, not too far away, there was a couple taking wedding photos. For a moment, both Peggy and Henry fell into silence, each lost in their own thoughts, the only sounds were those of the wind and waves interspersed with playful laughter from the other people on the beach.

"Henry, why did you start doing research on blockchain?"

"Well, you know I studied both computer science as well as banking and finance. After graduation, I worked in the finance sector for some time and that was when I was introduced to blockchain in general and cryptocurrencies in particular; I would say I had early exposure to blockchain in this respect."

"How long has it been?"

"Slightly more than two years."

"I was talking to you last night about the problems in the language services industry, and you said that blockchain has a solution, and you gave me a very graphic description of it. Is blockchain really that powerful?"

"You told me several stories about your industry yesterday, I will tell you one that's related to mine too," said Henry.

"Good, I love stories."

"There was a luggage company in Guangdong, which had been suffering from the impact of e-commerce for a long time, in short, its revenue was deteriorating. The boss of the company decided to issue an internal currency called 'god beans', to be given free to each department at the beginning of the year."

"What were the god beans for?"

"To put it simply, anyone in the company who asked a colleague to complete a task at work had to pay a certain amount of god beans to the other person. So…tasks like the changing of light bulbs, organisation of a company event, helping out with a drawing or doing something for a department were all paid for using god beans."

"I see, the god beans were confined within the company and used for internal corporate affairs, whenever there was a problem to be solved or task to be done, it was paid for in god beans; thus, whoever contributed more, would have more god beans."

"That is correct," replied Henry.

"What could the god beans be used for?"

"At the end of the year, the company counted the number of god beans that each person had accumulated. A part of the company's profits for the year was set aside to make a bonus pool, which was divided according to the total number of god beans held…The eventual result was that the company became more streamlined and managed to improve its performance."

"I see."

"This story illustrates two points, firstly, a token incentive mechanism is beneficial. Secondly, such a mechanism is possible without the use of blockchain, but with the use of blockchain, there would be a broader circulation and a wider scope of incentives to register these rights in the form of tokens."

"Okay…but you have not answered my question," Peggy probed.

"I am trying to add charm to the 'token'! The point I want to express through this story is that it is not difficult to understand how blockchain works, it is not that complex."

A pushcart vendor selling cold drinks and ice cream approached from a distance.

"The cart there is selling ice cream, do you want one?"

"Yes, the seaside is the best place to have ice cream," Henry replied.

"Still blueberry flavour for you?".

"You remember?!"

"Hah, I can't believe that your taste has not changed!"

"Let me continue, blockchain and tokens are very popular right now, particularly due to cryptocurrency like bitcoin. To be frank, there are not many people who truly understand what blockchain can do. Some blindly promote blockchain, but blockchain is not all powerful, and it does not only involve technology and businesses, in fact, it also involves politics, but let's leave that aside," said Henry.

"You say it is not all powerful, so tell me, what can it do?"

"Before I talk about what blockchain can do, let me give you another example. I am sure you know what a harvester is? Yes, a machine for harvesting crops. The productivity of farming can be greatly enhanced if a farmer has one. But do you know what conditions are not suitable for a harvester?"

"It cannot be used in the mountains and hills. It can only be used on flatland areas like in our hometown."

"Yes, the harvester can only be used for harvesting on paddy fields and on flatlands, definitely not for cotton."

"When I was a child, my mother used to take me to my grandmother's house. I would carry a basket on my back and help to pick cotton."

Henry continued, "The harvester is therefore not all powerful, there has to be some specific conditions under which it is used. It is the same for blockchain, by examining the existing cases, as well as conducting logical analysis, we found that an industry where blockchain can best deliver value should have one or more of the following four characteristics... the first characteristic is that business for this industry should be completely conducted online."

> Blockchain is not all-powerful, and blockchain technology can only exert transformative power in areas that are suitable for blockchain transformation.

"Why?" asked Peggy.

"It is because a token is virtual, and it has to be circulated and allocated online. If the business in the industry can be completely done online, then it will be easier for it to adopt the token-based model."

> The whole business process of translation, placement, acceptance, translation, proofreading, typesetting and payment can be done online.

"Well, the translation industry seems to be a good example. What we do is purely brain work and does not require any special equipment. With the support from modern technology, the translator and client do not even need to meet up if the job involved is a written translation assignment, they can just communicate and transact directly online. At present, although interpreters are required to provide services at specific venues, communication and transactions can be done online. Once the technology is further refined, I believe interpreters will not have to work on site either," Peggy said.

Henry nodded, "The second characteristic is that it must be directed towards a C-end scenario."

"This term sounds familiar, C is the abbreviation for consumer, isn't it? But why does it have to be directed towards a C-end scenario?"

"C-end is the client, as opposed to A-end, the development and B-end, the merchant."

"What is the main difference between them?" asked Peggy.

"Both the B and C ends constitute demand and are highly analogous, so let me explain the difference between these two ends first."

"The most fundamental difference between the B-end and C-end is that the former serves organisations while the latter serves individuals. While both are on the demand end, the former is the demand front, where all the demand points within and outside of the organisation in the same scenario are met, while the latter being the demand point, does not involve collaboration with others and only addresses individuals' needs," Henry continued explaining.

"Hence, ordering takeout on the phone is satisfying the needs of the C-end," Peggy said.

> The C-end has a high volume of users and varied scenarios for token circulation.

"Yes, that is an apt example. From this perspective, it is clear that there are many users and scenarios at the C-end, isn't it?" said Henry.

"Indeed, a large number of users spread across scenarios."

"The decentralisation of blockchain actually makes it very suitable for use on such fragmented scenarios."

"The translation profession is a typical example of fragmentation," said Peggy.

"That's right, we spoke about this last night."

"Although I have not been in Singapore for very long, I was approached for help with directions several times in the MRT by middle-aged and elderly Chinese ladies who could not speak English. I also accompanied my co-tenant Doreen to a parent-teacher meeting as an interpreter, and when Doreen's daughter was sick, she came to me for help to read the medication instructions. Small instances like these are common."

> Language services are part of our work and daily life, in fragmented scenarios.

"Strangers on the road approach you for help because you have a friendly face," Henry teased.

"It occurred to me that, although there are many occasions in life when a translator is needed, only a small number of them are large-scale and comprehensive. A lot of translation needs are small and fragmented, and they occur on an ad hoc basis, so people will not seek and pay for translation services unless absolutely necessary. Such scenarios are common but there is no corresponding service being provided," said Peggy.

"Remember the pictures of starlings and sardines? Their impact and charm lie in decentralisation."

"Oh, what does that mean?"

"Scientific research shows that these groups in nature do not have a fixed leader. Like I mentioned before, each animal basically watches the ones around it closely and maintains relatively similar distances to them. Thus, the individual animals are actually blind to the position and aggregation of the group," said Henry.

"In the case of human beings, forming large groups and acting collectively often requires the election of a leader."

> The natural language ability of mankind and the rapid transmission of language can lead to consensus and large-scale collaboration.

"Human beings are naturally intelligent and can collaborate through learning and using technology, and blockchain can facilitate human collaboration."

"The more you say the more amazed I am," said Peggy.

> Collaboration is the inevitable trend.

"In blockchain, financial disclosure is the goal, decentralisation is the means, trust building is the purpose, and facilitating collaboration is the result."

"Facilitating large-scale collaborations is the ultimate goal, I guess."

> Trust is the basis for collaboration.

"You are correct. Blockchain adopts the distributed ledger technology like the token, which allows unconditional trust between strangers, this is the basis for large-scale collaboration."

"This has indirectly led us to other topics as well."

"Ha-ha, that's right, from C-end to decentralisation and collaboration. Decentralisation is one of the core issues of blockchain. Next, we need to consider the third characteristic and that is, difficulties in determining values."

"It is not always difficult to determine the value of brain work but values that are difficult to determine always involve brain work. Am I right to put it in this way?" asked Peggy.

"Indeed, this is a very incisive conclusion which I have not thought of. The values of some forms of mental work are difficult to determine under current models, which in turn makes it difficult to achieve maximum value effectiveness."

> It is difficult to evaluate and reflect a translator's ability.

"It is such a coincidence. The translation industry also has difficulty determining the value of a translator, we had a lot of discussion on this issue yesterday."

"I remember, because of a lack of uniformity in measurement, a translator's personal branding is in a predicament of limited dissemination channels coupled with low levels of trust."

"The two examples on translations I gave for 'people in the golden age' and 'guest workers', these are valuable and creative output, but they could not be measured and be rewarded."

"Many have hailed blockchain as a revolutionary technology. Well, in contrast to previous industrial revolutions where new

> Translator's hard work does not equate to high returns, a situation that could be resolved in the blockchain era.

technology increased production capacity, the effect of blockchain is on production relationships. The production relationship is essentially one of power and authority, so a change in the production relationship is in fact a redistribution of this power and authority. The need for such a change arises from the fact that those who originally created value did not share it equitably to receive the deserving rewards, resulting in unequal rights and returns." Henry said.

"Finally, a translator's pain can be addressed effectively."

> Blockchain causes change in production relations which can redistribute power.

"It is not just limited to the translation industry, blockchain also has the potential to change production relationships in many industries. In summary, when distributed networks are realised and popularised, blockchain will be able to lead the world towards an outcome of great consensus, specific rules and clear order."

"Great consensus, specific rules and clear order. Hahaha, that summary sounds really lofty." Peggy replied jokingly, but she could not resist asking, "What is the last characteristic?"

"The fourth characteristic is fragmentation. In an industry that is monopolistic or dominated by just a few firms, use of the token will not be applicable at all. However, if an industry is large and very fragmented such as any business operating on WeChat, the adoption of the token will lead to greater prospects, token incentives will effectively expand operation boundaries."

"That is correct, the translation industry is also fragmented. Earlier on we talked about demand fragmentation at the C-end, in fact, translation services companies are fragmented too."

"What you mean?"

"The fragmentation of translation services companies is reflected in their workshop-style existence. The company that I am working for is very small with few staff, but it is one of the better ones in the local industry with its own office space. In this industry, many are husband and wife or father and son teams that do not even have an office but operate workshop-style from home," Peggy said.

"You have enlightened me. Prior to this, I had no understanding of this industry at all. In the internet model, almost all areas that can be exploited have been developed. Some of the industries that are not doing well in the internet-centric model are probably those where blockchain might be able to make a difference in."

"You are right, Henry. When I studied translation, I did my internship at Transn, the biggest language services provider in China. The concept of 'internet of language' originated from this firm. The company has a grand vision, but it is really hard to achieve that blueprint in a centralised model." Peggy continued, "Also, shortly after I started my current job, we had a meeting with the boss, who told us that even the largest translation services company accounted for only 2–3% of the domestic market, unlike some companies in other industries that constitute 20% of the market or even more. Translation services companies are basically small companies facing homogeneous competition, lacking scale and branding and a production chain. 80% of the business of a translation services company is outsourced to part-time translators, with blurred organisational boundaries."

"These data and descriptions have given me a rough picture of the translation industry," said Henry.

"Last night I told you about the difficulties I encountered in my job, you said that blockchain can provide a solution. Today you talked about the characteristics of industries suitable for the application of blockchain and it is amazing that the translation industry matches all of them!"

"You said earlier that the translation industry exists in the form of _____ workshops, which is actually due to the lack of capacity, and that bilingual and multilingual people form the core of that capacity. Blockchain-based tokens can make the value of bilingual talent recognisable and measurable, which can in turn spur changes in the translation industry."

> Translation industry is well suited for transformation with blockchain.

As the duo continued chatting excitedly, time passed without them realising it. The sun began to set and many visitors had already left.

"Peggy, let's go for dinner."

"Sure, time flew by while we were talking."

"Originally, I knew very little about language and the language services industry, but after two days of interaction with you, this quote just came to my mind," Henry said.

"What is it?"

"Perhaps we really do not exist until someone has witnessed our existence in the world; perhaps we do not speak until someone can understand our language."

"I suddenly recalled another quote: 'We shed tears for the sorrow of a bird, but never for the bleeding of a fish. Those species that are vocal are always happier.' This shows that mankind is indeed blessed to have the ability of language," Peggy said.

"Yes, I share that feeling after talking to you today. In fact, my earlier quote is continued with this: 'In essence, it is only when we are loved that we are truly given life'. Do you think that makes sense?"

"Perhaps." Peggy replied softly and did not comment further.

As they walked across the soft and undulating sand, their arms brushed together occasionally, each instance causing Henry to feel a tingling sensation, but Peggy did not seem to be affected, instead, she looked like she was deep in thought.

After dinner, they adjourned to the lobby of the hotel where Henry was staying for the night and continued talking.

"You are staying at Sentosa tonight?"

"Yes, principle of proximity, remember?"

The hotel lobby was brightly illuminated, like a beautiful castle. It was clearly a hotel for rock music lovers. Mesmerising purple lights and colourful graffiti on some walls created the atmosphere of a rock music lounge, and when Peggy and Henry walked in, a rock song was playing, involuntarily, they began to bop their heads to the music.

"Wow, the walls here are decorated with vinyl records, it also has a huge electric guitar pieced together with real jazz drum pieces for an artistic look," Peggy exclaimed.

"Peggy, do you know a lot about music?"

"Very little, but I love Mozart's music."

"Oh, why Mozart's music in particular?" asked Henry.

"It is because the professor I admired was a fan of Mozart's music, so I listened to it too and found that I enjoyed it."

"Well, you clearly love everything about that beloved professor of yours! So, what do you think is good about Mozart's music?"

"His music is for everyone. He may not have been the greatest musician, but he was certainly one of the least controversial, and although he died young, every one of his works was a masterpiece."

"What is the style of his music?"

"Believe me, his most prominent style is that there is no style to speak of, but once his music is played, anyone can immediately identify it."

"Oh, I must look for his music and listen to it carefully then," Henry quipped. The cider that they had ordered earlier on arrival were served then and they paused momentarily to sip their drinks. Peggy found the aroma of the cider very unique and the drink itself tasted both tart and sweet at the same time to her.

"We have been talking about how blockchain can generate values for languages. The more I think about it, the more I am amazed," said Peggy.

"In many cases the industry's dilemma is essentially a human dilemma. A token on the blockchain can address the non-measurability of the language services industry so that every bilingual and multilingual talent can be recognised and be leveraged upon."

"This is one of two points which our clients will usually highlight to us," Peggy said.

"Price, what else?"

"Price and time. Clients expect quality service at a low price and within a short timeframe, but because translation is a highly creative job, these requirements are difficult to meet." Peggy took a sip of cider and continued, "Sometimes, despite being willing to pay a high price, they may still not be able to find a translator who can guarantee their peace of mind and produce work that is worth that price."

"With blockchain, all these problems can be solved readily," said Henry.

> Language needs blockchain to harness the power of global communications.

"Yes, I think languages need blockchain! It is not just so that the value of language talents can be properly recognised and rewarded, but also because doing so can promote the spread and continuity of civilisation through the preservation of languages."

"In fact, the more I think about it, the more I feel that blockchain also needs language to develop more exponentially and fulfil its potential."

"What do you mean?" asked Peggy.

"In the course of my work in blockchain, many times we were bogged down by language. Most people in our field only speak Mandarin and English, so there is no way to communicate with professionals who only speak other languages."

"Communication barriers hinder further cooperation."

"In fact, many blockchain organisations are experiencing language problems. For example, when we set up a Telegram group with blockchain professionals from different countries, we will also have to hire blockchain-savvy translators. Another example, if the blockchain project has to produce white papers in different languages, then we will need people who have blockchain knowledge and relevant language skills to translate. It is very difficult to find such people," said Henry.

"It is indeed true that every industry has its own difficulties."

> Blockchain needs language to harness the power of global synergy.

"Blockchain itself is global in nature, and in order to achieve global synergy, the language barrier must be broken, otherwise, blockchain will only be able to revolve in separate language circles. At the moment, we can only call on some interdisciplinary talent to assist us."

"This reminds me of the phrase, 'a match made in heaven (天作之合 tiān zuò zhī hé)'," Peggy said.

"Yes, indeed! I am sure you are familiar with 'Internet Plus'."

"Of course, it is the application of the internet to empower conventional industries."

"As blockchain becomes more and more popular, there has been a new saying that blockchain will be the next big technology to empower industries. I do not think that is the case now, the biggest takeaway from my trip to Singapore is not from attending and speaking at the conference, but discovering in the process of our interactions, that language and blockchain are two-way empowerment."

"They are mutually inclusive, aren't they, it is not simply a union but a natural fit with each other," said Peggy.

"For over two years in the blockchain industry, I have not been able to figure out the path to take, now it is becoming clear to me. This trip to Singapore will be a turning point in my life."

"What plans do you have going forward?" Peggy asked.

"I have no concrete ideas yet. However, many people have been struggling to find deeper and wider applications in the blockchain field. After talking to you, I realised that the language we use every day fits so well with blockchain. This is indeed a situation that fits into the words of the poet Xin Qiji: 'as I suddenly look back, I find the one I was looking for, where the lights were waning (蓦然回首, 那人却在, 灯火阑珊处 mò rán huí shǒu, nà rén què zài, dēng huǒ lán shān chù)'."

"This reminds me of another phrase, 'same frequency, same resonance (同频共振 tóng pín góng zhèn)'."

"That is correct, given that they have the same frequency and resonance, can you imagine how powerful language and blockchain can become?"

Their conversation continued until Peggy realised that it was getting late and she had to leave.

"Let me walk with you to take the monorail," said Henry.

"Okay." They both stood up somewhat reluctantly and left the hotel.

The gentle night breeze caressed their faces and Peggy's skirt.

"The moon is so beautiful tonight," Henry said.

"It is the full moon tonight. Henry, when will you be going back to China?"

"The morning after tomorrow."

"I see."

"I would like to see you again tomorrow evening. Will you have time? I did not expect to meet you here and we still have much to catch up on," Henry said.

"Sure, I do not have any other plans, see you tomorrow, good night!"

Henry watched Peggy as her back view faded with the downward escalator, then he turned around and walked back to the hotel.

Summary:
A Perfect Match

Theoretically, blockchain can be applied in many areas, but the effectiveness varies. In areas where the value of blockchain can be demonstrated, it will of course play a greater role and have a more significant impact.

Blockchain is an upgraded version of the internet of information to the internet of value. It has the basic characteristics of the internet combined with the unique properties of blockchain. Blockchain is more likely to be of value in areas which are highly internet-based, has a richer role in consumer-end ecosystem, a higher contribution of human and intellectual elements, and a higher degree of industry fragmentation.

In fact, blockchain is not required for resolving most of the industry-related problems as many of them can be dealt with quite effectively through a centralised big data approach. However, if the entities that are collaborating are on equal footing but due to their lack of cooperation and the unwillingness to share data which resulted in inefficiencies and hamper progression, then blockchain with its specialised approaches such as encryption and integration of responsive data will be of great use.

The language services industry can be thoroughly transformed by blockchain. It is impossible for any translation company to cover the complete spectrum of languages and industries. Each translation company has its own specialised language pairs and areas of expertise, but these workshop-style translation companies and the bilingual talents are scattered all over the world. They are reluctant to share their language data as sharing is not rewarded. As such, the valuable language data which they have accumulated in the course of their work becomes isolated data and is unable to unlock any values. This is the situation that has led to countless repetitions of work taking place day after day, year after year, for prolonged period, making the industry inefficient and far from meeting society's need for rapid information translation.

In the era of blockchain, the language services industry is set to be transformed due to the following characteristics.

The entire business process of language services can be done online, from the initiation of customer needs, response of translators, translation, proofreading, layout, and submission to clients and payment. All these can be completed online, thus creating more scenarios for the circulation of token.

Language services are not only available to many C-end users, but application scenarios are also rich and diverse. Language is used by everyone throughout the life cycle and is used repeatedly in a variety of settings such as language learning, data search, business communication, travel, reading, dating, entertainment and more. There will be many different components within the ecosystem which will allow token to be circulated with greater frequency.

Language service is a form of creative labour, requiring not only language skills but also professional and inter-cultural communication skills which are highly intellectual. In the traditional centralised model, it is difficult to quantify intellectual efforts for their values to be presented at a reasonable price and this is an important aspect where blockchain can make a difference.

Language services companies are not only fragmented, but also small and unattractive, with blur organisational boundaries and most of the translators working on part-time basis. Language services is a segmented long-tail market, scattered and embedded in every aspect of our work and life.

SUMMARY

Translation is a profession that has been around for more than 3000 years and has undergone several technological revolutions, but the industry has not changed fundamentally. In the current age of internet, it is still a highly fragmented, workshop-based model for processing incoming information. The largest translation companies in each country account for only 2–3% of the local market share, and the combined turnover of the global top 100 translation companies is less than 15% of the total market share. The inherent attributes of language dictate that no translation company, under the centralised model, can cover all business scenarios while guaranteeing revenue. In the language services industry, there has not been, there is not, and there will not be, large leading companies. There will only be large ecosystems of co-existence, co-sharing and all-win situations.

The whole language services industry is in a weak centralised state where demand and supply are dispersed with obstacles to sharing of information and resources, and production is still based on a "labour intensive + information processing" model. Breaking down the fragmented and confined landscape is the way to change the language services industry.

On one hand, decentralisation and weak centralisation are the typical blockchain application scenarios, which are much in line with the characteristics and current situation of the language services industry. On the other hand, openness, transparency, and trustworthiness are guaranteed by blockchain from the underlying technology and cannot be manipulated manually, creating the possibility of opening access to industry-related information, and breaking the barriers for sharing of resources.

Blockchain and language are not only highly aligned in their natural properties, but they will also support each other at the application level. Blockchain requires language to harness the power for global synergy. The former is naturally universal, and each public blockchain, without language as support, is limited to only individual linguistic communities, which makes it difficult to reach consensus across different linguistic groups, and difficult to develop large-scale collaboration and value transfer on a global basis. Breaking down the language barrier is exactly what is needed in the blockchain era.

Language needs blockchain to reflect the values of linguistic talents in price which will increase language production capacity significantly and allow the charm of linguistic culture to be disseminated globally.

Blockchain and language empower each other to achieve and amplify their respective values.

———— Chapter 7 ————

The Born Child

Cross-Linguistic Capability as a Fundamental in the Blockchain Era

Henry's working partners called from China to inform him that their blockchain project, a multilingual website, had received another complaint. This incident prompted Henry to deeply ponder over the feasibility of a system that could generate linguistic capability, in the same way that the grid generates stable electricity, thus making consistent quality language services readily available.

Digital assets have become the fundamental resource driving social development in the internet era. Smart data that are being thoroughly exploited can enable human knowledge and wisdom to become the source material and driving force of the Intelligent Age. Human beings understand society through language and at the same time express wisdom through language. Language data is an important resource to reflect human thoughts and wisdom comprehensively. Blockchain + language equates to the ability to convert between languages, also known as, the cross-linguistic capability.

1. The basic resources for human development have shifted from surface and subsurface resources to data resources.
2. Cross-linguistic capability is the ability to convert between different languages.
3. Blockchain + language can generate cross-linguistic capability.
4. Cross-linguistic capability is a fundamental capability in the blockchain era.

The next day was a Monday. Henry was waiting for Peggy to get off work when he received a call from his colleague in Beijing.

"Henry, our multilingual website is having problems again."

"What happened?"

"A Thai user in the group complained about us. He was ranting in the group, he said that he could not understand the content on our website, his exact words were 'totally unintelligible'."

"We need to calm and reassure the other party, try not to let him rant in the group, it is bad for our team's reputation, but continue to communicate with him, user feedback and suggestions are important. Also, contact the team leader in charge of our website translation right away to feedback on the problem and request for him to review their work and make improvements as soon as possible."

"We paid a lot of money to get them to translate, and they pledged in all sincerity that they would do a good job, but we still ended up with complaints time and time again."

"Did they not make any changes to the website at all?" Henry asked.

"They did but it was all about fire-fighting only after receiving complaints."

"We just have to be more understanding. Afterall, blockchain is new and it is difficult to find someone who is good in both languages and also has knowledge on blockchain."

"Regarding the complaint from the Thai client, the translation team explained that the one responsible for translating the website into Thai does not know much about blockchain. The translator does not know Chinese too, so it was translated into the Thai language based on the translated English version by the teammates," Henry's colleague explained.

"I see, it was translated from a translation, no wonder meaning was lost…"

"That's right, the only thing we can really do now is to get them to review specific pages whenever we receive any feedback and also try to get them to do a comprehensive check of all the translation once more for the entire website."

"That is about all that we can do for now, do keep an eye on them, the website is crucial for our project implementation," replied Henry.

"I understand. By the way boss, when will you be back?"

"I will be back tomorrow."

"That's good, you are having a good time in Singapore while we are back at work here and dealing with all these problems!"

Henry could not think of a good reply, so his colleague continued, "Roche told me one of the interpreters is your childhood friend, that's why you extended your stay. Such a coincidence! I heard that your presentation in Singapore was very successful, the interpreters deserve some of the credit too."

"Indeed, good interpretation does much to amplify a presentation."

"The next stop for the road show will be Korea, let's hope the standard of the interpreters there will be good too."

"Yes, you're right, I will start the preparation with you when I get back. Besides hoping for the best, our effort is as, perhaps even more, important," said Henry.

"'Will do, will do, you can skip your philosophical sharing, I already know it well."

"You insolent fellow!" Henry replied in mock exasperation.

"Okay, thank you, boss, I just called to update you and vent a little. I will get back to work now."

"Go ahead, see you tomorrow."

Henry's team was in charge of a multilingual website that supported more than a dozen languages. The website had only been operating for a few months but had already been on the receiving end of several complaints. Those with a positive attitude would contact the team privately and would give specific suggestions for improvements. The ones who were less positive would simply complain about it.

The complaints received for different languages varied according to circumstances. The English website received the least complaints. There were several complaints for the Korean, Russian, Thai and Vietnamese versions however. In general, the less common the language, the more likely that the team would receive complaints about its version of the website. After all, people who were proficient in these languages and also in blockchain were a rare resource.

Henry put down the phone, leaned back on the couch and fell into deep thought.

On this trip to Singapore, he had realised through talking with Peggy that the language services industry and blockchain fit well together.

Blockchain allows language to share the insights of civilisation, and language allows blockchain to harness the power of global synergy. But how much of the same frequency do they actually share, and how high can they go together? Exactly how should such collaboration proceed? Henry did not have any answers yet.

Henry decided to think more laterally, he recalled what he had read previously about the historical process of discovery and resource utilisation by human society. Resources, including environmental resources, biological resources, land resources, and mineral resources, amongst others, provide the objective basis upon which human beings can survive and society can develop.

> The basic resources of the agricultural age were surface resources, and the basic resources of the industrial age were subterranean resources. These are the physical natural resources that have supported human society to this day.

Human societies began with the use of resources around us: air, water, animals, land, and plants. Later, as the population grew and society progressed, people's use of resources expanded underground, minerals and other underground resources were tapped and exploited. From surface to subterranean resources, agricultural and industrial societies have fully exploited our physical and natural world to ensure the survival and development of mankind.

In recent years, with the emergence and development of the cyber-virtual space, data has become the most important resource.

> Data is a fundamental resource for the age of information.

The traditional internet, the Internet of Things (IoT), cloud computing, blockchain and other concepts and technologies are developing rapidly as a result of "Big Data".

Just as some large modern corporations were formed around the excavation, processing and manufacturing of underground mineral resources, future industries must be built around data processing, knowledge processing and intellectual automation. Mankind can only build a new Smart Society through thorough exploitation of data and intellectual resources and with continuous intellectual stimulation to make data resources, knowledge systems and social wisdom the raw materials and driving forces for building a Smart era.

> The emergence of blockchain is a certainty in history.

Blockchain emerged from the larger context of the digitalisation of human society, driven by information technology. As information or digital migration of human society continues to intensify and advance, the original network technology structure has become inadequate for such high frequency, massive amounts of digital transmission, storage and usage; blockchain was thus created, utilising distributed technology.

However, in the current internet age, some data centres and large corporations have compiled huge volume of data resources and profited from them. People have contributed a lot of personal data, but can hardly receive anything in return for their data. In fact, the data provided by each individual can be recorded and transmitted on blockchain and connections of value can be made through the issuance and execution of smart contracts. This would radically change the collaborative mechanisms of human society and tag the ownership of data assets to the original value creators.

Our everyday behaviour, our body index, our words, our focus, etc. all of these are data that belong to us as individuals. The perspectives that Henry and Peggy inspired new ideas, and these could also constitute data resources. But at present, we do not have any corresponding applications for collecting, integrating, applying and cashing-in on these resources.

With the internet, a significant portion of data resources have fallen into the hands of others, more data resources like water and wind in the past, were wasted without serving any purpose. There was also a portion of resources that were being wasted in constant repetition.

For instance, taking the language services industry as an example, many people have been translating similar content repeatedly every day for years, these include fixed expressions in official correspondence and various types of academic materials. With many blockchain-related companies springing up, translation services are much needed, and many complaints about poor translations have been received. In fact, terms like smart contracts, tokens, distributed ledger, community autonomy, etc. are all generic translations. If these terms can be standardised, and given "one-time labour, shared forever" status, how good that would be, at least until better translations replace them. It is then that people will be freed from tedious repetitive jobs and more able to focus on creative work.

> Language asset authentication, language data sharing, contributors can reap the benefits, these will significantly increase language conversion capacity.

At this point, Henry recalled an incident involving one of his friends when he was doing his master's degree.

It was near the end of the second year, students doing their master's in many universities were either preparing for their graduation thesis or trying to think of topics for their graduation projects; it was the same for Henry. He was not very good with English at that time, so it was very tough for him to read and understand English-language materials. However, he knew that English was the dominant academic language and that the content at the forefront of many disciplines were only available in English, so he forced himself to keep reading and trying to comprehend as much as possible.

Henry had a good friend, Lucas, who was studying in a different discipline. Unlike Henry, Lucas had decided on his topic early and was very efficient — while Henry and the rest of their peers were still trying to decide on their topics, Lucas had already finished half of his thesis. However, Lucas was unable to revel in his lead for long.

When one of Lucas' seniors returned from a study trip to Russia, he told Lucas that the topic of his thesis had actually already been studied by a very renowned Russian scholar, who had done a much more in-depth and extensive research. However, since his achievements had not been translated into English, many people who did not know the Russian language also had no idea of them.

> Due to language barriers, information and knowledge (especially if it is not translated into English) is not circulated globally; when knowledge and ideas cannot be disseminated effectively, the result is a great deal of duplication in effort.

Lucas eventually chose to abandon his topic and start all over again.

Henry did not know why the Russian scholar's work was not translated into English, but he knew that in the academic field, such situations were actually common. Many scholars were keen for their research to be translated into English, after all, English is the dominant language in academia. But it is also a fact that high-quality academic translation is a form of creative work, many scholars have professional skills but not bilingual ability.

Why can't they engage someone to translate for them? The situation is not so simple and straightforward.

Translators face the reversed situation. They have strong language abilities but lack professional experience. Scholars would hence be hesitant to hand their research to these translators. Are there any translators that possess both qualities? Surely there are, but the chances of meeting someone suitable are low. Besides, some of these translators with dual abilities were being bogged down by repetitive work. The same content could have already been translated many times by many others, or even with better forms of expressions, but since these translations were not available, each translator had to work from scratch.

There were of course instances where academia cooperated and complemented each other's strengths and weaknesses, but such occasions were rare. In any case, outstanding academic achievements were ultimately confined for dissemination within the scope of the academics' non-English mother tongue.

In short, the low capacity in translation, results in the low capacity of production, mainly due to the lack of an incentive mechanism.

"Low capacity, low capacity..." This term began flashing across Henry's mind continuously as his eyes lingered over his mobile phone which was charging. An idea suddenly popped into his head: "Language data is a form of capacity and so is electricity, how can we make language work like electricity?"

Henry's eyes continued looking idly on the charging phone, but the thoughts in his head were moving at top-speed.

Without electricity, would there be mobile phones? No. He noticed the reflection of the lamp above his head on the phone screen and looked up, no electricity, no lights either.

It was electricity that had been discovered first, and that led to the invention of a wide variety of appliances and electronic devices, which in turn, catalysed tremendous changes to the way we work and live.

Electricity did not have a long history, in the long process of human civilisation, our ancestors had relied on the sun during the day and the faint moonlight and starlight at night to provide light.

Henry recalled that as a child his grandfather had told him stories about his own childhood. Living in a rural area, his grandfather had not had electricity at home when he was young. The only way that children could spend their time at night was to listen to adults tell stories. If the adults were moody or tired and not willing to tell any stories, the children would have to go to bed early in the dark.

When the village finally had electricity connection, individual household ownership of electrical appliances were uncommon. But over time, people began to acquire them, and in any household today, there are all kinds of high-end electronic equipment. The lives of people have changed radically.

As people started to own all kinds of electrical and electronic devices, they have forgotten that electricity is the foundation of it all. Today, there are a variety of electrical appliances, such as heating devices in winter, portable fans in summer, robot vacuum cleaners, and GPS watches…to meet the different needs of work and life, all owe their existence to the power of electricity.

> When mankind used technology to harness the energy generated by natural resources such as wind, water and sunlight, we produced standard and stable electrical energy through the grid to power various electrical appliances, thoroughly changing human society.

Then again, during Henry's grandfather's time, although there was no electricity, the wind blew, the water flowed and the sun shone daily, it is just that these resources were not put to good use, they were not transformed into electricity to change people's lives. Mankind subsequently developed electrical energy and various clean energy sources were also produced.

The natural resources that were not harnessed in the past are akin to the data resources we have today, they exist but are not being used effectively, resulting in low capacity.

> Bilingual talents, distributed across the globe, are the providers of language data. There has been a lack of effective incentives to assemble them, and pool them with machine capabilities to produce a consistent language service capability.

In terms of language data, many people are now bilingual or even multilingual, but scattered across industries. Since there is no real incentive for talents around the globe to gather, they will not do so and thus not be able to produce in term of capabilities and value.

Devices such as mobile phones, tablets and computers can be charged when plugged in. How nice it would be to have an interface like a charging socket that provides us with language services as soon as it is connected!

If that were the case, there would not be a need to struggle to have someone translate all aspects of websites, white papers, online communities, roadshows, conferences, etc., as is the case now with blockchain. The amount of money spent could be significant, but the quality of translation is inconsistent, resulting in the team receiving frequent complaints due to translation issues and an overall slowing down of progress for the entire project.

The more he thought about it, the more excited Henry became. He grabbed a pen and paper from the desk and began to note down his thoughts.

He started by writing "electrical energy" on the top left corner of the paper.

At the bottom he wrote nuclear, wind and solar energy, etc., transmitted through the power grid and exported in standard form, playing a variety of roles in both consumer and commercial applications. Consumer applications include: mobile phones, computers, televisions, refrigerators, washing machines and many others. Commercial applications include the whole range of production equipment such as cranes, lathes, and production lines, all of which make our work more efficient and our lives richer and more convenient.

At the bottom right corner of the paper, he wrote "language resources", which is transformed by blockchain and artificial intelligence technology into a standard form of energy like electricity, which can be used for both commercial and civil purposes.

In the commercial sector, websites, search engines, communication software, IoT and other applications can be connected to the system just as electronic devices are connected to the grid, thus enabling automatic multilingual presentation and eliminating the need to look for translators all over the place.

Developers in different fields would develop applications and software suitable for different scenarios with this system as a support. Henry did not have a concrete idea of how these apps and software could be developed, and what they would look like. The only thing he could be sure of was that these programs and software and even smart hardware, like all kinds of modern appliances, would be born out of real human needs, and would improve people's lives and break down language barriers. Just then, an idea flashed into Henry's mind, he quickly wrote the words "linguistic capability" at the top right corner of the paper, across from the words "electrical energy" in the left corner.

"Electrical energy, linguistic capability, this concept is becoming more and more concrete." Just as Henry was getting excited about his idea, he remembered a point that Peggy had shared with him earlier. Machine translation can be put to good use in languages with a similar structure, where meaning of a term in one language is easily matched by an equivalent term in the other, or in languages with a certain conversion pattern such as between European languages. However, for languages where the conceptual correspondence is not uniform and the structure differs greatly, machine translation has a lot of room for improvement.

Currently, there are several translation software available, and although there are so many languages in the world, translation software is still only able to translate between the few major languages that are widely used. Since the translation of language resources on the blockchain not only relies on systems and machines, but also requires human translation, is it possible to achieve a barrier-free translation between all languages on this system?

As Henry thought about it, he drew a big question mark next to the language resource conversion system, then put down his pen and sighed aloud to himself. This was an interesting projection and idea supported by reasonable grounds, but there was still a lot to deliberate over for this idea that also needed to be practically tested.

Henry was reminded of Zamenhof who had created an international language called Esperanto, and Earish, the new international language being researched by Taiwan's renowned AI expert, Farmer Lu.

In 1887, Polish doctor Zamenhof created a new language and named it Esperanto. Zamenhof was proficient in many European languages, he had ideas and ambitions and wanted to invent an international language to eliminate the language barrier between people from all over the world.

The rules for the use of Esperanto were not complicated, it only had only 28 Latin letters, each with only one pronunciation, the pronunciation of the letters in any word remained the same, and there were only 16 grammar rules, but Esperanto ended in failure. There were two main reasons for the failure.

Firstly, Esperanto, being an invented language, did not have the history, cultural connotations and context of other languages.

Chinese, English and other languages have long histories, and over time they have become not only tools for communication, but also bearers of culture. For example, in Chinese, ice and jade not only represent their respective objects, but also have abstract implications. The Chinese idiom "pure as jade and clean as ice (冰清玉洁 bīng qīng yù jié)" describes a person's character to be as flawless and uncorrupted as jade and ice. The Esperanto language, however, lacked such a cultural connotation and it often required several sentences to articulate a simple word in the source language, leaving much to be desired for depth and impact in the expressions.

Secondly, there was always a tendency to give priority to the use of one's mother tongue over the promotion of Esperanto, and the underdeveloped communication technologies of the time limited the strength and scope of Esperanto dissemination. Since then, with the advancement of globalisation, English, Chinese and other universal languages became more popular, and Esperanto was slowly forgotten until it was completely abandoned.

> Esperanto was born at a wrong time.

As compared to Esperanto being born at the wrong time, AI expert Farmer Lu's research on the new international language, Earish has greater prospects. By chance, Henry had heard Farmer Lu present on Earish and they had interacted briefly after the presentation.

In a nutshell, Earish is a new artificial language created by analysing the fundamental features of the world's languages through AI and bringing together the benefits of those fundamental features. In comparison to heterogeneous natural languages, Earish is superior in terms of ease of learning, avoidance of ambiguity, and language expressions can be expanded more effectively, etc.

There were two points in the speech by Farmer Lu that had left a deep impression on Henry. Farmer Lu had said that Earish is a basic middle language with a low learning threshold. Since it is based on precise algorithms, gathering features of the major languages can help humans to connect and convert between the various natural languages. Earish can accurately trace the origin and evolution of each language, as well as the correlation between natural languages, to reveal and restore the footprint of human language development and the relationship between languages.

Henry pondered further…Earish claims to have gathered the essence of all human language through precise analysis by AI, but depth and scope are generally difficult to reconcile. It might be able to build wide connections between languages, but this connection can only be preliminary and not thorough. It will probably work for day-to-day communications, but it will not be able to play an important role in professional fields. It is therefore not as functional and powerful as the language resource conversion system that he had envisioned.

But the two could actually be mutually reinforcing. Earish could act as a medium for basic conversion between different languages on the ecosystem. On blockchain, driven by the token and supported by technology, Earish could take flight given the dynamism of modern times. For instance, for a language that is less common, with the token incentive system on blockchain, there could be a high possibility that its speakers would be willing to learn Earish and transform their mother tongue

> The new artificial language Earish, emerged at an appropriate time as it is backed by blockchain.

into a parallel corpus on blockchain for paid usage by others. It could facilitate both the dissemination of the mother tongue and the integration of human civilisation.

Henry could barely wait to meet Peggy and share his thoughts and ideas with her. For the rest of the day, he was restless, checking the time on his phone again and again, feeling for the first time that time was passing so slowly.

In fact, Henry was so excited that he had no mood to do anything else, he messaged her on WeChat to ask for her company's address.

"Peggy, where is the exact location of your company?"

"Why do you need the address out of the blue?"

"I would like to pick you up from where you work later."

"Oh no, the company location is too remote, just tell me where to meet you and I will see you there tonight."

"I was doing some thinking at the hotel this morning and had some great ideas. You know what? Language and blockchain are not any average combination, this is something that can change history and can take human civilisation to the next level. I can't wait to share it with you, I don't even want to wait another minute!"

"Wow, okay, I look forward to your sharing then, here's the address, I will finish work at six." Peggy replied.

That evening, Peggy walked out of her office building and was greeted by the sight of Henry already eagerly waiting on the ground floor.

When they saw each other, they were a little surprised that they were dressed in the same colours.

A neat and tasteful dresser, Henry was wearing a pair of grey pants and a light-yellow polo t-shirt, which also had a tinge of light grey at the collar and sleeves. Coincidentally, Peggy was wearing a light-yellow dress in a similar shade.

"Hey, what a coincidence, we are in couple outfits today," Henry said half-jokingly.

Peggy looked amused but not sure how to respond, Henry continued, "there are two butterflies on your dress which are grey like my pants too. What I was thinking about at the hotel today also had something to do with butterflies."

"What?" Peggy was confused, and as they walked towards the MRT station together, she asked, "Have you heard of the butterfly effect?"

"Of course, it is about how a small change can lead to a huge, long-term chain reaction throughout the system."

"Yes, we were talking about the relationship between language and blockchain before. The language industry may seem like a narrow racetrack, but with blockchain technology behind it, the changes in the industry will be dramatic for the world. Almost like how a spark of passion between two people can be the start of a great and wondrous love."

"I don't understand, we simply came to the consensus that language and blockchain are a natural fit, like a match made in heaven, but how did it ignite a spark and cause a butterfly effect?"

"It is a long story. I will tell you slowly."

Looking at Henry who was in high spirits and clearly extremely excited, Peggy could not hold back her laughter, "Look at how excited you are, your hands are moving all over the place! Tell me slowly, I am listening."

"Oh, okay, okay I have to calm down and control myself, it is so quiet on the MRT in Singapore, I don't want people to give me strange looks and think I am crazy, hah..."

They arrived at the entrance of the MRT station. "Peggy, are you thirsty? Let's go and buy a soya bean drink." Peggy agreed.

In Singapore, one can get a soya bean drink from a franchise that has outlets at almost all MRT stations. Henry ordered a warm drink for Peggy and a chilled one for himself. He handed the warm cup to Peggy, "Here, a warm one for you. I know this young lady well, she has been drinking warm water since she was young, she will not drink anything chilled no matter the season."

Peggy's heart felt warm even before her first sip, after so many years, he could still remember this small detail about her.

After they finished the soya bean drink, they got on the MRT and sat down next to each other.

"People are probably thinking we are a couple on a date from the way we are dressed," Henry joked once more. Peggy's heart skipped a beat. She did not reply.

Due to China's one child policy, both Peggy and Henry had been only children. As Henry was two years older, he had always been like a big brother and the two of them squabbled and played well together like real siblings. Adults described them as "innocent playmates (两小无猜 liǎng xiǎo wú cāi)" and "childhood sweethearts (青梅竹马 qīng méi zhú mǎ)". When they learned the meaning of these two idioms later, Henry had already moved away with his parents.

Why hadn't they tried to reach out to each other? What fate led them to reunite at a conference in Singapore? How much had their paths diverged since then?

Peggy's thoughts were drifting aimlessly when Henry handed her a earpiece. It had not seem right to either of them to look at their phones on their own and neither was it appropriate to chat freely on the MRT, so Henry's gesture was a good alternative. The voice of the lead singer of the Taiwanese band, Mayday rang in their ears: "In the year I turned seven, I caught a cicada and thought I could catch summer, in the year I was seventeen, I kissed his face and thought I could be with him forever..."

By the time they reached their destination of East Coast Park, it was dusk, the lights along the beach flickered on one by one. There were rows of seafood restaurants by the sea, so one could either eat in the restaurant or al fresco. Henry had done some research and he knew that the indoor seating would close earlier, so he had made a reservation for outdoor seating at a table with an umbrella. He ordered the house specialty, the black pepper crab.

"Many people commented online that the black pepper crab from this restaurant is a must try signature dish," said Henry.

"The shells have already been cracked open, it does look pretty easy to handle."

"The flavours are better absorbed this way."

The crab meat was visible through the cracks on the shell, thick and fleshy and so tempting. Peggy put on the gloves provided, with a gentle twist, the tender, juicy crab meat appeared.

Peggy took a bite and realised that she could taste the black pepper in the fine and firm crab meat, it had absorbed the sweet and rich flavour of the black pepper sauce.

Henry's initial excitement over sharing his thoughts on blockchain had seemed to have abated and they enjoyed the food while chatting about random topics: their current hobbies, ideals, and whatever else came to mind. Their natural surroundings saw squirrels scampering past occasionally, leading to cries of excitement from overseas guests. The Singaporeans, on the other hand, appeared nonchalant, their expressions seemed to say, "What's all the fuss about some squirrels!"

After dinner, they sat by the sea and finally began to talk about blockchain and language.

"My colleague called from Beijing this morning, we received a complaint on our multilingual website again. It is a pain to have problems with language all the time," Henry vented, a downcast look on his face.

"Has the problem been solved?" Peggy asked in a concerned voice.

"I gave some suggestions over the phone and I received an email before I left the hotel that the client has been reassured and the translation team is working to improve the website."

"Well, that's good, regardless of industry, it is a hassle to run into obstacles because of language, not to mention the fact that our world is so globalised now."

"Exactly, after I hung up the phone, I started doing some free association thinking. You do realise that the human use of resources has gone from the surface to underground, and now into the scramble and exploitation of data resources, don't you?"

> Bilingual talent are value creators in the language services industry, but they have not been rewarded accordingly and a significant portion of their resources have been controlled and consumed by translation services companies that act as intermediaries.

"Yes, big data and cloud computing have been flourishing in recent years."

"However, a significant proportion of data resources are not used effectively, or their values are not returned to the original value creators, or there is a waste of resources," said Henry.

"Translators in the translation industry are often doing repetitive work, and it is this repetitive work that depletes their time and energy for creative work."

> Many professionals have strong professional skills but due to language constraint, they are not able to make the most out of the value they deserve.

"While I was studying, I realised that some highly professional academics, who had made very influential achievements in their home countries, were quite unknown internationally because they had not translated their research into English due to the lack of language skills. They probably did not know who to look for to resolve this issue, it is also difficult to find a suitable professional translator that can be a good match."

"Ultimately, it is still about low production capacity," Peggy concluded.

"You are right, these are my thoughts too. However, this is not just a simple issue of low production capacity but rather, how to pool fragmented capacity into stable capacity and scale up, with the former being a fundamental result of the lack of an effective incentive mechanism," Henry said.

"You were overflowing with excitement just now, do you already have a solution?" asked Peggy.

"I do have something in mind."

"Really? Tell me, quick!" Peggy was very eager.

"I have to start from electrical energy. Human society needed electricity before there could be electrical and electronic devices that improved and transformed human life. In modern society, people are enjoying these conveniences and have gradually forgotten that electricity is the foundation of it all. How did electricity come about?"

"Hydropower, wind power, solar power, and later nuclear power and clean energy generation," Peggy answered.

"That's right, but these resources had always been available since the time of our ancestors, it was just that they were not utilised to generate electricity. Is this not the same for a lot of data resources today? They exist, but are not being used effectively, resulting in a lack of capacity."

"This is true for bilingual and even multilingual talent scattered all around the world. What is your solution to this problem?" Peggy asked.

Henry pulled the notes he had made on the paper out of his pocket, unfolded it in front of Peggy, and explained, "This is what we just discussed on the left, where nuclear, wind, solar and other energy sources are transformed by grid technology into electricity for residential and commercial use, changing and improving people's lives and work."

"What about the right side? Linguistic capability, what is this?" Peggy looked at Henry, puzzled but feeling expectant.

> Language is a form of capability.

"Language is a form of capability. Language embodies the historical experience and wisdom of our human ancestors, which enables cognition to move from within an individual brain to other individual brains, from individual to group, and to continuously transfer its capabilities across time and space and territory, resulting in new scientific achievements and human civilisation." Peggy's eyes lit up upon hearing Henry's analogy.

The forces that have touched us, illuminated us, changed us, and are still affecting us through different forms of language, are these the ways in which linguistic capability has been working on us in real life?" Peggy asked.

"You have an excellent ability in understanding and expressing, you've accurately stated the point I am trying to make, with a vivid yet precise choice of words!" Henry began to get excited once more, "The linguistic capability that I am talking about is like the baby born from language and blockchain. To be precise, it should be known as cross-linguistic capability, which is the ability to translate between different languages, it can also be used like electricity. In fact, people do not need translation per se, what they need is effective communication and collaboration, just like they do not need electricity per se, what they need is the convenience brought about by various electrical appliances that are empowered by electricity."

Cross-linguistic capability is part of language capacity.

"My vision of this cross-linguistic capability, which will form the fundamental resource of the blockchain era, is that it will be plugged directly into the underlying blockchain application via a jack, enabling websites, search engines, communication software, the Internet of Things, etc. to automate multilingualism. At the same time, application developers from various industries will be encouraged to develop applications and software to fulfil language requirements in the different scenarios of people's lives and work," Henry continued without stopping to take a breath.

Cross-linguistic capability, the ability to translate between different languages, is a fundamental capability in the age of blockchain.

"Hold on, I have two questions," said Peggy.

"Sure, go ahead."

"Firstly, what is the difference between the application and software in these systems of language capability and the current internet apps? Secondly, can technology really eliminate the language barrier altogether?" Peggy asked.

"Good question! I thought about this too. I do not have a concrete idea of how these applications and software will be developed and what they will look like, but I am sure with human intelligence, they will be developed. Besides, human invention is profit-driven, as long as something is profitable, smart people would be willing to do it. For now, let's just call them distributed applications 'dapp'."

"That's true. When electricity first appeared, who would have thought that there would be mobile phones, computers, and all sorts of software that we are using now," said Peggy.

"When an open-source community is established, these problems can be easily solved."

"What is an open-source community?" Peggy asked.

"It is a network that publishes software source code under the corresponding open-source software licence agreement. It also provides a space for network members to freely learn and exchange ideas."

"I see, I guess some of the software that we are using now in our daily lives have been developed from the open-source community."

"That's right."

"What about the second question? Why do I feel that the picture you just painted is a language Utopia, too good to be true for language application?"

"Definitely not Utopia, it is definitely possible. Let me tell you two simple stories."

"Alright!" Peggy nodded.

"In 1887, a Polish man invented an international language called Esperanto, the rules for language formation and grammar were not complicated, but because it was a new language, it possessed no cultural connotation or context. You can see how some Chinese idioms can express complex and abstract meanings in just four words. However, translating these four words using a purely technical language like Esperanto would require a few winding sentences before the meaning could be clearly expressed. The other factor was the limitation of communications technology, when the common languages today, like Chinese and English, were popularised, the Esperanto language gradually disappeared."

"I did hear of this term 'Esperanto' before, but this is my first time hearing the story behind it. What about the other story?" Peggy asked again.

"An AI expert in Taiwan is now working on a new international language, Earish. In a nutshell, Earish is a new artificial language created by analysing the fundamental characteristics of the world's languages through AI and combining the merits of these fundamental characteristics. It is easier to learn and communicate using Earish than natural language."

"A universal language created by reconciliation and synthesis; will it be able to handle the issue of in-depth communication?" said Peggy.

"You are sharp, as expected from a linguist. We do not need it for in-depth communication per se, but with this middle language, it would make it easier for people to have in-depth communication across languages."

"I see your point. I am a little convinced. I think this is possible."

"I think Earish and blockchain go hand in hand. Earish can be used as the foundational corpus in this system, driven by the token and supported by technology, blockchain can equip Earish with the characteristics that a modern language needs and enable the basic conversion of languages that were previously unrelated to each other," said Henry.

"Wow, I feel like I am looking in on a whole new world."

"It is not an exaggeration to say that it is a new world, and I think that the convergence of language and blockchain will create wonders."

"I think this whole idea could be made even better," Peggy added.

Henry looked at Peggy with anticipation as she continued, "I am sure you will understand my thoughts because they have to do with AI. There is so much being said about Machine Learning these days, I wonder if each translator would be able to have a dedicated translation robot in the future, a robot that would constantly record and learn from the materials produced by the translators, thus improving the machine's own translation capabilities and achieving better and faster collaboration with the translators. The robot would then record and store the habits, feelings and thoughts of the translator, so that even the machine-translated content that it produces would have its own style."

> People provide big data to the machines, enabling them to become more and more powerful, while at the same time concentrating on creative work, resulting in higher-quality human-machine translation and a mutually reinforcing model.

"I would not have thought of that if you did not mention it. It is a great idea! People would then be able to focus on creative work and the capacity of the language field would be freed up considerably.

Moreover, with the help of blockchain, scattered bilingual talents can be gathered," said Henry.

"I would also like to give a name to this model, twin translators, where human beings and their own proprietary machines act like twin translators to each other, becoming more and more attuned and intelligent and creating value together," Henry added.

"They will be mutually reinforcing."

"Exactly. In the history of mankind, the human ranks number one in terms of production capacity of language, the machine is the second, but both of these will be a thing of the past in this new world. The third model of production capacity will be the mainstream in future, and that is 'human-machine translation,'" said Peggy.

"The best model for 'human-machine translation' is the one we just talked about, where the machine grows with the translator, thereby acquiring the same cultural background and ideology as the translator, and becomes the 'twin translator' of the human translator, i.e., the human imparts intelligence to the machine, and the machine empowers the human with capacity. This twin translator will be a core member of the new capacity we mentioned."

> Human imparts intelligence to the machine, and the machine empowers human with capacity.

Henry kept going, "For this product of human-machine translation, its frontend interface will resemble electricity delivery like the grid, empowering thousands of products. On the backend, its key capabilities are in organising and managing languages, integrating individuals, institutions, and translation machines with linguistic capabilities from around the world, to achieve unified deployment and create a third type of production capacity that is 'faster than human, with lower costs, and with better quality than machines'. With these two forms of capabilities and the innovation of the 'human-machine translator' model, people will be enabled to communicate, work and live their lives using their native language in all situations."

"It would then be truly possible for people to communicate without language barriers, to use language just like they use water and electricity," said Peggy.

"You are right. Besides this, there is another form of mutual reinforcement."

"Which is?" Peggy asked.

"It is the interfacing between applications and providers. Do you remember the voltage regulator that we used at home when we were young?" asked Henry.

"I have some recollection that, when the grid was not so stable, either because of power failures or because of tripping from time to time due to unstable voltages, voltage regulators were needed."

"Subsequently, as the voltage became more stable, the regulators were gradually phased out. I guess language resources will go through the same process, there will be a lot of problems at the beginning, and not many people will join in. However, this is surely a great Blue Ocean domain, the more people use it, the greater the demand for language capacities and the more varied the application scenarios; these will contribute to the enhancement and improvement of the supply. It is the same for usage of electricity, with varied usage scenarios, the usage volume became higher,

> Language use and language resources presented a model of mutual reinforcement. The more varied the scenarios, the higher the usage volume, which will facilitate increase and stable production capacity for language resources.

and this increased and stabilised the production of electrical energy."

"Fair point. And I want to add that some people may worry that these smart machines will gradually replace human translators. In fact, it will not. As the overall volume of business grows, there will be more and more areas where people can be of value. Human translators are not going to be replaced by machines, and because of the increased demand, human translators will have a brighter future." Peggy said, "I have the same feeling that the development of machine translation technology will lead to a growing market for human translation instead. For example, the localisation of some e-commerce websites, which might have been abandoned due to the high cost of human translation. The localisation may be initiated again under machine translation, and these, in turn, will create a new demand for human translators to review translation outputs by machines. This is similar to the increase in demand for quality control personnel due to the development of textile machinery, which in turn, contributed to the expansion of the textile market."

"An ancient text that I studied before has a passage that sums up the relationship between human and machine translation well," said Henry.

"What is the title?" Peggy asked.

"'Encouraging Learning' by the Confucian philosopher, Master Xun Zi (荀子)," said Henry.

"Ah, I know which part you are referring to:

'登高而招，臂非加长也，而见者远 dēng gāo ér zhāo, bì fēi jiā cháng yě, ér jiàn zhě yuǎn, If you climb to a high place and wave to someone, it is not as though your arm were any longer than usual, and yet people can see you from much farther away.

顺风而呼，声非加疾也，而闻者彰 shùn fēng ér hū, shēng fēi jiā jí yě, ér wén zhě zhāng, If you shut down the wind, it is not as though your voice were any stronger than usual, and yet people can hear you much more clearly.

假舆马者，非利足也，而致千里 jiǎ yú mǎ zhě, fēi lì zú yě, ér zhì qiān lǐ, Those who make use of carriages or horses may not be any faster walkers than anyone else, and yet they are able to travel a thousand li.

假舟楫者，非能水也，而绝江河 jiǎ zhōu gēn zhě, fēi néng shuǐ yě, ér jué jiāng hé, Those who make use of boats may not know how to swim, and yet they manage to get across rivers.'"[18] Peggy could not help reciting what she recalled.

"'君子生非异也，善假于物也' jūn zǐ shēng fēi yì yě, shàn jiǎ yú wù yě, The gentleman is by birth no difference from any other man; it is just that he is good at making use of things.'"

Henry recited the concluding sentence when Peggy paused to catch her breath, then said, "Human technology development will not halt, the constant use of machines to further empower human beings and unlock productivity is an inexorable trend. I think it is also inevitable that the human translation industry will embrace and leverage on machine translation."

"In conclusion, linguistic capability is not only for communication, but also to bring about unexpected transformations and development. Just as electricity was first invented only for lighting, it subsequently became a basic resource that human societies can no longer do without," Peggy summarised.

---

[18] As translated by Burton Watson, an American translator, and writer known for his numerous translations of Chinese and Japanese literature into English. https://wenku.baidu.com/view/3ed0dfb25901020207409ca1.html

> Language data is the most comprehensive and profound reflection of human intelligence and thinking, and it will be the raw material and driving force of a Smart Society.

"Furthermore, the Smart Society of the future needs to be supported by Smart Data, and language data is the most comprehensive and profound reflection of human thinking and Smart Data, it will be the raw material and driving force for the development of a Smart Society," Henry added as he and Peggy exchanged satisfied smiles. They looked around and only then did they realise that all the surrounding patrons and tourists had already left.

Henry suggested a walk along the beach before going home and Peggy agreed readily. The warm wind, carrying the scent of the ocean, rustled the leaves of the trees by the shore. Looking out to sea, bright lights from vessels of different sizes blinked and from time to time, a siren could be heard, it was a bustling scene that set off the tranquillity along the shore.

Henry and Peggy walked without speaking for a while in easy companionship. "Singapore is such a beautiful city," Henry remarked to break the silence.

"'A garden city state', it definitely lives up to its reputation. Having been here for some time, I have been several places, everything feels good," Peggy replied.

"Will you stay here permanently then?"

"I am not sure yet, it depends on the opportunities available. My thinking was that Singapore is multi-cultural and multi-racial, suitable for people like me who learn languages, that is why I decided to look for a job here."

"It is good to venture out into the world while you are young. But a lady like you must protect and take good care of yourself since you are alone."

"I will. What about you? What are your plans? To continue working on blockchain with your current partners?"

"Yes, blockchain will be an integral part of the future, I have no intention to let go of it. On this trip to Singapore, after speaking with you, I have realised that the interaction between language and blockchain is definitely a promising Blue Ocean."

"And this is where you want to start a new venture?"

"That's right, you have just reminded me, since we already have such specific and detailed ideas, shall we start a business together?"

"Aren't you going to continue working with your current partners?"

"It is not likely, these pals of mine have their own projects on hand." After a momentary pause, Henry asked again, "If I do go into business in this area, will you join me?"

Just at that moment, Peggy tripped on her heels and almost fell. Fortunately, Henry swung his hand out quickly which helped her break her fall. For a split second, they were holding on tightly to each other. As soon as Peggy regained her balance, Henry hastily let go of his hand. The embarrassment in the air was palpable.

"Thanks...Um...I don't know, starting a business is a very arduous and challenging task," Peggy stammered, quickly returning to the topic.

"Yes, it is...I have seen and heard many stories of business failures. There are only very few who took the path of entrepreneurship and succeeded. However, the idea of integrating language and blockchain to produce cross-linguistic capabilities was something we discussed together, that's why I think it would be great for us to start a venture together," said Henry.

Peggy smiled but she did not say anything when she saw that Henry's eyes were filled with anticipation and enthusiasm.

They continued the rest of their walk along the shore in silence, listening to the waves lapping rhythmically against the shore, as the stars and a full moon shone down on them. Finally, Peggy looked at her watch and saw that it was already two in the morning.

Henry suddenly felt very reluctant to part with Peggy. He would be flying home later that same morning and he did not know when they would be able to meet again. He quietly looked at Peggy from time to time on the taxi ride back to her home, but did not know what to say. After they bid goodbye, Henry continued to linger below her block, staring blankly into space for a long time.

Summary:
The Born Child

Language is dynamic. It carries the rich life experiences and wisdom of our ancestors since the beginning of human civilisation. Language influences our cognition to progress from within the human brain to beyond, from an individual to a group, and continues to transmit capability across time, space, and territory, leading to new scientific achievements and progress for the human civilisation.

The power of language is palpable and has been felt by everyone. The forces that have touched us, illuminated us, changed us, and are still affecting us through different forms of language, is a manifestation of language capabilities acting on us in real life.

As human civilisation evolves, language capacities are accumulated. The process of our growth and learning is a constant exchange of capacities with our predecessors and others. As technology advances, particularly with the development of internet and artificial intelligence, language information is unprecedentedly rich and varied and has generated tremendous capacity.

The capacity that language possesses on its own and those derived from different forms of language work are summed up as Linguistic Capability. The ability to convert from one language to another is known as Cross-Linguistic Capability. Cross-linguistic capability is a part of linguistic capability.

Blockchain and language are strikingly similar in their natural attributes. The combination of blockchain and language could resolve the long-standing problem of having large amount of information remaining in the world of native language due to insufficient capacity for language conversion.

The greater the cross-linguistic capability, the stronger the ability to convert between different languages. The faster the conversion, the more stable this capability will be. The more accurate the conversion, the higher the quality of the conversion.

The value of linguistic data does not lie in the data itself, but in how these data can be linked to knowledge, society, culture, behaviour, and people, and using scientific approaches such as mathematical and statistical methods to uncover the hidden patterns behind the data regarding human cognition, behaviour and interaction with society and nature.

Linguistic capability is made up of language data resources, which are different from other behavioural data. Language data reflects the full spectrum of human thoughts and wisdom. They are the raw materials and driving force of the age of intelligence.

The basic resources differ for different eras. In the agricultural era, surface resources were the basics — land, forests, rivers, etc. were the target of competition; in the industrial era, as technology evolves, exploitation of resources went underground — oil and mineral deposits were the objects of competition. Today, the surface and underground resources have been thoroughly developed, and they drove human civilisation to a new phase — the information age. The basic resources of the society have shifted from the physical world to the artificial world where data resources are now the basic resources of the information age.

Language data resources have been widely dispersed and there is no mechanism to effectively gather and utilise these valuable data. Every day, people are doing huge volume of repetitive work. They are racking their brains to translate countless sentences and expressions that have already been translated. This is because the best translated output cannot be reflected on any platform and be shared for a fee. Blockchain can authenticate an individual's data assets so that the creator of quality corpus can get a fair return relative to the market. It can address the key challenge of data aggregation and timely provide high-quality solutions for the third-generation neural machine translation which is hampered by insufficient data.

Human and machine translation are mutually reinforcing in providing linguistic capability. People provide big data to machines, making them smarter to enhance productivity, quality, and efficiency of translations. In turn, machines provide technical support for data to be shared efficiently so that people do not have to spend time and energy on repetitive tasks. Instead they may focus on creative work to improve the quality of translations. This model of positive and mutual reinforcement of human and machine translation can unleash huge cross-linguistic capability, so that translations can attain the speed of a machine and the quality of a human.

At the same time, we will also see mutually reinforcing development between linguistic capabilities and end-users. Motivated by profits, there will be more technology developers who will develop language services according to people's needs in different scenarios. A wide variety of end products related to language will be available, making language services readily accessible. Demand stimulates supply, and language capabilities will be boosted as well.

Comparing this model to electricity, it is like natural energy sources such as water, wind and sun being left untapped for electrical generation for the benefit of mankind. With the invention of electricity, this technological development allows people to gather electricity generated from various resources such as water, wind, sun, coal, oil, etc. and integrate them through the power grid to produce stable supply of electricity. Electricity is a fundamental capability of the industrial age, and various appliances can be supplied with electricity by simply plugging into a standard socket, providing convenience for people in their daily living. In fact, their lives have been changed radically by the availability of electricity. The power of electricity has pushed human civilisation to the next level.

The capability of electricity is derived from the basic resources of the physical world, while linguistic capability is derived from the basic resources of the artificial world. This cross-linguistic capability arises because token allows exchange and circulation of individual's linguistic creations in the form of linguistic data. Token is the soul of the blockchain system. Although there is no standardised definition of token, it is made up of three elements namely, proof of interest, cryptography, and negotiability. In the blockchain system, token is the bearer of the rights and interests owned by different subject. Token is the unified bearer of core values such as responsibility, rights, and interests of individuals.

Every day, across the globe, people translate in massive repetition the excerpts and content that have already been translated. With blockchain, everyone's linguistic data will be identified, shared, and circulated as language assets, and there will never be a need to do repeated translations. Moreover, everyone will be happy to contribute their own linguistic data and focus on work of creativity. The capacity for translation will increase, and the quality will be higher too. This cross-linguistic capability will bring about a profound change in the development of human civilisation.

Linguistic capability is the spark that erupts when blockchain and language meet. It is the love child of blockchain and language. Based on artificial intelligence and blockchain technology, comprehensive and profound linguistic data reflecting human thoughts and intelligence can be shared abundantly and receive recognition through the value tagged to their contributors, after a systematic compilation and circulation. This will greatly stimulate human creativity and trigger widespread application of linguistic capabilities, opening a new era of application for the internet of value.

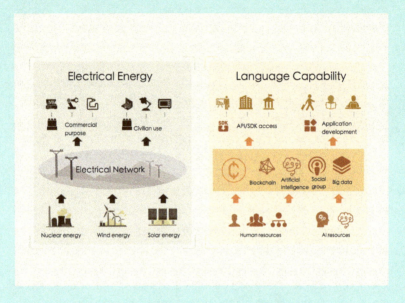

Chapter 8

A Beautiful Evolution
A New World Free from Language Barriers

Peggy quit her job resolutely and went to Beijing with the intent to set up a new business with Henry. They reunited with their two childhood friends, a technology journalist and an e-commerce entrepreneur. The foursome reminisced about the past but also excitedly discussed the future that Peggy and Henry had envisioned: a new world with language barriers eliminated. The friends came up with several possible scenarios, in the fields of communication, e-commerce, university education, and research collaboration; eventually Brenda, the technology journalist, was convinced to join in the business venture as well.

Blockchain and language will generate a new foundational capability to empower different industries, this will result in more parties becoming involved in communications, expansion of commercial boundaries, multi-dimensional perspective for problem solving and a strengthening in the forces of collaboration. The seamless global circulation of knowledge and value will dramatically reduce marginal costs and restructure business and communication models in many industries. The world will be presented with a new landscape.

1. Linguistic capability will empower different industries.
2. Restructuring of business and communication models will follow.
3. A new wave of innovation begins.
4. Civilisation enters a new phase.

***

Peggy's life returned to its routine after Henry left Singapore. More than half a year passed before Peggy finally felt settled in and familiar with her job. She still received complaints from time to time, but the problems were resolved quickly, and she got along well with her boss and colleagues. Her boss was a generous person, he would prepare small gifts for the staff and invite them to have dinner together to celebrate festive occasions.

While she was still studying, Peggy had always worried that she would not be able to adapt well in the workplace due to her forthright personality, and even more afraid that she would not be able to handle 'office politics'. However, this first job allayed her fears, the simple interpersonal relationships that she shared with her colleagues made her feel comfortable, and her concerns about working also faded away.

As always, her co-tenant Aunt Doreen took good care of her, and she lived a well-paced life, keeping a regular routine, and continuing to read and think about what she read. The only thing that was different in her life was that she no longer posted so much on her WeChat public account.

Nevertheless, she felt at times that something was missing in her life, but she could not tell exactly what it was. It gave her a feeling of emptiness and weariness, and it made her question herself: "Is this a normal downturn of emotions or because I am not passionate enough about what I am doing? Is this really the career and life purpose that I am willing to work for, for the rest of my life?" Unfortunately, she could not find an answer.

Occasionally, she would think of Henry, the images of Henry as a child and as an adult overlapped in her mind, until the former became blurry and the latter became clear. The way he had walked into the interpreters' booth so smartly dressed, his intelligent and witty responses whenever they had talked, the twinkle in his eyes when he smiled and looked at her, and how he had caught her elbow when she nearly fell…All these memories caused Peggy to feel both happy, but also a little melancholic for some reason.

After Henry returned to China, he contacted Peggy from time to time on WeChat. During their chats, Peggy learned that Henry's team would be travelling to Korea for their next roadshow after Singapore, and she casually obtained their detailed itinerary from Henry.

After that, Peggy did not sleep well for days, she would dream all night and would sometimes wake up from her dreams in the middle of the night, but she was not able to recall the contents of her dreams.

Finally, one night, she awoke in the middle of the night again and whilst she was still in a dreamy state, a thought of Henry and his invitation to start a business together just crossed her mind. Peggy decided at that moment that she should take the plunge.

"Mum, I'm thinking of returning to China to work," Peggy confided in her mother the next morning.

"What? Did something happen in Singapore? I thought you have always felt that working in Singapore is good?" Peggy's mother had always been supportive of her, but this sudden announcement was a little unexpected.

"It is very good in fact, the job, my boss and colleagues are all good, but I somehow feel that this is not the kind of life that I would really like to have."

Peggy's mother was not surprised to hear this from her daughter, "Then have you figured out what you really want to do with your life in China?"

"I am thinking of setting up a business with a friend in Beijing."

"Oh?!" Peggy's mother was taken aback. Given Peggy's temperament, it was not surprising to her mother that she would want to work in a big city like Beijing. But with no experience in entrepreneurship, why would she suddenly think of starting a business, and who was the friend she was talking about?

"Mum, do you remember Henry who lived right next to us when I was young?" Peggy asked quietly.

"Of course, I remember, both of you were the best playmates, he subsequently followed his parents back to their hometown, didn't he?"

"I was working as an interpreter at an international conference on Blockchain in Singapore and it turned out that he was a guest speaker, we were reunited in Singapore after many years!"

Peggy's mother did not know what Blockchain was, but she could hear the excitement in her daughter's voice, "So you will set up a business with Henry?"

"We met a few times when he was in Singapore and had several intensive conversations. We realised that the combination of language and blockchain is a vast Blue Ocean market. Before he left Singapore, he told me he would like to set up a business in this field, and asked if I wanted to join him. Well, I cannot explain all about blockchain in a few words, so please don't ask me too many questions about this."

"I am not worried about you being cheated since it is a business venture with Henry. But is he really planning to start a business?

Does he know you intend to go to Beijing to start a business with him?" queried Peggy's mother.

"From what I know of him and how I felt when I met him, I think he really wants to do something in this field. I did not give him a definite reply when he asked me to start a business together, and I have not told him that I am thinking about it."

"Peggy, it is tough to set up a business, I am sure you know this, do consider carefully. But then again, if this is something that you want to do, Mum and Dad will support you."

"I understand, thank you Mum!" Peggy was relieved.

Peggy wasted no time and submitted her resignation the day after her conversation with her mum. Naturally, everyone was taken by surprise.

The boss asked with concern, "Is it due to anything that happened at work or an emergency at home?"

"It is neither," Peggy answered in all seriousness.

"Then why this sudden decision to resign? I've always thought we work well together." David looked puzzled.

"Indeed, I have learned a lot in the past six months, thanks to all of you. I feel very grateful and happy to be working with you, but I found something else that I would like to do." Peggy was already looking ahead into the future.

The boss did not probe further, he replied reluctantly, "Well, I am sad to see you leave, you are the only employee in the company with profession training. It has not been easy to expand the business and now I am about to lose a trusted worker."

At this point, the rest of her colleagues who had inadvertently overheard their conversation gathered around with concerned looks.

Jason was the first to speak, "As a Singaporean, I have yet to play my role as a tour guide to show you the unique sights of Singapore!"

"Thanks! I have been to quite a few places, one or two of them were with you guys, working here is an experience I will always remember, Singapore is great!" Peggy looked sincerely at Jason.

Juliana was rather shocked, "Peggy, it's such a pity, many people who want to get a work permit in Singapore are unable to get one, why have you decided to quit?"

"I know that it is not easy to get a work permit in Singapore, but I think I have found what I want to pursue more than anything else. As the saying goes 'whatever the heart desires, press forward courageously'," Peggy could barely conceal her excitement.

"In that case, let me wish you all the best!" Juliana replied with a smile.

Lily's reaction was the most dramatic, she had always treated Peggy like a younger sister and Peggy had interacted most with her in the company, "Peggy, can't you tell us why have you resigned so suddenly? I will miss you! Will you continue to stay in Singapore?"

"No, I will go back to China, thank you for helping and taking care of me during this period of time, and be sure to come look for me the next time you go to China," Peggy replied in a regretful voice.

"I will, if you come to Singapore again, you must come and visit us too." Lily held on tightly to Peggy's hands, tears welling up in the eyes of the both of them.

To bid farewell to Peggy, the boss gathered everyone for dinner that night. Amid the toasting and laughter, Peggy suddenly felt a little reluctant to leave Singapore.

Doreen was equally surprised and upset when she learned that Peggy was returning to China. Nevertheless, she helped Peggy with the packing and sent her off at the airport on the day of her departure. They embraced and bid farewell to each other. As the plane slowly lifted off the ground in Singapore, Peggy murmured to herself, "A brief encounter. Farewell, Singapore."

After landing at Beijing Capital International Airport, Peggy took a taxi directly to the studio in Jianwai SOHO where Henry and his team worked.

Peggy had already confirmed the exact location of the office and the timing of her arrival was planned. If there were no last minute changes, Henry and his team would have ended the roadshow in Korea and also arrived back in Beijing.

"Hello Peggy, why are you calling me at this hour? What is the urgency?"

"Henry, can you guess where I am?"

"Hmm…Your boss took you out for fun today and you are somewhere in Singapore with beautiful scenery, you miss me while admiring the view and hence decided to give me a call?" said Henry.

"Who misses you? I think you are the one who misses me," retorted Peggy.

"Of course! I was thinking of you, you sensed it? So, was I right in guessing where you are?" Henry teased.

"I am very close to where you are now actually," Peggy replied softly.

Henry looked around subconsciously, there was no one else except his busy partners.

"Young lady, stop fooling around, only my colleagues are around me, you're saying that you are beside me, is this a confession?"

"You are the one who should stop fooling around, go to the window and look down," Peggy looked up as she spoke.

Henry hurriedly walked to the windows and looked down, immediately, he saw Peggy standing at the ground level of his office building with two pieces of luggage beside her, one big and one small. She waved to him with the hand that was not holding her phone.

Henry immediately muttered, "I'm coming down." He hung up and rushed to the lift. Henry's swift reaction alarmed his colleagues, they looked at each other, wondering where Henry had gone in such a hurry. "He took a phone call and went down in a hurry." "Gone in a flash, was it something urgent?" "No, he didn't take anything with him, he just ran out, I think someone is waiting for him down there. Didn't he just look out of the window?" Everyone rushed over to the windows.

At that moment, Henry was standing in front of Peggy, almost frozen in shock but also feeling a sense of excitement and anticipation running through his veins.

He stared at her for quite a while and she too looked back at him, smiling brightly without saying a word. Peggy did not know that she had been constantly on his mind after he left Singapore; he even dreamt of her often. However, they were so far apart from each other, he didn't think it was appropriate to mention it on WeChat.

In a state of mixed emotions, Henry suddenly opened his arms and hugged Peggy tightly. Peggy was caught off guard by Henry's embrace and stood frozen, not knowing where to place her hands.

"Aww…" There were loud cheers and whistles from the junior colleagues watching from the windows upstairs. Henry let go of

Peggy, looked up and signalled for them to stop and go away, the gleeful crowd dispersed.

"Why are you here? The company gave you a holiday?" Henry had regained his composure but was nevertheless puzzled.

"I resigned," Peggy replied in a calm and composed voice.

"Oh, did something happen in the company? Did something bad happen in Singapore?" Peggy had mentioned that she would work for a few years before returning to China, so upon hearing that she had resigned, Henry was concerned.

"Don't worry, I did not run into any trouble. I just figured out a few things."

Henry seemed to have guessed what Peggy wanted to say, but he did not respond and waited for Peggy to continue.

"I decided to come back and start a business with you, to explore blockchain applications in languages."

"Really? Really? That's great!" Henry was thrilled to have his thoughts confirmed by Peggy. They looked at each other with delight on their faces.

"You came directly from the airport?" asked Henry.

Peggy nodded, suddenly she began to feel the fatigue from her journey.

"Silly girl, why didn't you find a place to settle down and take a rest first? You do not have a place to stay tonight, do you?"

"I wanted to see you right away," Peggy wanted to say, but she thought it was not appropriate, so she merely answered, "No."

"Come on, there is a decent chain hotel near where I live."

After calling to confirm that there were rooms available, Henry took Peggy to the hotel. Henry kept talking on the way to the hotel, at one moment he asked Peggy if she was hungry and what she wanted to eat and at the next moment he said perhaps she should take a nap first if she was tired. He kept on chiding Peggy for not telling him about her plans earlier, he could have picked her up at the airport...

Peggy responded softly, on and off. She looked at this guy who was showering her with great concern, it made her felt warm and at ease; it felt good to be home, good to see him again...

Just as Peggy and Henry were talking, she received a phone call from their old playmate Fanny, who dropped a bombshell of her own: she was getting engaged to her foreigner boyfriend and planning to emigrate to live with him after marriage.

"Oh my, why are you getting engaged so suddenly and quietly?" Peggy was surprised.

"Hey, fate is unpredictable and besides I didn't do it suddenly or quietly, I shared our loving moments on WeChat!" Fanny's voice was bubbling with bliss.

"Are you still in Beijing?" asked Peggy.

"I am, I will still be in Beijing for a while, unless I am on business trips."

"Guess where I am now," Peggy asked.

"Are you not working in Singapore? I am not sure if I will get to see you again before I go abroad," Fanny replied, sounding a little disappointed.

"You surely will, because I am in Beijing now."

"Oh?!" it was Fanny's turn to be surprised, "How did you end up in Beijing?"

"It is a long story. Let's talk about it when we meet. Isn't Brenda in Beijing too? Let's arrange a time to catch up. Will you call her, or shall I do it?" Peggy asked.

"I will call her and also tell her about my engagement."

"By the way, another person will be joining us," said Peggy.

"Your boyfriend?"

"Don't be absurd, I am not like you, about to go away with someone else. I am sure you remember Henry?" Peggy said jokingly.

"Of course, I remember! We were the 'innocent gang of four'! How did you manage to get in touch with him?" Fanny asked curiously.

"This is another interesting story, I'll tell you when we meet," Peggy replied with a smile.

"Alright, alright, you will have many stories to tell!" Fanny quipped.

Peggy and Fanny chatted for a little longer before hanging up. Peggy told Henry that she was planning a gathering for four and Fanny also got in touch with Brenda. Without further delay, the four of them quickly fixed a time and place.

The venue was a private room at a restaurant with a canopy boat, located at Beijing Houhai, an area in central Beijing that is surrounded by a lake.

Peggy and Henry went together. As they pushed open the black wooden door to enter, before them was a gravel path under the bamboo forest. In an instant, they felt as though they were back in their hometown of Jiangnan, among the apricot blossoms and spring rain.

"This is very nostalgic…I feel like I am back in Jiangnan, a place I have not been for years." As he looked around at the mantles, grey tiles, wooden windows and screens in the restaurant, Henry could not help but feel impressed.

"I specifically chose this restaurant, it focuses on sharing Jiangnan's culture and its unique atmosphere is what makes it so appealing to the patrons," said Peggy.

Shortly after they had settled down in the private room, Brenda and Fanny arrived. After so many years, everyone had changed a lot, whether it was in terms of appearance, demeanour or attire; so much so that they were hesitant to acknowledge each other at first sight.

"Wow, look at how much you have grown, Henry! You're no longer skinny, short and dark like you used to be when you were little!"

"Indeed, you look so impressive and handsome now." Brenda and Fanny marvelled when they saw Henry.

Henry was caught off guard by the compliments and felt a little shy but he replied, "Well, you two ladies have been pretty since young and now you have become even more beautiful, graceful and radiant!"

"Come on, we have just met again, and you all can't wait to lavish praises on each other?" Peggy joked as she gestured for everyone to sit down. A waitress dressed in a small blue printed top with a small blue printed square scarf on her head entered the room and handed them the menu. "Let's order food before we catch up, I've heard the dishes in this restaurant have an authentic Jiangnan flavour."

"Do they have Dongpo pork (braised pork)?" asked Fanny.

"We have the rice plant flavoured Dongpo pork," the waitress replied.

"West Lake vinegar fish and stir-fried shrimps with Longjing tea, are these available? I feel like having the vinegar fish," said Brenda.

"Yes, yes, these are available."

"What about vegetable dishes?" asked Henry.

"How about trying stewed bamboo shoots and deep-fried stinky tofu?"

"All right, we will have one of each," said Henry.

"What would you like to drink?" Peggy asked, "Is everyone keen to have some wine?"

"Sure, we have not seen each other for so many years, we must drink and chat to our hearts' content," Brenda replied.

"In that case, we shall have a bottle of Shaoxing wine too," Peggy said with a smile; the waitress acknowledged it and repeated their order before leaving the room.

Looking around, the table and chairs were covered with Jiangnan-style wax-dyed printed tablecloths and cushions, the cutlery provided were bamboo chopsticks and porcelain tableware in the native blue and white Jiangnan style. There were a few blue and white porcelain flowerpots containing arrangements of elegant orchids and blooming chrysanthemums. A Shaoxing wine jar with carvings of flying Apsaras and various kinds of porcelain were tastefully arranged on the long narrow table and some calligraphy and paintings hung on the walls.

"Peggy, you are good at choosing places, this place makes me feel like we are back in our hometown," Fanny seemed to be feeling emotional as she looked around.

"Exactly, I have been in Beijing for many years, how is it possible that I have not been to this place before..." Brenda added.

"Peggy, are you not working in Singapore? Why have you come to Beijing?" asked Fanny, "Why did you come with Henry, how did you meet each other?"

"Wait! Don't tell me that the both of you have good news for us?" Fanny exclaimed, as a thought suddenly occurred to her.

Brenda and Fanny exchanged looks and immediately began bombarding Henry and Peggy with questions. Peggy suddenly felt anxious that Fanny had misunderstood her relationship with Henry, she interjected quickly, "Fanny, stop talking nonsense, Henry and I just happened to bump into each other in Singapore."

"Oh, I didn't mean anything, why are you so anxious?" Fanny winked mischievously.

Henry came to Peggy's rescue, "Alright, my dear Miss Fan, please stop joking around. We have not seen one another for years and it so happens that we are all in Beijing. Aren't you getting married and emigrating soon? That's the main reason for this gathering, but coincidentally, Peggy and I also have a serious matter to share with both of you."

"Are you together?" Fanny blurted.

"Oh dear, this engaged woman associates everything with romantic love! Why must a man and a woman always be considered a couple? Henry and I are not a couple, we will tell you everything slowly if you'd just let us talk," Peggy replied laughingly.

The food arrived then and the four of them tucked in before continuing their conversation.

"Recently I went to Singapore to attend a conference on blockchain and met Peggy who was the interpreter. We talked for a few days and discovered a business direction with great prospects," said Henry.

"You all know that I studied language, Henry has an undergraduate degree in finance, a master's in computer science, and now he is working on blockchain. Our exchanges revealed that language and blockchain are a match made in heaven. After much consideration, I quit my job and came back, we are planning to start a business together," said Peggy.

"Wait, you guys summarised everything in just a few sentences, I don't get it, what is blockchain? How is it a match made in heaven with language?" Fanny was confused.

"It is difficult to provide a comprehensive explanation of blockchain in the time we have, let me just briefly explain the concept," Henry continued, "basically, the internet age is about point-to-point information transmission and blockchain is about value transmission. Let's look at online shopping, take-out and online booking of transport, we are essentially transmitting information according to our needs and suitable sellers will receive this information and provide services for us, do you agree?" Fanny nodded her head in agreement.

"The transmission of information for such transactions are very centralised. For instance, when we send an order for our online shopping, our payment will first be deposited into the account of a third party. After we receive the item, the system will transfer the money to the account of the seller," Henry continued.

"What is blockchain all about then?" Brenda cupped her chin in one hand, a serious thoughtful look on her face.

"Blockchain is a form of information technology that gives impetus to the digitalisation of human society. Its core feature is decentralisation, which not only enables direct transactions to reduce transaction costs, but also expands the scope of transactions to enable optimal allocation of resources on a global scale," Henry explained.

"This is still quite abstract. Can you give us a more specific example?" Fanny still seemed confused.

Peggy stepped up to do so, "as you know, I majored in translation. After graduation, I went to Singapore to work as a project manager with a translation services company. In the course of my work, I felt deeply the agony of the translation services companies, the clients and the translators, all of whom do not have it easy. The whole industry is still adopting the workshop model by processing work as and when the clients supply them. Take the translators as an example, on one hand, their capabilities cannot be measured and acknowledged effectively, it is therefore difficult for them to receive enough projects that match their professional ability. On the other hand, they are not adequately rewarded for their effort, thus their creativity is not exactly stimulated, and they are not motivated to share their creation of high-quality language data."

Henry continued, "With the help of blockchain, all these problems can be resolved. Blockchain is decentralised, any translator can use it to disclose or update their information which would include personal details, professional skills, transaction details etc. This is equivalent to setting up an extensive personal profile for unconditional search when the information is needed. In addition, the fact that blockchain builds trust based on cryptography, the trust we have in each other will not be based on emotions but based on a shared belief in mathematical algorithms. With regard to the issue of inadequate rewards for efforts put in as well as the unwillingness to share high-quality language data, blockchain will allow validation of each translator's contributions, those who need the information can access directly after paying a small fee, the contributor will then be rewarded accordingly, with more people using the data, the returns will be higher. This will in turn encourage active contributions of language data and more focus on works of creativity to accumulate individual linguistic assets."

The expressions on Brenda's and Fanny's faces did not inspired confidence that they understood any better, so Henry continued.

"As a result, Peggy and I came up with the concept of 'Cross-Linguistic Capability'. We intend to use blockchain as a basis to set up a public chain for language information and launch human-machine translation products on the chain. On the front end, it will be presented like the power grid delivering electricity to empower thousands of products. On the back end, the main function of this chain will be to organise and manage language data. It will link up individuals with language capabilities, institutions and machine translations from all over the world, standardise control to create linguistic capabilities that are faster and cheaper than human translators on their own, but with better quality than machine translation."

"Linguistic capability is like electrical energy, it can transform some of the language data that already exists, but is not being effectively utilised, into a standard, stable capacity to be of service to us in our work and daily lives. In terms of work, various websites, search engines, communication software, IoTs, and other applications can be connected to this system in the same way that electronic devices are connected to the power grid, thus automating the multilingual presentation without having to rely on human translators. As far as daily life is concerned, with this system as a support, developers can develop applications, software for different scenarios, and of course that includes hardware too," Henry explained further.

"I kind of get it now!" Brenda was enlightened, "It seems like an integration of language and blockchain, but it can in fact trigger changes in many domains because language is required in any activity, and in the context of globalisation, the inconvenience of language barriers is becoming more apparent."

"Bingo, Brenda, you nailed it!" Henry exclaimed.

"During my grandparents' generation, long-distance communication was mainly through letters. Sending a letter took several days to weeks and not all places were reachable. Communication with foreigners was almost a fantasy. For our parents' generation, there were no mobile phones when they were young. Although mobile phones and internet access are now widely available to facilitate communications, the language barrier still restricts everyone's 'circle of friends' to people who speak the same native language," Brenda replied, smiling at Henry's excited response.

"Yes, the younger people of our generation who have studied foreign languages and have wide social circles are better off, our elders' generations could only communicate mainly with people in China. If there were no language barriers, one could actually make friends from all over the world," said Peggy.

"We would then be able to see the social media postings by friends from abroad, photos of sceneries and food they have enjoyed, as well as their native living environment." For Brenda, beautiful sceneries and good food were the tenets of a true and genuine life.

> The world is on the edge of a new wave of business innovation with linguistic capabilities empowering different industries.

"I understand now. It would not just be limited to the living environment, but also the working environment, the educational environment, etc., as long the other party is willing to share, we would be able to be exposed to all aspects of life in other places," Fanny added.

"Linguistic capability is about empowering all kinds of scenarios. Hopefully one day, we will be able to generate hundreds and thousands of scenarios on our language information public chain, with each scenario directly connected to a language capability solution, thus making it possible for any of the characters in this scenario to communicate in their native language," said Peggy.

"Allow me to be bold and envision this, Virtual Reality (VR) and Augmented Reality (AR) are now very popular, is there a possibility to link them up with languages? Anyone with a wearable device, be it a wristband, or an accessory worn on the neck or some other similar device, only has to put it on and tune it to the channel of individual mother tongue language. No matter what language the person encounters, he will always experience it in his native language. In short, no matter what language people speak, we will hear them in our native language," Brenda said.

"Yes, thus, no matter which country we travel to, all the text and audio information displayed in shops, tourist attractions etc., will be presented in our native language, we will then be able to tour meaningfully instead of perfunctorily walking around taking pictures and just shopping," Peggy gave her a thumbs up.

"The world will truly be flattened then, and the term global village will become a reality," Henry continued, "If the internet deals with information, then blockchain deals with value. Blockchain supports the two basic functions needed to process value in the digital world: value representation and value transfer."

> The token allows for value representation and value transfer.

"Blockchain allows us to take control of our data assets and prevent them from being arbitrarily taken away by large centres and institutions, protecting the value of our data and content on the internet," Henry added.

"Therefore, with blockchain, everyone will be more willing to actively contribute to creating our own linguistic data, we will be contributors of linguistic capability and be paid in tokens. At the same time, we will also be consumers of linguistic capability and pay in tokens, is this correct?" Brenda asked and Henry nodded his head vigorously to show agreement.

"By the way, have you all seen the video that is being circulated on the internet recently? It was posted by a tourist who bumped into a boy in Cambodia selling souvenirs. The boy could speak more than eight languages." When the other three said they had not seen it, Fanny searched for the video on her phone to show them.

The little boy was cute and lively, with a dark complexion and a smile that showed off his white teeth. In the video, he was walking barefooted on the beach with a basket of things in his hand whilst simultaneously filming himself with a mobile phone camera. He claimed he could speak Cantonese, Mandarin, English, Thai, Japanese, Korean and French and some other languages.

The tourist who took the video then put the boy through a language test, and indeed, he responded well. As part of his sales pitch to the tourist, he sang a modified version of "We are Different" in fluent Chinese: "We are different. Everyone is in a different situation and we are here to sell things to you. We are different. We are going through different experiences, but we hope that we will meet again in the next life."

Towards the end of the video, when the tourist asked the boy, "Who taught you all this?" He answered, "I learned from the tourists before you."

The four friends watched in amazement and sighed collectively in disbelief afterwards, they were moved by the little boy's cuteness and intelligence, but also felt sorry that he was not getting an education in school like other children of his age.

"It is only because this boy used different languages to solicit for business that people were attracted to buy from him. If he had depended on gesturing, it would have been tough to strike any deals. In fact, that is essentially what we do in cross-border e-commerce, don't you agree?" asked Fanny.

Without waiting for a response, she continued, "The cross-border e-commerce business that my company does is actually benefitting from the information gap. Each country has its own e-commerce platform, their target customers and goods are mainly within their own region. Due to language barriers, they do not gather market information and try to meet customer needs in other countries, but if you want to engage in foreign trade, you will need intermediaries. We provide them with services such as information gathering, connection to overseas platforms, handling of enquiries, customs clearance and cross-border payments. Our company is the equivalent of an agency that integrates this one-stop service."

"The plug-in of linguistic capabilities will magnify global e-commerce platforms, goods can then come from anywhere in the world, goods will also be distributed globally, e-commerce platforms will focus on remodelling their competitive advantage." Henry, ever wise and far sighted, summarised further, "If the age of blockchain does come to pass, there will be no need for businesses to set up companies to issue shares. The founders of a business would simply set up a foundation based on a cryptographic protocol that would pay all the parties involved in this product or service, such as developers, users, investors, etc. by issuing tokens corresponding to this protocol, and this corresponding blockchain network will connect together to form the collective entities for all future business activity."

The future of e-commerce is cross-border, and every one of us will be in a world of commerce that breaks borders.

"This sounds wrong, it feels like those of us in cross-border e-commerce are going to lose our jobs," Fanny quipped.

Henry quickly consoled her, saying, "Don't worry, if you reposition yourself in the new economic structure, you will be able to make a big difference. When I was in school my mentor shared these quotes with me: 'respond to changes by adapting to changes, respond to changes by remaining unchanged'. The first sentence refers to keeping an eye on the big picture and being ready to adapt to change, while the second sentence is a reminder that no matter how much the outside world changes, as long as our desire to keep up with the times remains unchanged, we will be able to cope with anything."

"A very philosophical and profound quote, I will note it down!" Fanny activated her phone memo and noted it down.

"Language is powerful indeed. Whether I am feeling positive or depressed, this quote has always kept me motivated, encouraged me and given me strength when I was depressed," said Henry

> **Language is so powerful.**

"I agree totally, language is so powerful, as the saying goes 'a kind remark gives warmth in winter, but evil words send chills in June (良言一句三冬暖，恶语伤人六月寒 liáng yán yī jù sān dōng nuǎn, è yǔ shāng rén liù yuè hán)', especially when the words are spoken by someone you love, their power is magnified," Peggy thought of her teacher again, "The philosophy teacher I admire believes in 'accepting adversity and adapting to different circumstances' which fits the two quotes you mentioned perfectly."

"Hah, why have you all started a discussion on language? I was just thinking, after eliminating the language barriers, businesses conducted by my friends on WeChat platform will be expanded," Brenda suddenly jumped in.

"How could you actually tolerate receiving all those promotional messages from your friends who are doing business on WeChat?" Peggy exclaimed.

"Well, I blocked those that would never be of interest. It is inexplicably exciting to think that in future, before I make any purchase through an agent, I can first enquire online from friends in different countries. Hahaha, I feel that future purchases will be smoother, and I will have less anxiety."

When she saw Brenda talked about shopping with such delight, Peggy could not hold back her laughter. She thought to herself, "Indeed there is something for everyone! Brenda immediately thinks about shopping, whilst I am thinking about education..."

As the thoughts passed through Peggy's mind, she said, "The education industry is expected to undergo dramatic changes too. I recall that as an undergraduate, I was particularly interested in learning an analytics software. I even had the software downloaded and installed and had my account registered. When I found out that the course was only taught in English, I was fearful and procrastinated as I was not confident learning in English so I ended up not taking it. Their customer service staff wasted much effort emailing me continuously..."

"Nowadays, universities are more like independent sites with their own characteristics, and in China it would probably be increasingly common for several universities in the same region to jointly offer inter-university electives for a double major or other programmes," Henry echoed.

"There are also online course platforms that offer a wealth of online resources but users are still limited to courses from their own countries." Peggy casually clicked on an online course platform to show everyone.

> "A university is not about a building, but about having good professors (大学者，非大楼之谓，大师之谓也 dā xué zhě, fēi dà lóu zhī wèi, dà shī zhī wèi yě)."
>
> The professors will then be able to share their wisdom globally.

"If the education industry can be empowered by the network of language capabilities, it will then be possible to attend courses and lectures from universities all over the world, listen to quality lectures of all genres, and share every library's electronic resources with the world," Henry envisioned.

"There will be a big change in the way talents are trained and the way universities are managed," Peggy continued, "The physical campus is still important, but technology has made education truly borderless."

"Not only will education be borderless, scientists will also collaborate extensively; innovations and technological achievements would occur globally." The discussion about the education sector reminded Brenda, a technology journalist of her work experiences, "This reminds me of an interview I did once with an old scientist, I was very impressed by him."

"Tell us more?" Fanny's curiosity was aroused.

"He had developed a new heat-generating coating but experienced some problems with his product. He wanted to look for similar products in other countries to find out what he could learn from international counterparts about the methods and progression in product development. However, as he was not proficient in English, despite putting a lot of effort into research, he remained uncertain about international developments," said Brenda.

"Did he approach anyone for help?" Henry asked.

"After we reported on his research, someone approached him for collaboration and that helped resolve the problem. Subsequently, a team was formed and they applied for an international patent together, thus allowing their research results and technology to be promoted to the world. The old scientist was fortunate to find a partner with language skills and a good understanding of his field of research. In many cases, one can only find people who meet a condition but not the other," said Brenda.

"Oh! I attended a seminar on 'Nobel Prize and Collaborative Co-creation' in Singapore. The speaker's statistical analysis revealed that collaborative co-creation is the trend for Nobel Prizes. In the discussion session, I said that civilisations and knowledge are still limited by national boundaries because of the language barrier. We had no answer to that at the time, but it is just a few months later and we have found the answer," Peggy was excited.

"That's right, the collaboration of scientists is now based on a common language. For example, if a Russian person wants to learn acupuncture in China but does not know the Chinese language, no matter how good he or she is, there is no way to learn the skill. The first step for many Chinese students working overseas is to overcome the language barrier, which requires a certain level of language ability and professionalism before collaboration can take place. The collaborative threshold is thus very high. If the language barrier is broken and everyone can communicate comfortably in their native language, the scope for collaboration will be greater and efficiency will be enhanced," Henry was clearly experienced and knowledgeable and he could relate personally to the situation.

> Breaking down language barriers lowers the threshold for global collaboration and enables people to collaborate freely to create value, thereby accelerating technology development.

"Yes, in the course of my work, I came across some news stories about foreigners. They had developed new technology overseas and hoped that the Chinese media would help promote it in China so that they would be able to find companies in China to work with and convert these scientific and technological findings into actual products," Brenda continued to share.

"With linguistic capabilities, these researchers and developers will not have to search so hard for localised resources," said Henry.

"People will be able to watch news reports of other countries directly to learn more about the local situation, there may be less prejudice and misunderstanding as a result," Fanny was excited.

"Wow, it did not take us long to paint this sweeping picture of a new world," Brenda took a sip of water from her cup.

"Indeed," everyone echoed the sentiment.

Henry grabbed the opportunity to conclude, "Essentially, blockchain is about a change in mindset, reconfiguration of organisational formations, and the transformation of social collaboration mechanisms, brought together to form a new concept."

"Earlier on, both of you mentioned serious business to discuss with us. With all the discussion we had and Peggy's resignation from Singapore to move to Beijing, I am guessing that the two of you are planning to start a blockchain business together?" Brenda noted.

"We are indeed childhood playmates, although we have not met in years, we are still connected in spirit. You are right, we intend to set up a business." Henry looked at Peggy before turning towards Brenda and Fanny.

"So, are you asking us to join the partnership?" Fanny was direct with her words.

"Well, of course we cannot force you to join us, we just wanted to share our ideas and information, if you are keen, then you are most welcome to come on board too!" Henry hastily explained, fearing that Fanny's misunderstanding would spoil the mood.

"I can't, I am about to get engaged to my Prince Charming and departing for Chile." Fanny looked instantly happy when she mentioned her fiancée.

"By the way, I would like to say this, do not miss the right person once you meet him or her," Fanny looked at Peggy and Henry earnestly. Henry turned to look at Peggy who was blushing and did not know how to react.

Brenda grinned and said, "I am keen to join you guys in the business venture. I have been a journalist for years, although the content of reporting is different, the style of reporting we use for every piece is similar, and I am quite tired of it. I am interested in what you guys have said, and since we grew up together, I have confidence in starting a business together."

"You are more than welcome to do so! One of the biggest advantages you have as a journalist is your connections, starting a business requires not only capital, but also connections!" Peggy rejoiced upon hearing that Brenda was keen to join them.

"Oh dear, as one of the four playmates, I am missing out on such a good opportunity for a partnership with all of you," Fanny suddenly felt that it was a shame that she was not able to join them.

"Don't think so much, getting married is more important! Afterall, marriage is for a lifetime," Peggy smiled at Fanny who smiled back blissfully.

"All of you must work hard on it then!" Fanny exclaimed.

"Okay, we know, don't worry too much," Peggy and Brenda burst into laughter as they looked over at an also grinning Henry.

After a good reunion over a satisfying meal, the four of them bid farewell and headed home.

Summary:
A Beautiful Evolution

To imagine a world without language barriers is the same as to imagine 30 years ago, when the internet would make "clairvoyance" and "clairaudience" a reality. It is a wonderful aspiration of mankind, and a dream that is long overdue.

Human have become accustomed to being separated by the invisible net of language. The boundaries of our practical life experiences are the boundaries of language. Unless there are no alternatives, we will not turn to a translation services company.

When the boundaries of language are eliminated, the greatness of the world, its beauty, and its renewal, will be presented to us at an accelerated pace. A new world without language barriers can give us a real sense of the magnitude of the world. For many people, no matter how many friends they have in their contact list, they are basically friends from their own native language. If they have foreign friends, it would not be possible for their friends to be from all language groups.

In a new world without language barriers, we can have customer information from different countries on our mobile phones and deal with these customers in our native language. We can send and receive any product information in our native language, just as we communicate with our friends and customers in the provinces and cities in our country every day. Our circle of friends and customers will be expanded, and the products and information can reach any country in the world without any obstacles. Everyone can inquire and shop on any e-commerce platform in their native language or sell their goods to any other countries with ease.

A new world without language barriers can give us a real sense of the beauty of the world. The history and heritage differ in different countries with distinctive beauty in their thoughts and cultures. When the language barrier is broken, we can read books that we could not have read before, listen to stories that were completely unfamiliar to us, and see things that we could not possibly experience before. We can enjoy the beauty of human civilisation accumulated in different parts of the world. The folklore, cultural heritage and customs of each country can be disseminated around the world, realising the fact that whatever is national can be universal too. For courses at universities around the world, regardless of the language in which they are taught, students from any country will be able to learn and listen in their native language, tremendously increasing the number of people that will benefit from new knowledge. The greatness of a university lies in its intangible presence.

A new world without language barriers can instil the feeling in us that the world is genuinely new. Different languages represent different ways of perceiving the world, such dynamics can spark new ideas in many ways. When scientists from different countries with different mother tongues form joint research teams, a prerequisite is that everyone needs to use the same language; otherwise, there is no way to comprehend each other's ideas and conduct scientific explorations. It is inevitable that some scientists will need to work harder, not just to reach a certain level of scientific research competency but also to attain a certain level of linguistic competence. The language threshold will no doubt exclude some scientists. If scientists from all over the world could be grouped flexibly into scientific research teams according to the required expertise, they can then work together to overcome global issues such as cancer treatment, global warming, water security, etc. There will be no language barrier to hamper the gathering of the world's best human talents to find solutions for the benefit of humanity.

SUMMARY

285

When the language barrier is broken, we will usher in a new world where business and communication models are reconfigured, and human civilisation is accelerated.

Note

——— Chapter 9 ———

The Journey with Language
A Mutually Fulfilling Partnership

"A day in the world of cryptocurrency is a year in the human world." Once they immersed themselves in the world of blockchain, the team saw for themselves the greed and ugliness of human nature. They encouraged one another when faced with setbacks, never forgetting their original aspirations and insisted on doing only meaningful work that they believed in. In this way, they attracted a few other like-minded people to their team. They decided to dedicate themselves to product creation, with the firm belief that by doing good for the society, they would have a bright future.

Freedom from language barriers has been a common human desire since time immemorial. Blockchain can provide the underlying technology support to assemble artificial intelligence and human intelligence to enable the convergence of human civilisation. The first successful application of blockchain was in the field of cryptocurrency. Currency and language are the respective products of human material exchange and spiritual communication. We have reasons to believe that the second phenomenal application will occur in the language field. This is a once-in-a-millennium historic opportunity.

1. The common nature of currency and language.
2. The differences between currency and language.
3. Linguistic data thoroughly reflects human thought and intelligence.
4. The phenomenal growth of applications for blockchain in the language field is inevitable.

**

Since the decision to set up a business venture had been made, the three friends wasted no time getting started.

Brenda used her connections from being a technology journalist to shortlist and find a reliable incubator firm. After renting a small open-plan office, the trio plunged headlong into writing white papers and business plans.

Henry, who had the most ideas and insights in this area, coupled with actual entrepreneurship experience, took on the role of main writer. He managed to find quality white papers and business plan templates for reference, so the entrepreneurial novices, Peggy and Brenda could read and learn from them. Subsequently, they all came together to brainstorm for ideas.

"Before we start to write the white paper, we should be clear about the vision and mission of our business," said Henry.

"Do we have to differentiate between vision and mission? Are they not the same?" Brenda asked.

"There is a difference, vision focuses on an objective and the outcome, it is a description of the purpose. For mission, it identifies the activity for the business, it is about the job," said Henry.

"Yes, the language we use must be easily understood and as precise as possible," added Peggy, "Let's refer to the vision and mission statements of some of the world's leading companies, give it some thought separately and meet again in the afternoon to discuss,"

In the afternoon, the three of them sat down for a meeting armed with their notes and ideas.

"The most striking quote I saw was 'No business is too difficult to handle'. Can we state our vision as 'No language is too difficult to understand'?" Brenda was the first to present her idea.

"This may sound slightly demanding, but I do not think that is the right way to phrase it, each language itself is still difficult to understand, after all, it reflects the characteristics of its respective country and ethnicity, with a myriad of history and culture behind it, we are just providing a great system for language conversion," Henry shook his head.

"How about my idea? 'Let every language be understood', modified from 'Let everyone be happy'," Peggy suggested.

"This is possible but does not reflect our unique feature," Henry was still not convinced.

"Unique feature?" Peggy and Brenda asked simultaneously.

"Yes, unique feature. It is not only human translation combined with machine translation. We are going to leverage on blockchain to deliver this."

"Then the other one I was thinking of would not be appropriate either," Brenda was a little discouraged after hearing Henry's explanation.

"What is that?" Peggy asked.

"Change the world in your language," said Brenda.

"I got it! Your idea has inspired me, how about 'Chain the world in your language'? Chain is reflective of our unique feature; it is easily understood. The Mandarin expression of the phrase would be '母语链通世界 mǔ yǔ liàn tōng shì jiè'. There is dual meaning in this Mandarin expression, the first being 'mother tongue chain — reach out to the world' and the other one 'mother tongue — connect with the world', said Peggy.

"This is great! The idea of blockchain is ingeniously incorporated!" Peggy and Brenda applauded.

"For our mission, how about 'Make language no longer a barrier'?" Brenda shared her thoughts.

"Let's modify it a little to 'Break down language barriers'," Henry suggested.

"That is fine with me," said Peggy.

"I agree too," Brenda and Peggy gave each other high-fives.

"In that case, all our work from now on will focus on these two core objectives." Henry brought up another important issue, "Besides this, we have another important matter to discuss. We must form a strong team to create our product with research and development. Many so-called start-up teams in the blockchain field only have ideas and are looking to raise money without doing anything concrete, these are the fraudsters."

"Specifically, what should we do?" asked Peggy.

"Since the three of us are not technical experts especially with regard to language related technology, we must look for someone who is highly familiar and proficient in this field to spearhead the team," said Henry.

Suddenly, Brenda thought of a suitable candidate, "Hey, when I was conducting an interview previously, I met a technology expert named Steven. He is highly competent, holds several patents, is low-key and persistent, and had led technical teams. The last time we interviewed him, he was paying attention to blockchain, he could be a good candidate, I will get in touch with him tonight."

"What a coincidence!" "That's great!" Henry and Peggy exclaimed simultaneously, the three friends exchanged excited smiles.

After defining the core objectives, they discussed the framework and the key elements of each section before finally writing the first draft of the white paper.

In the process of writing, they started to learn more about the industry. At the time, digital currencies were the only popular product on the blockchain, so a lot of material focused on understanding the cryptocurrency world than understanding the technology of blockchain per se.

> Blockchain has a promising future, but the reality at the initial stage of development is a state of total disorder.

Amid the frenzy of proxy voting, fundraising, open outcry, and initial coin offerings (ICO), there were tales of both impulsiveness and restraint, as well as successes and failures. The stories they encountered through their research left the three of them feeling both shocked and undecided, not knowing the direction to take on their path to entrepreneurship.

One day, as soon as the three of them arrived at the office, Henry shared the story of how one of his WeChat friends, Casey, had "struck gold". "It seems that those stories we read of overnight riches in the cryptocurrency world really does happen around us."

"Which of your friends became rich overnight?" Peggy asked out of curiosity.

"We are not exactly friends, we only met on a WeChat group a few days ago," Henry replied, shrugging indifferently.

Brenda asked, "A guy or a lady?"

"Make a guess," Henry refused to answer.

"Middle-aged man, with a wealth of experiences, good observation and reflection skills and has a keen eye for any business opportunity," Brenda presented her analysis.

"That is a stereotype, and that was what I thought initially. However, when I looked at Casey's friends list on social media, I found that she is an average post-90s girl just like you both," Henry tapped the table with his pen.

"Why do you think that she is an average girl?" Peggy could not hold back her laughter.

"I saw the postings on her WeChat Moments, they were all about eating, drinking, making merry and life's trivia, nothing at all about ideology or values or anything like that," Henry replied, seemingly having fun spinning his pen.

"Hah, that's because postings on WeChat Moments are one-sided, there must be some kind of secret since she is so successful in the crypto world, did you try to find out more from her?" Brenda was indeed an experienced reporter.

"I had a chat with her, she said that she learned about bitcoin from a paid reading app and was 'brainwashed' into buying two bitcoins when it was not as popular, and the price was not high. Subsequently when the price of bitcoin skyrocketed, she immediately decided to participate in a chain-only private placement. In less than half a year, she sold all of them and received more than $6 million. After buying a house and a car and spending another million on lightning bitcoins, the rest of her money was presumably spent on food and drinks based on her social media sharing," Henry answered nonchalantly.

"Based on your description, I can see that this person Casey has a good sense of propriety, she is not greedy and knows when to stop," said Peggy.

There were not that many people like Casey, and it was the chaos in the cryptocurrency world that Henry and the others heard about the most.

As a journalist, Brenda was sharp in identifying information sources and had the capability to search for and organise them.

On another day, she came to the office with the "breaking news" that had happened the night before. The chat content of the crypto world tycoon, Soar, about his experience in cutting "chives", had been leaked by accident. The term "chives" refers to individual crypto investors who were vulnerable to big selloffs. The chat content broke the hearts of numerous "chives".

Soar was a well-known figure in the circle of cryptocurrency with countless fans. He was often invited to participate in large-scale events and to give speeches. In the chat records that was circulated, he was very different from his usual public image, he used coarse language repetitively and most importantly he was very blunt about the truth which the "chives" were unwilling to admit.

"In fact, the 'chives' were not actually sure of the many things that were said in the cryptocurrency world, after all, a lot of income from these people who were propagating information was actually cut from other 'chives'. When they finally heard the truth leaked from their trusted guru of cryptocurrency, it was a mental blow for them," Brenda sighed.

"From 'pretending not to know' to now being 'unable to pretend not to know'," Henry hit the nail on the head with his remark.

"The truth always hurts," Peggy added.

"The circulation of the recording caused an uproar among the fans of Soar." Brenda continued, "Although I do not know much about blockchain and bitcoin, I have always felt that the various digital currencies had deviated from what bitcoin founder Satoshi Nakamoto had intended. He was trying to decentralise transactions through bitcoin, but it appears now that people are caught up in a frenzy of cryptocurrency speculation and profiteering, with a desire to become rich overnight."

"We must stay true to our original intention. The more I hear of such stories, the more I think we made the right choice to skip the crypto world and go further into the language field," said Peggy.

In the process of drafting their white paper and business plan, Henry and the team sourced for opportunities to attend various blockchain conferences and closed-door meetings. These allowed them to accumulate knowledge and materials for writing the white paper and to prepare for financing at a later stage.

At one such conference, a giant of the cryptocurrency circle, Bryan, shared his experience on blockchain investment as one of the keynote speakers. Bryan was from the northern part of China, he had graduated from the Special Class for the Gifted Young, and had made a good living after joining the blockchain field with his extraordinary talent; his nickname was "The knight who escaped to the top".

At the beginning of his speech, Bryan sounded the alarm to the audience — all investments are risky and that finance is essentially a game of buying and selling risk.

Following this, Bryan explained how to select blockchain investment projects and how to raise funds.

Towards the end of his speech, Bryan offered another piece of advice: "Do not borrow money to speculate in bitcoins, and do not dream of getting rich overnight".

On the way home from the conference, the team had a discussion revolving around Bryan's presentation.

"From his presentation, it's clear Bryan is still active in the circle of cryptocurrency," said Henry.

"Yeah, the discussions at blockchain conferences and closed-door meetings will never break away from cryptocurrency." Peggy agreed, "When he talked about methods of financing, it was clearly about cutting off the 'chives'. All that talk about 'using blockchain ledger technology to turn your business into a true public company' literally just means that 'since all small businesses like yours lack access to financing, why not sell high-tech packaged blockchain chive coins to the public to raise money in the name of internet investing and fool people who are more stupid than you'."

"I can imagine this scam penetrating into the Tier 3 and 4 cities targeting the middle-aged and elderly," Brenda was concerned.

"Whatever we do, we must keep our conscience clear." The trio exchanged nods as they confirmed their common understanding.

"Yes, we should only do what is meaningful and make honest money. Let's get the white paper and the business plan finalised," said Henry firmly.

The writing of the white paper and business plan proceeded smoothly, after all, the three of them had already had clear goals and ideas in mind since the early stages of planning. It was only because they had high self-imposed requirements, which saw them making multiple rounds of changes, without being able to finalise the proposals. Peggy finally suggested putting aside the two proposals for a while, since burying themselves in uninterrupted discussions and amendments was not likely to be the best thing to do. The trio agreed to do so, in the hope that they would be able to come up with new ideas after a break.

"We should design a company logo in the meantime," Henry suggested.

"I have an idea regarding the company logo, this is related to a story that I have read from the Bible," said Peggy.

"Oh? Tell us," Brenda's curiosity was piqued.

"There is a story in the Bible about the Tower of Babel, the gist of the story is that mankind once spoke the same language. The people then decided to work together to build a tower to the sky so that mankind would not experience the devastation of another flood from god. The move prompted god to change and differentiate the languages of humankind so that they could no longer gather and synergise their efforts because of language barriers and thus the tower was left unfinished. I thought the design of the company logo could start with the Tower of Babel since what we are doing is trying to remove the language barrier," Peggy said.

> Any new technology that succeeds in bringing about social changes must not be amoral, but embody values that can bring benefit to society, and blockchain is no exception.

"What does the Tower of Babel look like?" Henry had never heard of it.

"Well, the tower was not completed, so no one really knows, but I think we can refer to the pyramids. The pyramids stood for over 4000 years, it is a symbol of ancient Egyptian civilisation and also signifies human civilisation."

Brenda searched for a picture of the pyramid on her computer, "Hey look, doesn't the shape of the pyramids look like the Chinese character 'gold (金 jīn)', and it looks the same from any side. In Chinese, gold represents wealth, and gold is an auspicious colour, so perhaps it would be a good idea to use the pyramid shape and earthy yellow."

"I agree." Henry stood up, "The product that we want to develop is equivalent to an amplifier, it will expand business opportunities and market capacity by amplifying the value of information, thereby increasing people's wealth."

"That is correct. Language contains history and culture, our product will extend to every corner of the world, using each individual's mother tongue to link-up with the intelligence of mankind, in order to create more wealth and to form an inclusive and coexisting landscape for human civilisation. Peggy, what do you think? Do a quick mental scan of your previous experiences in reading and attending seminars to see what useful information you can draw from them," Brenda urged.

> Language acts as the basis for people to draw on the wisdom of their predecessors and collaborate with them.

Peggy rested her chin in her hand and pondered for a moment before speaking, "In the book 'The Classic of the Virtues of the Tao', the ancient philosopher Lao Zi said that 'one begets two, two begets three, three begets all creations', I think we can design three pyramids, which signify that our product will stimulate and connect the wisdom of mankind to change the mindsets of people through cultural aggregation and exchange and also enable creations of new business models in different fields. To be specific, we can have a bigger pyramid in the middle and two smaller ones on the right and left."

"This idea to combine tradition and culture is brilliant!" Brenda exclaimed, "I have something else in mind, also to draw wisdom from traditional culture and that is 'Yin and Yang'. We can have a solid design for the upper part of the logo and leave the lower part hollow."

"There is a saying I heard, 'all things bear the yin and embraces the yang, to achieve balance and harmony', the energies of yin and yang will intersect to form a favourable condition for creation, and they will stimulate each other to form a new harmonious body," Henry was also thinking hard.

"Yes, the solid section equates to our explorations and discoveries and the hollow section is an implication of what is yet to be known and explored by mankind. It is the same for the pyramid, they are more amazing than we can imagine, and there is a great deal of wonder beneath the horizon," replied Peggy.

"I already have a graphic in my mind," Henry opened the image processing software on his computer and quickly came up with the first version of the logo, "Different languages represent different ways of thoughts and accumulation of the different elements of civilisation. Our product not only breaks down the language barrier, but it also connects people from around the world with their mother tongue and amplifies the value of information to expand business opportunities. It also encourages explorations to activate the dormant culture of mother tongue to gather the best cultural heritage of all nations and races, pushing human intelligence to a higher level."

"Now that we have the logo, don't we need a slogan as well?" Brenda pondered for a while before suggesting, "This is easy, how about, 'Be Free'. The fact that language barriers hinder communication on a spiritual level, our ideal is to allow people to communicate at any time and in any situation freely and with ease, without being troubled by languages."

In blockchain circles, many already knew that Henry and his team were preparing to raise funds for their start up, and the team was hence approached regularly by both familiar and unfamiliar investment teams, for no other reason than to hurry them to finish their white paper as soon as possible in order to raise funds.

Henry and his team handled this with prudence. From the beginning, they had reached an agreement to "do what is meaningful and make honest money". Having experienced the madness in the world of cryptocurrency, they were all the more careful not to commit to anything on impulse.

One day, Brenda suggested it was time for them to look for someone to design their website.

"Why look? We have one readily available," Peggy replied, turning to look at Henry with a grin.

"Precisely! Brenda, have you forgotten that I studied computer science? I know how to set up a website, but I will need suggestions from both of you on the content and layout."

The framework of the website was quickly set up; with a completed white paper, filling in the content was not difficult. But when Brenda looked at the first draft of the website, she felt something was wrong.

"I have a feeling that something is not right. There is no problem with the content, but I feel that the website does not stand out, users will know what we are doing but will not be moved."

"What are your ideas then?" Peggy asked, with some anticipation in her voice.

"Let's write a letter and post it on the website, as much as possible, try to be sentimental and artistic. We should make known our purpose for doing this, what we are doing now, as well as our visions for the future," said Brenda.

"This is a good idea, but you must be the one to pen this. You are an effective writer with exquisite writing style and together with your media experiences, you will definitely be able to touch the hearts of many with your writing." Henry felt satisfied, Brenda's experience in the media was indeed a great asset for the team.

"I shall gladly accept this responsibility, hah! Any objections if I write about the three aspects I mentioned?" Brenda was all ready to start writing.

"No problem, actually, why don't we quickly discuss the key points of the letter now?" said Henry.

"One more point to add, if we manage to keep going with the business, we can write a letter every year as part of our annual report," Brenda added, her eyes sparkling as the ideas came flooding into her brain.

"That seems so far away, but I think it is a good idea," Peggy was impressed.

"The first part of the letter will describe the difficulties faced by the three parties namely: language talents, users and language services providers."

"The second part will focus on what we are doing, we have to be clear about the operations of our ecosystem and who we will be inviting to the system."

"The third part will be world building, that is, a showcase of our visions in different scenarios. Remember the scenarios that emerged from our unfettered imaginations when we were at

Houhai? I feel that we only need some modifications here and there before we put them to use."

Feeling inspired, the trio jumped into a brainstorming session before Brenda commenced writing. She very quickly completed the first draft and after Henry and Peggy offered suggestions for some simple amendments, a letter filled with affection and 'faith' was posted.

Today is the ground breaking day for the launch of our company's website.

You will realise that this is relevant to you after looking at our website. Going forward, we will do a yearly review, every year on this same day, you will discover that our relationship will become closer and closer.

The first report will be divided into three sections:

I   *Awareness Checklist: What Can We See?*
Between our first contact with blockchain and the time the system began to take off, the length of time was not long, but the system also did not appear overnight. In fact, it took us some time to develop and consolidate our ideas in the background, our thinking just happened to coincide with and be expedited by the rising popularity of blockchain. The following are observations we have made:
1. *There are numerous talents with professional knowledge and language capability, the system names these talents 'linguists'. The value they can provide could not receive proper reflection previously as there were no platforms for anyone to appreciate and also be able to pay for them to provide this value.*
2. *It is difficult to gain access to valuable information from around the world. It is true that information from respective countries*

can be presented to us via computers, it is no further than the distance from the computer screen to your eyes. But the boundaries of language have kept us confined within the empires of our native languages.

3. *Despite several industrial revolutions, the field of translation, which has been developing along with human civilisation for more than three thousand years, has not seen any significant changes. It is also difficult for Artificial Intelligence to reach its full potential in this field because the big data are scattered across the individual domains of each and every translator and AI lacks an effective model to gather these data.*

II *Action Checklist: What Are We Doing Now?*

The purpose of translation is to disseminate information and to communicate. We are building a global and public language information chain. This will allow anyone to obtain desired information globally using his/her own mother tongue language, and also to release information in his/her mother tongue language to be disseminated to the whole world. We are doing the following:

a. *With blockchain as the basis, we have set up a system to validate the expertise and language assets of knowledge providers. Each and every provider who uses and provides language translation service will receive token incentives. We will ensure that the first batch of users and providers will share the joy of success in the days to come.*

b. *We have also successfully invited a batch of top global language services providers to move their businesses and translators to the chain to carry out business transactions and be among the first to apply and integrate our system with their business ecosystem.*

c. *Thirdly, we have designed a system for repetitive use of language assets which will allow idling language data in the computer to present their value in the process of exchange to build our translation engine. We welcome anyone with linguistic capability to get on the chain to activate dormant resources in their possession and create value from them.*

III   *Blueprint Checklist: What Have We Envisioned for the Future?*
The future is not too far away. We will, in the near future, realise our vision: "Chain the world in your language", to enable mankind to communicate without language barriers, to have access to language services as easily as access to electricity, to communicate with the world in one's native language. Towards the fulfilment of this wonderful vision, we are putting the following into action:

1. *Incubating and building more ecosystems in businesses, tourism, education, media, trading and other areas to develop their applications on the system. Anyone with knowledge and capability will be both consumer and contributor within the system, in coexistence and cooperation.*
2. *Combining blockchain technology and distributed Artificial Intelligence to accumulate individuals' intellectual creations. Translated phrases will not be re-translated all over again to allow energy to be focused on creative work with machines as assistants to human beings.*
3. *Building an ecosystem of language services to form the infrastructure of human civilisation, empowering the global demand for information dissemination, communication and collaboration in different contexts, and becoming a value amplifier in the era of the token economy.*

Since this is an open letter, we shall be honest and unrestrained about the thoughts in our minds: not just our visions for the future but also our innermost apprehensions.

We know well that we are definitely not the first in this explorative endeavour. Translation occupies a high ground in the domain of human wisdom, yet, its transformative power has not been able to be properly harnessed for thousands of years. This is despite many predecessors working and struggling for it all their lives. We are now making another attempt. Not from the starting point of thinking that we are smarter than those before us, but rather, because we have been presented with a once-in-a-lifetime historic opportunity. In the age of the internet, we are persistently exploring ways to gather language talents who are scattered all over the world, and link them up with each other and users, using the unique characteristics of credit build up and token incentives enabled by blockchain technology; we truly believe this is a match made in heaven between blockchain technology and the language services industry.

We have a dream, but at the same time we are also extremely cautious, fearing that we will fail in this great age. Let us go forth and journey together, and support one another even as the challenges against us loom. May our affinity never cease!

However, the highly anticipated spring that the team was expecting did not come. Instead, they were faced with policy changes and increasing government regulation. Rather than the common saying of "a day in the cryptocurrency world, a year in the human world" coming to pass, the reality they faced was that of "a day in the cryptocurrency world, ten years in the human world". One by one, blockchain enterprises began closing down.

Like these other blockchain companies, Henry and the team received notification to move out of their rented co-working space. Given this precipitous situation, many people from these companies quickly turned around and went back to their original fields or switched careers.

"Let's work at my place, we can save on rental," Henry noted the expressions of loss in Peggy and Brenda's eyes, but he tried his best to appear unperturbed. Steven, despite his smiling response, could not hide his concern as well.

The four of them packed up their business into boxes and took a taxi to Henry's quarters. Upon arrival, Peggy's eyes welled up with tears. Although Henry had not elaborated on where he lived before, she was expecting more than a semi-basement room with windows level to the ground. The room was shabby but neat and tidy, it was furnished like a dormitory, with two double-decker beds, a wardrobe and two desks.

"Hey, don't look down on this humble room, my buddies love to chill out here. Look, their clothes are still on the upper deck," Henry joked as he motioned for Steven to help him join the two together.

"Look ladies, we have a pretty big office table," Stevens quipped in response, taking his que from Henry.

Henry took a portable projector from a box and projected his file onto a small section of one of the white walls. The document he prepared for presentation was entitled "Accelerate Landing Via the Coin Valley".

"Let's have a meeting now," Henry rallied, "you have seen the current situation out there. It is an opportunity for us, a rare opportunity in fact." Henry looked at everyone calmly and firmly as he began to speak.

"We know from history that everything has its rise and fall. Right now, we are in a similar situation as experienced by technopreneurs in the early days of the internet, after the burst of the dot com bubble. But let us not forget, there was a new wave of robust growth and a group of internet magnates that emerged, new and robust business models were created which have changed lives irrevocably. After this severe winter season, we will be able to embrace the spring of blockchain and will definitely be able to present a project of real value to our users."

Seeing that his team still looked morose, Henry continued, "We must take advantage of this window of opportunity to accomplish two things: one, we need to conduct in-depth theoretical reflection and compilation to figure out the connections between language and blockchain, why and how the language services industry can be integrated with blockchain, and the path to do this; two, we must identify the point of penetration, to genuinely and devotedly come up with a good product that is of value to users."

"Our product must be built upon the basis of solid theoretical research and not based on subjective feeling or blind following of trends. Once we are firm on our product direction, we will conduct a comprehensive competitive research to find a point for breakthrough for product penetration in the shortest time."

"I have withdrawn all my savings accumulated over the years and mortgaged the house that my family had set aside for me for my marriage, this is to guarantee the salary of the research team. You all can contribute as much as you can manage, I will not impose any minimum requirement," the words seemed to tumble out of Henry in a single breath.

Peggy looked up met Henry's eyes, she looked away immediately. In her mind was the thought that, in addition to contributing her limited savings, she could also approach her parents for help.

The team continued their discussion based on the projections on the wall. Subsequently, they drew up a plan for job distribution, a budget and a schedule for progression.

After hours of working continuously, Peggy and Brenda regained their motivation and Steven's bright smile also made a reappearance.

From that day on, each of them worked individually during the day to complete their own work assignments, both in and outdoors. Every day in the evening, they gathered at Henry's quarters to discuss solutions for any issue that they encountered.

After working hard for three months, Henry's keen eye for detail became even sharper, Steven's tummy seemed to grow rounder as he got busier. The ladies also changed. Peggy no longer dressed like an executive. She cut her hair short, wore t-shirts and jeans and travelled everywhere with a backpack, on the subway. Brenda no longer projected an aloof professional image, but one that was more down-to-earth and affable.

To save on time and costs, the team members often took the night sleeper trains to travel to another city. They would arrive in time for a quick wash up in the morning before starting work for the day. With every minor breakthrough, they rewarded themselves with barbecued skewers and beer.

Within this short timeframe, the team managed to become totally immersed in the language services industry. They were able to deeply engage and communicate with clients, translation services companies, translators, professionals, institutes of higher learning, companies engaged in machine translations, associations, communities and others, and also participated in overseas online community activities. Seemingly overnight, they honed their knowledge and skills to become an industry expert. At the same time, they followed closely the latest developments and research outcomes relating to blockchain. The whole team also took an online course on the token economy to ensure their knowledge was updated and they made sure to maximise their insights by gathering together to study and discuss what they learnt.

By combining the data from various surveys and studying the statistics of the language services industry, they gradually developed a clearer direction for their product and reached a consensus. They were ready to work on two products: The first product would provide a means to identify bilingual talents so that their capabilities would be genuine holographic portraitures and would have the ability to win public trust. The team understood that trust is important, it is the foundation for large-scale collaborations between strangers. The second product was a multilingual platform for human-machine translation. The integration and innovation of online assisted translation and machine translation, along with the knowledge base system, would enable bilingual talents to work while the engine of machine translation continued to grow with them. The platform would be an integration of assisted online translation, exclusive machine translation engines and blockchain, in order to create an exclusive engine for every bilingual talent which would comprise of individual's cultural background, thinking modes, language style etc. Finally, through intensive interfacing of these two products, in the near future, the team's vision was that bilingual talents would be able to work, share and collaborate simultaneously to accumulate a strong base for their own credit and language assets. Those with capabilities would be able to rise above others, and their income would also be raised significantly.

"Let's name these two products. The names must reflect the product functionality and allow users to visualise it." Henry suggested, feeling excited and inspired after a beer.

"The one for identifying translators can be named 'Yi Nuo' (译诺, literally, a translator's promise), to convey each translator's promise to himself and to others." The name that Steven suggested was as straightforward as his character.

"That's what we hope for but it should not be so straightforward," Brenda shook her head.

"I got it! Ours is an era that places importance on attractiveness ratings (颜值 yán zhí), the capabilities of our bilingual talents in the industry should then be rated by their language values (言值 yán zhí)!" Peggy's eyes shone brightly as she offered her suggestion to the team.

"You are a distinctive wordsmith indeed! 'Looks (颜 yán)' and 'words (言 yán)' have the same pronunciation in Chinese, this name is apt, and since blockchain is a perpetual record (录 lù), I think we can name our product 'Wordpower (言值录 yán zhí lù)'," Henry responded excitedly.

"Yes!" The team made a toast in agreement.

"As for the second product, the data of every translator will be stored in the Cloud system which will be the equivalent of a virtual translator. What do you guys think of 'Cloud translator (云译员 yún yì yuán)'?" Steven asked.

"How about 'Cloud translation geek (云译客 yún yì kè)' instead? In the internet era, exceptionally intelligent people capable of creating new business models, frontier technologies and trends are known as 'geeks (极客 jí kè)', can we also refer to translators as 'translation geeks (译客 yì kè)'?" Brenda's suggestion reflected her background as technology journalist indeed.

"When we were in Singapore, Peggy came up with a very appropriate name called 'Twinslator', which means in future, each and every translator will have their exclusive translation engines, just like a twin translator," Henry recalled suddenly.

"We…?" Brenda raised her eyebrows and winked at both Henry and Peggy with a mischievous look on her face.

"Cheers!" Henry was too excited to notice, he stood up to propose a toast and the four of them emptied their glasses in one gulp.

Thus, their first two products "Wordpower (言值录 yán zhí lù)" and "Twinslator" were born.

Steven and two other junior partners for research and development (R&D) moved in with Henry. There was a collegial atmosphere and with everyone working very hard, it felt like they were back to their days as students preparing for their examinations. The team recruited a few other part-time R&D junior partners who were spread out across other cities and it became a norm for everyone to meet up virtually at their daily product video conference at 1am. Within less than half a year of intensive work, product development was completed and launched online.

A good product speaks for itself. "Wordpower" and "Twinslator", though still in their pilot run, began to be spread quickly through word-of-mouth among translators.

Wendy, a millennial from Tianjin commented, "this product has indeed touched our hearts! I can be a volunteer for you, I want to introduce these two products to more translators."

After Jay, an American student at Beijing Language and Culture University started promoting the products on his Facebook account, more than 2000 translators from all over the world signed up within a week, all of them actively interacting online to share their experiences on the use of the products.

Allan, the boss of a translation services company in Shijiazhuang, Hebei, told the team directly, "My translation services company is small in scale, I was contemplating on how we could make swift progress in this era of blockchain, whatever that I can do to be part of this, let me know, I will do my best!"

From Singapore, Susan, the Programme Head at the Department of Translation and Interpretation, sent a message, "Will you consider allowing the products to enter university classrooms to connect students with the latest blockchain technology?" It was indeed a remark that invigorated and energised the team, it felt great to know that both teachers and students at institutes of higher learning had such great desire for and acute sensitivity to new technology!

Subsequently, Peggy attended a few international industry conferences in America, Canada and Singapore and presented as the keynote speaker on the topic of "Blockchain remodelling the language services industry". Personnel from renowned global translation services companies expressed interest since this was the first blockchain project in the language services industry.

But the best encouragement by far came from the biggest language services provider in China, Transn. It was the first to respond positively and express interest for in-depth cooperation, as well as offer to be the first node on the public chain of language information.

The flattering response from translators, the recognition by people in the language industry and the anticipation of higher learning institutions boosted the confidence of Henry and the team. The R&D team led by Steven was especially excited when they saw the overwhelming response from the market.

One day, Brenda sent a shocking piece of news to the team's chat group: Bryan, the key speaker at the conference they had attended some time back, had committed suicide. It was suspected that he had drawn on thousands of clients' bitcoins to short-sell and to leverage on them multiple times. But in the end, the waterfall decline did not happen, and Bryan was greeted with a 3% rise in bitcoin futures.

"The media reported that Bryan had committed suicide in desperation," Brenda commented.

"He was just slightly over forty years old, it's such a pity," Peggy lamented.

"By leveraging so many times, he was also extending the risk by a hundred times; with just a 1% rise in bitcoin, he lost everything he had and more. Just a momentary slip led to such serious consequences. He behaved like a gambler who was totally out of control! I wonder what was on his mind then," said Henry.

Involuntarily, they all recalled what Bryan had said in his speech, "Do not borrow money to speculate in coins, and do not dream of getting rich overnight", unfortunately, he had not heeded his own advice.

The death of Bryan affected their morale somewhat and the ensuing chaos in the cryptocurrency circle also made a small dent in the confidence of the team. But they rebounded quickly and reached a consensus over the following: The era of blockchain that could be funded by merely presenting white papers and bragging rights was over. The air coin items that were advancing rapidly based on the pump and dump mechanism were gradually disappearing. The digital currencies that dominated the screens once upon a time had started to see downturns. However, blockchain was still going strong. In the end, the blockchain project that would be able to stand tall and firm amidst big waves would be one that can truly move society forward and one that has a grounded application scenario. The team had a strong conviction that convergence of language and blockchain was already a winner on the starting line, given its strong values as a foundation.

However, it was also a fact that their business venture had not obtained any financing, the three founding partners were hence depending on their savings to pay the salaries of the R&D team, the going was really tough.

> Blockchain is an irresistible force.

Just when they were least expecting it, a piece of big news boosted their morale. Libra Network, the subsidiary company of Facebook, based in Switzerland, released a white paper of its cryptocurrency system.

"This is such an important piece of news!" Henry who was usually calm and collected appeared excited, "The usual practice for digital currency projects is to release a white paper first, and between six months to a year later to start circulating the digital currency. The release of the white paper signals the countdown to the Libra project."

"Why are you so excited about others issuing currency?" Peggy teased.

"I am definitely excited, the project was launched by Facebook, and there is more to it than meets the eye, a compilation of analysis articles written by the blockchain expert Meng Yan and other pundits are spreading like wildfire all over the internet."

"Tell us the details then," Peggy was curious.

"Well, the article I read described in detail the reasons that prompted Facebook to issue Libra, the values of Libra, the mechanisms of the currency, applicable scenarios, the impact of Libra and how the different levels in the society should respond, from the government down to the individuals."

Henry continued, "All I know is that this project is 'ambitious'. Look at this, my WeChat Moments has been flooded with comments. The project will create a digital economy consisting of a hundred Cooperative Alliance nodes, Visa, Mastercard, Uber, PayPal, among others who have already signed up and affirmed that they will be the founding nodal points. Over time, a total of 2.7 billion global users of Facebook and WhatsApp will be included in this economy structure."

"There are lots of speculations out there about why Facebook decided to launch Libra. There is no doubt that Zuckerberg wants to leap over from the internet to blockchain and to also become a leader in the world of blockchain," Henry continued.

"Is there anything special about Libra? What is the difference as compared to other digital currencies?" asked Brenda.

"Oh, there are many. For example, Libra collateralises a basket of low-risk assets and is not limited to US dollar-denominated assets, allowing it to hedge the risks associated with a single dollar-denominated asset, creating more financial openness and offer greater profitability," replied Henry.

"What is its relationship with legal tender and US dollars?" asked Peggy.

"To put it simply, Libra is an expansion of the legal tender system, it will value-add to the US dollars but will not replace it," said Henry.

"What are its applications?" Peggy asked again.

"Professionals analysed and feel that Libra will be rolled out in cross-border remittance, Facebook-based and digital economy payments, investments, offline payments, etc.," Henry replied swiftly.

"It does seem that the circulation of Libra will have a great impact on, or even replace, the sovereign currencies of small countries. After all, between the sovereign currency of a randomly increasing number of small countries and a world stable currency anchored by a basket of high-quality fiat currency government bonds, the latter would be a better choice," Brenda clearly understood the implications.

"That's right, the impact of Libra is multifaceted and enormous. It will have significant impact on traditional currencies and financial systems, digital currencies and blockchain, the general public and other internet companies. There is great room for imagination with regard to Libra's financial openness," Henry was getting more excited as he spoke.

"Tell us more about financial openness," Brenda asked, diligent always to beef up her knowledge of the industry.

"The financial world we face today can be imagined as a four-tiered inverted pyramid, with the dollar issued by the Federal Reserve at the bottom, central bank currencies issued by national central banks, and securities issued by investment banks at the top. But this system is highly centralised, monopolistic, not transparent and confined. Financial openness translates to the integration of technology with the financial infrastructure through the internet and blockchain. In this way, everything becomes more transparent, monopoly rights are broken and confined situations reduced, the effect is an increase in financial inclusion that allows for public usage, sharing and common governance," said Henry.

"What is the connection between financial openness and the token economy?" Brenda questioned further.

"Good question! Earlier I mentioned that the top tier of the inverted pyramid is 'securities' and these are issued by investment banks on behalf of enterprises, this is a right that belongs to the enterprise. These companies will issue 'securities' to raise capital, and with the raised funds, companies will set up a structure beneficial for its ecosystem, production, and operating environment. This is known as the 'token economy' and it is right where we are." Henry explained clearly in a few words.

Brenda gave him a thumbs up. Henry waved off her compliment.

"After listening to your explanation, it does appear that Facebook's launch of Libra is indeed a big thing!"

"Although Facebook's launch of Libra is a movement within the cryptocurrency circle, it indicates that blockchain is unstoppable. Blockchain has great prospects, we must have confidence in our business project. The road may be tortuous, but the prospects are bright!" Peggy and Brenda were thus encouraged by Henry's explanation and evidence to keep going.

> Singapore's legislation is viewed as the beginning of the implementation of digital currency payments.

It did not take long before they received another buzzworthy piece of news: Singapore had started to legislate digital currency.

"I've just read news that the Inland Revenue Authority of Singapore has released a draft on goods and services tax (GST) for payments done through digital payment tokens," Brenda shouted across the room.

"In terms of digital currency, Singapore is quick to act as always, as to be expected of a country with strong legal awareness. Exposure, acceptance and use are rapid, and regulation by legislation is also prompt," Peggy commented.

"Although the draft still needs to be revised on the basis of extensive public consultation and there is still some time before it is officially implemented, it is indeed comforting to know that Singapore is taking the lead in legislating digital currencies," Henry concluded.

Meanwhile, the product development team had been working round the clock on the two products, "Wordpower" to establish credit assets for translators and "Twinslator" to build language assets for translators. After several iterations, they were progressing at an amazing speed, all of these helped to boost the confidence of the team further.

Henry and Peggy started to run roadshows and their first stop was Hangzhou. Both of them were excited to be back in Hangzhou and they talked about revisiting the West Lake afterwards.

At the site of the roadshow, Henry analysed the relationship between currency and language and explained to listeners why language would be the next successful application of blockchain.

Currency and language play unique roles in the development of mankind. Currency satisfies material exchange between people while language is formed to enable intellectual and emotional communication. They share the three characteristics of universality, randomness and contextuality; furthermore, both currency and language are symbols of nationality.

> Currency is rational and quantifiable. Language is perceptive and non-inferential.

Currency is rational and quantifiable. While the conversion of different currencies can be done precisely, conversion between different languages is not always smooth and unhindered. At the same time, because national interests are at stake, digital currencies have encountered resistance to their widespread and extensive application due to the intervention of national policies. Language, on the other hand, carries the culture and history of a country, thus every country is keen to encourage the export of its own language and culture to promote cultural exchange. The human desire to be free of language barriers is a powerful underlying force behind the application of blockchain in language services.

The first roadshow was extremely successful, in fact unexpectedly so. Many like-minded people were attracted to "Wordpower" and "Twinslator", given Henry's logical and inspiring presentation and the intuitive interfaces and comprehensive functionalities of the products. When Henry told them that the company had not received any funding, some expressed interest to join the team regardless, expressing their belief that the business was very promising, and that they saw Henry and Peggy as ideal working partners. They were even willing to forego their salaries for the time being.

Henry and Peggy were encouraged by the response. To them, everything had become clear, including the business prospects.

They resolved to lead their small group of like-minded partners and dedicate themselves to improving their products and simultaneously sorting out the theoretical compilations; they were determined to do a meaningful job, in an honest way.

When the roadshow ended, they realised their wish to revisit the West Lake after more than ten years. It was July and all of nature was in full bloom. Looking into the distance from the broken bridge, the golden rays of the sun shone on the lake and the water reflected them like a million sparkling diamonds. The water birds soared in the blue sky and in between the clouds, swooping down at times to the water surface. It had just rained, and the air was very fresh. The breeze created little waves on the blue waters, making it seem as if countless transparent ribbons were fluttering in the water.

"The landscape of Hangzhou is such a big part of our history and culture, but it is not especially outstanding; the scenery is almost surreal yet so closely linked to actual events and works," said Henry.

"Indeed, historical stories about the West Lake are abundant and for thousands of years this place has been well-loved by writers and scholars as a place for them to create their masterpieces." Peggy acknowledged. At that moment, she suddenly felt the urge to recite a poem that the poet Su Dongpo had written about the West Lake:

"The brimming waves delight the eyes on a sunny day,

水光潋滟晴放好，shuǐ guāng liàn yàn jīng fàng hǎo

The dimming hills present a rare view in a rainy haze.

山色空蒙雨亦奇。shān sè kōng méng yǔ yì qí

West Lake may be compared to the lady of the West,

欲把西湖比西子，yù bǎ xī hú bǐ xī zǐ

Whether she is richly adorned or plainly dressed.

淡妆浓抹总相宜。dàn zhuāng nóng mǒ zǒng xiāng yí"

"Do you remember Xu Xian and Bai Niangzi in the story 'Legend of the White Snake'?" asked Henry.

"Of course!" Peggy nodded.

"I think you are just like the little white snake spirit," Henry said with a smile.

Upon hearing herself being compared to a snake spirit, Peggy was a little upset, "What are you talking about, what makes you say that I am like the snake spirit?"

"No, you have misunderstood, the term 'snake spirit' may not sound good but this is in fact a compliment. I have always felt that you are a very perceptive person, perceptive not sensitive, your ability to perceive changes around you and the emotional reactions of others is a very good trait, and snakes are such animals," Henry was quick to explain.

"Why do I feel that you are twisting words with forced logic?" Peggy was still not convinced.

"In ancient times, many believed in snake totems in China, and many of the most famous gods in Chinese folklore were hybrids of humans and snakes. In Han dynasty artwork, Fuxi, (a cultural hero in Chinese legend) and his sister, Nuwa, were depicted as creatures with the faces of humans and bodies of snakes. Many famous people from ancient times like Qu Yuan (屈原), Liu Bang (刘邦), Xiang Yu (项羽), Hua Tuo (华佗), Zu Chongzhi (祖冲之), Lu You (陆游) were all born in the year of the snake. There are also great men from modern times who were born in the year of the snake, I believe you know who they are without me listing them. When I say that you are a snake spirit, I meant to compliment you."

"Alright, alright, I get it," Peggy replied with a slightly more relaxed smile.

Henry let out a sigh of relief and teased, "If you were a little snake spirit in your previous life, I might be Xu Xian. Why else would we be able to reunite after so many years apart and now start a business together?"

Peggy did not reply. Looking out at the beautiful scenery comprising the lake and mountains, Henry suggested, "Shall we each come up with a three-liner love poem on our mobile phones?"

"Oh, I didn't think you would be in the mood for this…?" Peggy was surprised, but she took out her mobile phone and agreed.

After a short while, Henry saw that Peggy was done, he could not wait to read it. "Peggy let's look at yours first. I am afraid mine might intimidate you," he said jokingly. She scoffed at him but obliged.

"Three lifetimes of love affair, only to be enthralled in this life,

三世情缘今生醉，sān shì qíng yuán jīn shēng zuì

Two hearts longing for each other, obstructed by the heavens,

两心相映天作凭，liǎng xīn xiāng yìng tiān zuò píng

Hand in hand with complete devotion, to practice and perfect as one.

一意执手同修行。yí yì zhí shǒu tóng xiū xíng"

"Wow my lady, a good poem! This three-liner poem is profound indeed, the initial characters are all numerical, 'three, two, one', is this a countdown to a vibrant spring?" Henry's eyes were filled with admiration.

Peggy grinned, "Correct interpretation! You are perceptive and able to comprehend well too."

"You flatter me, now it's my turn to show you what I have."

"I am ready to lend you my ears," Peggy made a funny face in mischief.

"At first sight,

一见, yí jiàn

I am in love,

便钟情, biàn zhōng qíng

Fate is indestructible.

缘起不灭。yuán qǐ bú miè"

"Your three-liner poem is indeed clear and concise," Peggy praised.

Peggy somehow sensed that this poem was a confession from Henry and was slightly shaken, but she did not want to think any further or say more, she took some steps forward and they continued with their stroll along the lake in silence.

The gentle wind by the West Lake continued to blow.

At that moment, Henry told himself, "There is ample time, I will confess to her when the opportunity arises."

Summary:
The Journey with Language

It is a common human desire to be free from language barrier. Blockchain is the dawn of the new era to the realisation of this wonderful desire. In the era of blockchain, the Tower of Babel can be constructed on the basis of preserving history and culture to enable the convergence and dissemination of human civilisation.

People are discussing, searching, and anticipating, what will be the next phenomenal application of blockchain after bitcoin. The consensus is that it should not be in a field that has already been tapped by the internet. After all, the underlying logic and the most compatible applications are different for both the current internet of information and the internet of value that is blockchain-based.

Any new technology that succeeds in bringing about social changes must not be a "cold technology" that is purely rational and instrumental, but one that embodies values that will benefit the society. Blockchain is no exception. The first successful application on the blockchain was the digital currency Bitcoin, which is the result of a group of aspiring cypherpunks using cryptography as a weapon to protect privacy and promote social change.

Currency and language are two things that are significant in the course of human history, which have arisen naturally in different countries one after the other. Currency was created to satisfy material exchange between people and language was created to fulfill the spiritual aspect of communication between people.

SUMMARY

323

Currency and language share several common characteristics which include firstly, universality — currency and language are needed by everyone throughout the life cycle. Secondly, randomness — the amount of money spent, and how much is said each day, most of the time, is not predetermined and is mostly random. Lastly, contextuality — the use of currency and language occurs in certain scenarios, money will not be paid, and words will not be mumbled for no reasons.

Currency and language also have their unique characteristics. Currency is rational and can be measured with precision; language is perceptual, it reflects the collective consensus of a linguistic community and has width, depth, and warmth. As a result of the diversity of linguistic expressions and the richness of national cultures, it is difficult to determine how language can be measured. It is also due to such differences that currency and language, with their special values reflected in the history of human civilisation, have varying results in transnational applications.

The exchange of different currencies is now done extensively with precision, and global exchange of materials has been smooth. However, the conversion from one language to another has not been as convenient. Most people still communicate primarily with people of their own mother tongue, and most of the information still flows only within the world of their mother tongue. The translation industry has remained a workshop-style industry since its inception. It is an industry that has not been truly transformed despite several industrial revolutions.

Currency and language are both symbols of national sovereignty. It is understood that countries are sensitive towards the creation of digital currencies and therefore, they are cautious in their polices. Language, on the other hand, embodies history and culture. Every country will encourage all forms of cultural exchange, and adopts a relatively open attitude towards language, so that their cultures and civilisations are enriched by exchange and mutual appreciation.

The world has become increasingly unified. The need to break down language barriers is more important than ever, and this is a strong internal driver force for the application of blockchain in language services. In the initial stage, the blockchain industry may experience some chaos and mingling of the good and bad players; however, it will eventually be restored to its true nature.

The internet enables efficient transmission of information, while blockchain enables quantitative interconnection of values. Blockchain allows communication and transmission of language and text to quantify value. We have reasons to believe that the love child of blockchain and language — Cross-Linguistic Capability — will be the next phenomenal application to impact human life and work significantly.

The Conclusion: Once in a Thousand Years

Constructing towers like that of Babel to be high among the clouds and building a world free from language barriers have been common desires of mankind throughout the ages.

The developments in technology has realised the visions of humanity one after another. Over a hundred years ago, the Wright brothers invented the airplane that allowed us to cruise at ease through the clouds; the rise of mobile connectivity more than two decades ago allowed us to see our loved ones and communicate with them, anytime, anywhere, despite being thousands of miles apart.

In this new age where Artificial Intelligence, 5G, the Internet of Things (IoT) and blockchain work hand-in-hand, the future is set to be even more exciting and colourful. Language and blockchain, the divine couple from a previous incarnation and bound in this life, have created Linguistic Capability that will make it possible for people around the world to work together closely and happily, to create a new world without language barriers.

Tokens are like little busy elves on the blockchain, they are impartial, tireless and faithful in their work. They measure every individual's abilities, accumulate their wisdom, track their achievements, record their contributions and realise their values, the results derived from individual languages will then be shared and rewarded. This will encourage everyone to actively explore the beauty of their country's history and culture, actively utilise their ability to create and innovate, and enjoy the fruits of wisdom that they have jointly gathered.

I am thankful to live in a time where I can witness the birth of blockchain, a technology that has transformed production relations, and to be fortunate to work in the wonderful field of language services and be pleasantly surprised to discover that language and blockchain can create such a beautiful love and synergy together.

This is truly a once-in-a-millennium historic opportunity and privilege!

Epilogue

I had never thought of writing a book. It was He Enpei who proposed that I turn my thoughts on language and blockchain into a book, otherwise, I would not be gazing at the bright moonlight outside the window tonight thinking about this epilogue.

It was with He Enpei's apt advice, time and again, that I finally decided on the style of the story and the visuals, and finally completed this book. Over the years, his caution in times of pride, encouragement in times of frustration, guidance in times of uncertainty, and support in times of crisis have helped me see a better version of myself.

I must also mention He Zhengyu, who seems to have some kind of magic in his head, he can spontaneously quote interesting examples to enlighten me on any technical problems. This guy with a great sense of humour is a treasure as a friend.

This book was completed at the Jiusi Bookstore of Huazhong University of Science and Technology (HUST). Zhu Jiusi was the President of HUST, and it is an honour to have been under his mentorship. In the beautiful campus of HUST, I could still feel the clock turning back, and I would be reminded of the light in the hallway thirty years ago, the windowsill on the first floor of the hostel and the concrete bench in the open-air cinema. Those were the springtime of life, a record of our youth and passion.

It is destiny that has linked our hearts together for more than thirty years. Our common ideals and pursuits supported us in overcoming many difficulties. We complemented each other's success and together we strive to create a promising future in the field of language services.

After I completed the first edition of the manuscript, the renowned linguist, Professor Chew Cheng Hai from the National University of Singapore and Professor He Guixiu who is my best friend, amazingly connected me to The Commercial Press in China. Since then, it was love at first sight between this book and The Commercial Press, the origin of modern publishing in China. The drive and commitment of the management at The Commercial Press is admirable. It is not difficult to comprehend why The Commercial Press has been hailed as a cultural miracle of modern China, spanning three centuries, with its motto of "promoting education and enlightening the people".

After the publication of the Chinese version of the book, which was the time of the global outbreak of Covid-19 pandemic. Winnie spared no effort in helping me with the translation of the book. It was a difficult task, and I was very touched by her full commitment and conscientiousness.

What was unthinkable was that when I was at a loss in finding an English publisher. Professor Phua Kok Khoo, the chairman of World Scientific Publishing, gave his recognition and support to the book and promptly decided to publish it. I was overjoyed.

They are the valuable people in my life, appearing magically one by one when I needed them most.

Everything went so unexpectedly well that there must have been some sort of help that transcended time and space. My parents, who voluntarily and unconditionally donated their bodies to medical scientific research after they passed on, are two silent stars in the sky, lovingly shining down on me and guarding me; my elder sister who stashed half a baked bun in her pocket for me during kindergarten and now insists on stuffing apples in my bag; my little sister who loved making up nursery rhymes and carried tales to our mother, is now frequently checking on my well-being; my beloved son, who is now assuming a key role in his job, treats me like an elder sister and pours out his emotions at times, and at other times criticises my inadequate consciousness on environmental protection, I am blessed with so much love from all of you. I am truly so lucky and blissful.

Peng Zhihong
25 August 2021

Index

agricultural age, 221
  surface resources, 221, 251
air coin, 312
artificial intelligence (AI), 82, 83, 102, 106, 128, 143, 167, 169, 170, 229–231, 241, 242, 302, 303
Augmented Reality (AR), 273

behavioural data, 181
big data, 167, 169, 171, 175, 176, 179, 182, 236, 242, 252
bilingual, 5, 9, 40, 44, 58, 65, 95, 97, 105, 109, 110, 117, 124, 130, 133–135, 139, 140, 143, 144, 148, 170, 175–177, 179, 180, 182, 183, 207, 209, 213, 224, 227, 238, 243
  recognition, 143, 172, 179, 180, 181, 183, 253, 311
  remuneration, 183
  value creators, 222, 236, 237
Bitcoin, 137, 138, 292, 294, 311, 322
  lightning, 293
blockchain, xxxv, xxxviii–xl, 37, 70–73, 105, 106, 113, 114, 137, 138, 143, 144, 149–158, 160, 161, 163, 170–177, 179–184, 197–200, 202–207, 209–218, 221, 222, 251, 252, 263, 269–271, 273–275, 280, 287–291, 294–296, 299, 301–308, 310–317, 322–324
authenticate, 252
authentication, 180
authenticity, 113
autonomous, xxxviii, xxxix
autonomy, 177
consensus, 152, 158
credibility, 113
cryptography, 270
decentralisation, 150–152, 173, 202–204, 215
decentralised, xxxviii, xxxix, 270
distributed ledger, 152, 204
encrypted ledger, xxxix
encryption, 213
immutable, xxxix, 179
industrial transformations, xxxviii
integration, 213
mathematical algorithms, 270
non-tamperable, 174, 175
openness, 152
open system, xxxvii–xxxix
shared distributed ledger, xxxix

system ontology, xxxviii
tamper-proof, xxxix, 143
technological innovations, xxxviii, xl
time-ordered cryptographic ledger, xxxix
token incentive system, 231
traceable, xxxix, 174, 175
transparent ledger, xxxix
validate, 302
value transmission, 269
Blue Ocean domain, 248
buzzword, xxxviii

central nodes, 106
China, 1, 3–11, 13, 15, 17, 19, 26–28, 31, 33, 35, 36, 118, 119, 131–133, 139, 257, 258, 260, 261, 263, 272, 277, 279, 280
  Beijing, 255, 258, 259, 261, 264, 265, 268, 280
  Hangzhou, 4, 21, 30
  Hunan, 109, 116, 117, 120–123
  Jiangnan, 266, 267
  Qingdao, Shandong, 11
  Shanghai, 4, 29, 30
  Wuhan, 10, 22
  Xinjiang, 25
Chinese communication platforms, xxxvii
  Baidu Tieba, xxxvii
  Weibo, xxxvii
Chinese fork art, 121
  Hunan Tanci, plucking rhymes, 121
cloud computing, 221, 236
Cloud system, 309

cognition, 75, 81, 96, 179
cohesion, xxxv
collaborate, xxxv, xxxvi, xxxviii, 82
collaboration, 69, 152, 159, 166, 181, 183, 184, 193, 194, 202–204, 215, 255, 278–280
  recognition, 143, 172, 179–181
communication, 39, 42, 45, 56–58, 73, 81, 84, 97, 100, 183, 184, 201, 214
  gestures, 56
  language barrier, 56
  sketching, 56
  translation tools, 57
consumer-end (C-end), 201, 202, 204, 205, 214
context, 222, 230, 241
corresponding expression, 64
credit assets, 143, 144, 176, 179, 180, 181, 316
cross-border remittance, 314
Cross-Linguistic Capability, 217, 251, 271, 324
cryptocurrency, 137, 287, 291, 293–295, 299, 304, 312, 315
  chives, 293, 295
cryptographic protocol, 275
cultural connotation, 230, 241
culture, xxxv, xxxvi, 45, 57, 58, 61, 67, 69

data assets, 222, 252, 273
deadlock, 75, 104
digital assets, 105, 152, 217
digital economy payment, 314
dissemination, xxxvii
distributed applications (dapp), 240
dot com bubble, 305

INDEX

e-commerce, 190, 198, 255, 275, 276, 284
electrical energy, 226–228, 238, 245, 271
electricity, 217, 225, 226, 228, 238–240, 243, 244, 246, 252, 253
empower, 211, 216, 243, 246, 255, 256, 271
encrypted digital certificate, 157
ethnic groups, 58, 63
evolution, 255, 283
expertise, 302

financial openness, 314, 315
Friedman, Thomas, 81
fundraising, 291

globalisation, 83, 134, 230, 272
global synergy, 211, 215
global village, 273
Google, 45
   AdWords, 45

Hangzhou, 316, 318
   West Lake, 4, 316, 318, 321
heritage, xxxvii
history, 3, 16, 24, 27, 36
   educated youth, 27
   Old Three Grades, 26, 27
holographic digital identity, 174, 179
holographic portraitures, 307
human civilisation, xxxix, 287, 297, 302, 303, 322, 323
human intelligence, 287, 298
humanity, xxxvii
human-machine translation, 242, 243, 271

human material exchange, 287
Hunan cuisine, 116
   Dongpo pork, 117

incubator firm, 288
industrial age, 221, 253
   subterranean resources, 221
information age, 251
   data, 217, 218, 221–223, 225, 227, 236, 238, 242, 247, 251–253
information asymmetry, 106
information sharing, 94, 106
infrastructure, xxxviii
initial coin offerings (ICO), 291
instrumental value, 110
interface, xxxix
International English Language Testing System (IELTS), 131
internet, xxxviii
internet buzzwords, 33
Internet of Things (IoT), 221, 228
interpretation, 44, 75, 89
interpreter, 143, 149, 155, 159, 160, 163, 173
isolated data, 214
isolated language data, 141

Language, xxxv– xl, 1, 2, 5, 6, 9–12, 16, 18, 22–25, 30, 31, 33, 35, 36, 39, 40, 43, 47, 50–52, 56–59, 61–64, 66–73, 75–77, 79–81, 83, 88, 89, 95–97, 100, 102–106, 109, 110, 117–119, 124, 126, 127, 130–132, 134, 135, 140, 141, 183, 184, 192, 194, 198, 203, 206, 207, 209–225, 227–231,

233, 236, 237, 239–244, 247,
248, 250–253, 255, 258,
269–276, 278, 279, 283–285,
287, 297, 310, 317, 322, 323
accent, 31, 32
agreement, xxxvi
Arabic, 71
Bahasa Melayu, 5
Chinese, 219, 230, 241, 246
cognitive image, xxxv
common understanding, 40, 68
communal resource, 70
community autonomy, 2
consensus, xxxvi–xxxix, 1, 35
culture, 1, 4, 17, 22, 25, 36
decentralised, 1, 36
dialects, 21, 30
distributed storage system, 1, 36
diversity, 58, 64, 70, 73
Earish, 229–231, 241, 242
economic value, 9, 11
emotional resonance, xxxv
emotions, xxxvi
English, 5, 9–12, 18, 23–25, 28,
  31, 33, 219, 220, 223–225,
  230, 237, 241, 246
Esperanto, 229, 230, 241
expandable, 70
expression, xxxvi, xxxvii
fineness, 63, 64
French, 52, 71
fundamentals, xxxv
global context, xxxv
granularity, 63, 64
group memory, 36
Hindi, 5
historical footprint, xxxvii
hypotactic, 72

intangible net, 72
integrate, 57, 66, 72
Japanese, 52, 57, 58, 66
Mandarin, xxxvii, 5, 6, 11, 12,
  15, 23, 25, 30, 32, 33, 35,
  39, 50–53, 56–61, 63, 66,
  67, 71, 72
national symbol, xxxv
native, 302, 303
open system, xxxvii–xxxix, 1, 2,
  30, 36
operating system, xxxvi, 31, 35
paratactic, 72
proficiency, 66
profundity, 11, 16, 24, 39
resource, xxxvii
Russian, 71, 220, 224
Sinitic, 57
social forms, xxxv
Southern Min, 57
Spanish, 71
Tagalog, 58
Tamil, 5, 61
tone, 9, 31
transmit information, xxxv
Uighur, 25
universality, xxxv
language assets, 143, 144, 175,
  176, 182, 253, 302, 308, 316
language data, 143, 154, 180, 181
  terminologies, 143, 155
language barriers, 75, 81, 146,
  183, 184, 194, 224, 228, 244,
  255, 272, 275, 276, 279, 283,
  284, 287, 290, 296, 298, 303,
  317, 323
language capability, 301
language chain, 39, 40, 58, 67

INDEX

language conversion, 289
language data, 106, 223, 227, 247, 251, 270, 271, 302
language requirements 62
   fragmented, 62
language talents, 105, 106
Lao Zi (ancient philosopher), 297
Libra Network, 312
linguistic, 70
linguistic ability, 35
linguistic community, xxxvi, xxxvii
linguists, 301
localisation, 245
long-tailed market, 100
Lu, Farmer, 229–231

Machine Learning, 242
machine translation, 57, 82, 83, 88, 228, 229, 242, 243, 245, 246, 252, 289, 308
mode of thinking, 58
mother tongue, 58, 59, 67, 225, 230–232, 290, 297, 298, 302, 323
multicultural, 1, 11, 18
multilingual, 1, 11, 109, 207, 209, 217, 218, 220, 227, 228, 236, 238
mutual reinforcement, 244, 252

natural person, 35
neural machine translation, 171, 180, 252
Nobel Prize, 90–95
   collaboration, 82, 95, 96, 106, 107
   collaborative co-creation, 90–93, 95

Nobel, Alfred, 93
Nobel Prize winner, 92
   Bohr, Niels, 94
   Curie, Marie, 91, 92
   Einstein, Albert, 93
   Joliot, Frederic, 93
   Yousafzai, Malala, 92
node, xxxviii, xxxix, 36, 40, 71, 158, 177, 311

online assisted translation, 308
open outcry, 291
open-source licence (open-source software licence agreement), 240

parallel corpus, 232
perceptions, xxxvi
perspectives, xxxvi, xxxvii
polycentric, xxxviii
power grid, 227, 253, 271
power of value transfer, 183
proxy voting, 291
psychological, xxxvi
public blockchain, 70, 71
public chain, 311
public chain for language information, 271
pump & dump, 312

Qian Zhongshu, 196, 197

read, 54, 62
   enunciation, 54
   tone, 43, 52, 54, 59, 68
replacement terms, 64
resonate, 36, 37
rule-based translation, 171, 180

Satoshi Nakamoto, 294
sight interpretation, 154
simultaneous interpretation, 149, 157, 167
Singapore, 1–16, 18–21, 23, 26, 28–33, 109–116, 128, 129, 131–133, 136, 138, 139, 145, 146, 149, 165, 171, 178, 185–188, 202, 211
    Garden City, 14
    Henderson Wave bridge, 111, 128, 129, 136
    Marina Bay Sands Expo and Convention Centre, 149, 155
    National Library, 90
    Orchard Road, 185, 186
    Sentosa, 187, 192, 208
    Tekka Centre, 84, 85
smart contracts, 152, 222, 223
smart data, 217, 247
Smart Society, 222, 247
social man, 35
source language, 150
spiritual communication, 287
statistical translation, 171, 180

talent mobility, 134
target language, 150
Test of English as a Foreign Language (TOELF), 131
text messaging service, 56
    WeChat, 57, 64
    WhatsApp, 56
The World is Flat, 81
token, xxxix, 105, 143, 156–159, 172, 199, 201, 202, 204, 205, 209, 214, 231, 242, 253, 273
    cryptography, 253
    identity-based, 158
    incentive mechanism, 105
    income-based, 158
    negotiability, 253
    proof of interest, 253
    rights-based, 158
    value-based, 158
    value representation, 273
    value transfer, 273
token economy, 156, 303, 307, 315
token incentive mechanism, 199
token incentives, 302, 304
Tower of Babel, 2, 296, 322
    confound, 2
    congregate, 2
translation, 1, 5, 10, 11, 21, 23–25, 39, 40, 43–48, 57, 62–64, 67, 73, 75–83, 85–89, 95, 96, 100–106, 109, 110, 117–119, 121, 123–128, 137, 139–141
    ambiguity, 63
    Commercial Translation, 39, 50, 62, 65–67
    conciseness, 140
    context, 64, 72, 139, 140
    job of creativity, 77
    licence translation, 44, 45
    terminologies, 79
    translation services company, 1, 5, 10, 11, 23
    vividness, 140
translation services company, 39, 46, 47, 77, 81, 85–89, 95, 104, 117, 123, 140, 148, 166, 173, 174, 206, 236, 270, 283, 310
    centralised system, 105, 106
    endorser, 174

INDEX

fragmented, 183, 202, 203, 205, 214, 215
freelancers, 40, 84
intermediary, 46, 107, 173, 174, 236
interpreter, 97
outsource, 206
outsourcing service model, 105
project manager, 39, 43–48, 148, 166, 270
translator, 46–48, 61, 75, 80, 82–89, 102, 104, 106, 270
Transn, 206, 311
trust building, 86
workshop-style, 75
workshop-style existence, 206
transliterate, 102
Transn, 206
 internet of language, 206
Triple Principle of Translation, 83
 Elegance, 83
 Expressiveness, 83
 Faithfulness, 83
tweets, 67

Twinslator, 309, 310, 316, 317
twin translator, 243
two-way empowerment, 183, 211

university, 9–11, 19, 23, 24, 26, 32, 50, 51, 57, 68
 adult learning institute, 23, 25
 adult learning institution, 49, 66
 city campus, 50, 51

value exchange, 105
Virtual Reality (VR), 273

white papers, 288, 312
window of reflection, 18, 22
Wordpower, 309, 310, 316, 317
wordsmith, 308

Xun Zi (Confucian philosopher), 245

Yang Jiang, 196, 197

Zamenhof, Ludwik Lejzer (Zamenhof), 229

CPSIA information can be obtained
at www.ICGtesting.com
Printed in the USA
BVHW090156270422
635143BV00002B/89